THE MAKERS OF CHRISTENDOM

General Editor: CHRISTOPHER DAWSON

THE WESTERN FATHERS

THE MAKERS OF CHRISTENDOM

General Editor: CHRISTOPHER DAWSON

The
Western Fathers

Being the lives of SS. Martin of Tours, Ambrose,
Augustine of Hippo, Honoratus of Arles
and Germanus of Auxerre

TRANSLATED AND EDITED

by

F. R. HOARE

SHEED AND WARD

NEW YORK · 1954

CONTENTS

PREFACE

THE biographical writings in this volume are the primary sources for the Lives of the five Western Fathers with whom they deal. If the purpose of this series were to convert the contemporary pictures of the makers of Christendom into biographies of the modern type, each of them would have to be pulled to pieces, supplemented from other sources, interpreted in the light of later knowledge and reconstructed on quite a different plan. Since in actual fact the purpose of the series is largely to enable the twentieth-century reader to see these makers of Christendom as far as possible as their contemporaries saw them, it would seem that the task of the translator is to preserve as far as possible the feeling and manner of the original, and that the task of the editor is as far as possible to put the twentieth-century reader in possession of the knowledge of the setting of the Lives which the contemporary readers had and which the writers took for granted.

As regards the translations, they have been made on the principle that, though the primary duty of the translator is to reproduce the precise meaning of the original, the mentality of the writer is only half conveyed if the quality and idiosyncrasies of his style, the peculiarities of his vocabulary and so forth are all flattened out under the steam-roller of the translator's own English. And when, as in the present case, five or six contrasting styles are involved, representing five or six quite different types of mind and literary levels, the principle gains in importance.

But it is not only the certainty of at least partial failure that dogs the footsteps of translators who follow this road. All sorts of tiresome problems arise. How far, for example, should patches of really bad Latin, such as occur in two or three of these biographies, be reproduced in really bad English? · Here I have been inclined to fall back, perhaps weakly, on the good old tag that " one must draw the line somewhere " ; and I have been all the more inclined to draw one because the reproduction of such faults would be mainly wasted labour, since they would in most cases quite reasonably be attributed, not to the original, but to the translator, whose own English can make no claim to be impeccable. Nevertheless, here and there I have taken the risk.

Again, I have noticed that most previous translators of these Lives (and not only of these Lives) frequently and silently correct in their translations inconsistencies and illogicalities in the wording of the originals. I am bound to say that I can find even less justification for smoothing out inconsistencies than for smoothing out unevenness in style. It seems to be an unwarranted falsification of the original and, incidentally, results sometimes in an over-confident corrector altering the original when the original was perfectly right.

Speaking of previous translations (of which full particulars are given in the Introductory Notes to the Lives), it is right to say that, although I have often referred to them and, on rare occasions, borrowed a phrase, I have never taken them as a basis for my own version, even for a single clause. It is one consequence of adopting the principles I have described, that it rules out that procedure altogether.

Lastly, I must explain three details in the arrangement of the volume. First, the biographies are printed in the order in which their subjects were born. This order, which has much to recommend it in any case, has in this case the incidental advantage that it is also very nearly the order in which the biographies were written, the only exception being that the Life of St. Augustine, who was born before St. Honoratus, was written a year or two after the Discourse on the Life of the latter. Second, for convenience of reference, the footnotes to the Lives are numbered according to their position in the section, not according to their position on the page. Third, as regards references to Holy Scripture, when the numbering of chapters or verses differs as between the Vulgate (and the Challoner version) and the Hebrew or Greek and the Anglican versions, the figure in the Vulgate is given first and the other figure follows in brackets.

INTRODUCTION

This volume contains translations of short biographies of five makers of Christendom, written by men who knew them. It is an essential part of the plan of this series that these Lives should be allowed as far as possible to " speak for themselves " ; and only in one instance in this volume, and then for very special reasons, has it been thought desirable to make more than the briefest comment on the technique or the value of the biography.

But in order that contemporary biographies written in the fifth century of our era may speak for themselves intelligibly to readers of the twentieth century, the reader must know something of the state of the world and the Church in the fourth and fifth centuries. Otherwise he will not understand the conditions under which the subjects of the biographies lived or the special problems that they had to face. For the writers, naturally enough, alluded to these things and to the great personages of their day without explanation, just as biographers do now. Moreover, almost all their geographical terms need explanation, for few of them are now in use and, if they are in use, they have in most cases acquired a new meaning in the course of time.

The period surveyed is the hundred years from A.D. 350 to A.D. 450, within which the active lives of these five makers of Christendom were lived.[1]

---

[1] It is difficult, in the case of a survey like the present, which makes no pretence to great learning, to indicate very precisely its indebtedness to works of authority. Of the general histories covering the period, volume I of the *Cambridge Medieval History*, vols. III and IV of Fliche and Martin, *Histoire de l'Eglise* and vols. I and II of Hughes' *History of the Church* were kept at hand for consultation or reference as I wrote ; and there are several passages in this survey that are recognizably based on some passage or other in one of those. Of special studies, Mr. Dawson's chapters on St. Augustine and his Age in *A Monument to St. Augustine* were particularly helpful. Where I am aware of specific borrowings of any significance, I have indicated them in a footnote ; but there will probably be many cases of borrowings from past reading of which I am quite unconscious.

I

THE CHURCH

WHEN our period opens, with the young Hilary in the army and the young Ambrose at school, the Church as a body had been exempt from persecution within the Empire for nearly forty years. For the first time since her foundation she had been able to legislate for a period of peace and had done so under imperial auspices at the General Council of Nicaea in A.D. 325. There she emerged from the catacombs with a structure recognizably identical with her structure today and there she took the first steps to devise regulations adapted to life above ground regarded as a normal condition. By the middle of the century the adjustment was reasonably complete and, on the geographical side, included, as was natural, a certain degree of approximation to the administrative divisions of the Empire, especially in the East. (The Church was never confined to the Roman Empire—she flourished greatly in the Persian Empire, for example, in the third century; but the Lives in this volume do not bring us in touch with Catholics beyond the frontiers).

Everywhere the unit of her structure was the bishop's see, which was normally a defined territory centred upon a city. In Egypt and in Roman Africa there were many bishops in villages; and a century or two later, in Ireland and Celtic Britain, bishops were frequently attached to monasteries; but these were exceptions which died out. In Gaul, a land of many towns, where the spread of the Church was very rapid during the second half of the fourth century, there was an almost exact equivalence between towns and bishoprics at the end of it: there were three or four bishops in villages and three or four towns without bishops; the rest of its 115 towns were episcopal sees.[1]

The bishop's office had two distinct aspects, embodied in the two names for him that run side by side throughout these Lives.

[1] See J. R. Palanque in Fliche and Martin, III, 462

On the administrative side he was the *episcopus* or " superintendent " and in the sacramental order he was the *sacerdos* or
" priest ". Around him were grouped his assistants, who likewise
had a dual capacity. Their constitutional and administrative
position in the Church's organization was denoted by the term
presbyter or " elder ", a name coming down from the Synagogue,
by which they were generally known at the beginning of our
period. But they, too, had a share in the priesthood of Christ
and, before the end of the fourth century, the term *sacerdos* is
sometimes applied to them as well as to the bishop, in spite of
the ambiguity involved. A little later it became their usual
designation in Latin, while in the vernacular the word *presbyter*
itself, in such forms as " priest " and *prêtre*, acquired the
essentially sacramental associations that it carries today.

The shift in terminology corresponded to an actual change, not
in sacramental realities, but in the day-to-day administration of
the sacraments in the Church during this period, a change
following naturally upon the conversion of the countryside. At
the beginning of the period, when in most countries there were
few Catholics to be found outside the towns, the bishop was the
sole minister of the great sacraments of initiation—of baptism
and confirmation (which was so closely associated with baptism
as to form with it practically one rite) and also of the Holy
Eucharist.[1] Then, as Christianity became more widely diffused
and many village congregations came into existence, it became
usual (outside Africa) for the priests to become the ordinary
ministers of all the sacraments necessary for the daily Catholic
life of the village. In particular, they had to celebrate the
Eucharistic sacrifice.

It was an inevitable consequence of this development that the
terms *sacerdotium* and *sacerdos*, at first reserved for the fullness of
the priesthood and for *the* priest *par excellence* of the local
Church, were increasingly applied to all whose share of the
priesthood was sufficient to enable them to take the bishop's
place in the central rite of Catholic worship. Before the end of
the fourth century the possible ambiguities of this terminology

[1] See P. Hughes, *A History of the Church*, I, 145.

were clearly resolved by a writer used by St. Jerome, in a passage relating to bishops and presbyters : " Both are priests, but the bishop is first ; so that every bishop is a presbyter but not every presbyter a bishop." [1]   Similarly St. Jerome distinguishes between the bishop and the presbyter as *summus sacerdos* and *sacerdos* respectively ; and his contemporary, Pope St. Innocent I (401-417), speaks of presbyters as " secondary priests." [2]   There is nothing arbitrary, therefore, in the rendering of *presbyter* by its later form " priest " consistently throughout these Lives.

It was a corollary of this necessary clarification that, in the writings from which these quotations are taken, it is made extremely clear that deacons, as compared with either priests or bishops, stand in a wholly different relation to the sacraments. Nevertheless, they constituted during our period, and for long after it, an order of great importance. So far from the diaconate being regarded as merely a step to the priesthood, many deacons were content to remain deacons all their lives. For, besides taking an important part in the Eucharistic rites, they handled, under the bishop, all the business and financial side of the Church's administration and this provided a full and absorbing occupation for those with an aptitude for it, besides giving them an influence with the laity on which St. Jerome makes some caustic comments. These Lives are full of stories of them.

Much the same is true, in its degree, of the minor orders. We read in the Life of St. Ambrose of exorcists who really exorcised and formed a distinct group and, in the Life of St. Martin, of what might happen when the *lector* was late whose turn it was to read the " lessons " at Mass. Similarly the " porters " or " door-keepers " really stood at the church door and saw to it that only qualified persons were present at the Mysteries.

In one aspect the whole of this hierarchy could be regarded as grouped around the great Sacrament of the Mass. (The term *missa* was used as the equivalent of *missio* in formulae for the dismissal of the catechumens, that is to say, intending converts

---

[1] " Uterque enim sacerdos est, sed episcopus primus ; ut omnis episcopus presbyter sit, non tamen omnis presbyter episcopus ", quoted from Ambrosiaster by C. H. Turner in the *Camb. Med. Hist.*, I, 155, 156.
[2] " secundi sacerdotes ", *ibid.*, p. 157.

who were " under instruction ", and was just beginning during our period to replace for everyday purposes the more theological terms such as *oblatio* and *sacramentum* used, as a rule, in these Lives. (It occurs twice, for example, in the last Life, that of St. Germanus, section VII). This rite was the centre of the Church's corporate life and was celebrated never less than weekly and, to an increasing extent, daily. Its outlines were identical with those of the modern Mass in the Western rites, in which the non-essential parts are much abridged. There were the chants, the " collected prayers " of the congregation and the *lectiones* or readings, all more lengthy and varied than now. We read in the Life of St. Ambrose of his introduction from the East of antiphonal or alternate chanting under somewhat unusual circumstances. Then followed the sermon, ordinarily preached by the bishop if he were present, after which the catechumens left. This preliminary section was known as the Mass of the catechumens. In the Mass of the faithful, the congregation made their offerings in kind for the Sacrifice and, after the Consecration, received Communion under both species.

The dismissal of the catechumens was a survival of the secrecy originally preserved concerning many doctrines of the Church, particularly those concerning the Eucharistic Sacrament. It was still very much of a reality during our period. In the fifth century St. Augustine could write that only the baptized Christian could know what was meant in speaking of eating Christ's Body in the Sacrament.[1] The tradition is still traceable in the publicly recited creeds, none of which expresses explicitly the sacramental teaching of the Church, though its acceptance is, of course, implied in the acceptance of the teaching of the Church. Similarly, the Mystery of the Trinity is not set out explicitly in the earliest " symbols ".

All this, however, is perfectly intelligible if it is borne in mind that these first symbols were not " creeds " in the sense that came afterwards to be attached to that word, namely written documents devised for the purpose of providing a standard of reference regarding the teaching of the Church on disputed

[1] *Tractatus in Ioannis Evangelium*, XI, 3 ; the date was probably A.D. 416.

points. They were essentially baptismal formulas, in which the neophyte proclaimed his adhesion to certain fundamental truths that separated him from paganism and, in doing so, accepted the Church as his teacher in whatever more he needed to know of his religion.

Thus baptism was a very great event, not only interiorly, which it has never ceased to be, but in its externals also. Not only was it approached through a long period of oral instruction, given particularly during the Lenten fast, but everything was ordered so as to emphasize its uniqueness as the beginning of what was to be in every sense a new life. It was ordinarily administered at the two greatest Feasts of the Church, Easter and Pentecost. The candidates formed usually a large group set apart, for a spell, even by dress, from the rest of the Christian people. Tremendous stress was laid on the innocence conferred by baptism, including (as it did) the blotting out both of " original sin "—the absence of sanctifying grace shared by all the human race since the Fall—and also of the sins actually committed by the candidate himself. All this has left a deep impress upon all the Lives in this volume.

So vividly, indeed, was it all realized and felt, that it had given rise to a misguided practice, very prevalent during our period, not only among intending converts from paganism but even among those brought up in the Catholic families, and illustrated in every one of these Lives. The reception of baptism was frequently postponed until mature life, or even until death seemed to be approaching. Sometimes the motive was a sincere dread of committing sins after baptism that could not then be forgiven, for the Church had not yet made it clear just what sins could be forgiven after baptism and how often. Sometimes the motive was a low one and indeed gravely sacrilegious, namely to be able to go on sinning for a while longer, secure that all would be forgiven at the font. So much St. Augustine makes very clear in his *Confessions* (I, xi).

Thus baptism, both in the right understanding of it and in the wrong understanding of it, was given prominence in every possible way as the great dividing line between the " Saints "—the souls rescued from the common doom of fallen man and " consecrated "

by the waters of salvation—and those still unredeemed. Nevertheless, the catechumens had also a certain status in the Catholic
community. They formed a recognized grade of which a high
standard was expected and we read more than once in these Lives
of some sort of formal admission to the catechumenate by a laying
on of hands.

Over this ordered community the bishop presided in his dual
capacity of its superintendent and its " chief priest ". Furthermore, his jurisdiction extended far beyond what we should now
regard as ecclesiastical matters, for the members of his flock were
encouraged to bring their disputes before him instead of to the
civil courts. Moreover this judicial work was to an increasing
degree recognized, and even positively encouraged, by the civil
authorities, especially in the West when the civil administration
was beginning to break down. It might even be extended to jurisdiction in disputes outside the congregation. We find St.
Augustine oppressed beneath the burden of judicial work that fell
upon him and St. Germanus besieged by his flock with complaints
of their ill-treatment by the civil authorities and undertaking long
journeys to seek alleviation for them.

The bishops themselves were more and more coming to be
grouped in Provinces corresponding to the civil administrative
Provinces, of which there were about 120 in the Empire. This
principle had been laid down by the Council of Nicaea and had
been applied fairly completely in the East and in Italy by the time
that our period opens. It was not until 398 that the conversion of
Gaul had proceeded far enough to allow of its systematic application there.[1]

The bishops of a Province were bound together in a close unity
under the authority of their " Metropolitan " or chief bishop.
One of the most frequent and important occasions for collective
action by them was in filling vacant sees. They were all summoned
to take part in the choice of the new bishop and also in his consecration. When, as sometimes happened, the people intervened
to choose a bishop by acclamation and insist upon their choice, it
was still necessary (as is particularly well illustrated in the story of

[1] See Fliche and Martin, III, 462, 463.

St. Martin) for the assembled bishops of the Province to give their consent, reluctantly or gladly as the case might be. (This was necessary, also, on those occasions when, after the Empire had become officially Catholic, the bishops virtually stood aside and allowed the Emperor to nominate).

In this connection the reader should be warned that the more or less violent intervention of the people in episcopal elections was by no means as common as might be inferred from its prominence in these five Lives. Doubtless, however, we can reasonably infer from the Lives that it was always recognized to be an ever-present possibility. At the same time, no one ever disputed the fact that no choice, however made, could become effective until the bishop elect had become the *sacerdos* through consecration by a bishop, and Canon Law required the presence of three bishops at a consecration. (At this period the transfer of a bishop from one see to another was forbidden).

The Province was also the unit for the Provincial Synod, or Council of bishops, presided over by the Metropolitan. The Synod acted as a Court of Appeal from the judgements of individual bishops, settled inter-diocesan disputes, and so forth. The Council of Nicaea had laid it down that these Synods should be held twice a year. It should be borne in mind, however, that canons passed in Councils in the East, even ecumenical Councils, often remained for a long time a dead letter in the less highly organized West, sometimes for the simple but sufficient reason that they had not been heard of.

There was a growing tendency during this period for the ecclesiastical Provinces themselves to be grouped (in the interests of ecclesiastical unity) in still larger units, corresponding to the civil Diocese, which might comprise ten or a dozen Provinces. In this system was the germ of the later Patriarchates in the East. In the West during our period the process made little headway except in the cases of the Diocese of Africa (the coastal strip from Tripolitania westward) which was united under Carthage, and of Italy, which was united under Rome. We can infer from the Life of St. Ambrose that during his episcopate the combination of his personality with the use of Milan as the imperial residence in the

West gave Milan a temporary primacy in northern Italy, and beyond the Alps to the Danube.

The jurisdiction of the see of Rome was not limited to its primatial authority in Italy. Without being formally defined, it was in actual fact exercised intermittently, as occasion arose, in widely separated territories far beyond the civil Diocese, and it was exercised as something not requiring justification beyond the appeal to Scripture and tradition. " The Roman pontiffs ", says an accepted authority writing of this period,[1] " exercise outside Italy a regular and traditional authority which at this period takes new forms more precisely defined than in the past."

In so far as these interventions related to matters of discipline, they differed in extent rather than in nature from those of some of the other great primates within their civil Dioceses. There were other pronouncements by the see of Rome, however, that were wholly unique, namely those on questions of doctrine ; and resort was made to it, to obtain such pronouncements, such as was made to no other see. Even heretics condemned as such by the hierarchies of their own countries, such as Priscillian, of whom we hear in the Life of St. Martin, came to Rome to put their case.

There was, indeed, no other see to which such an appeal could be made. Eastern sees, jealous of Rome's ecclesiastical prestige, or individuals with good reason to know that Rome would condemn their theories, might refuse to submit disputes concerning doctrine to Rome, but no see ever offered itself as an alternative. There was, of course, always the possibility of an appeal to a Council but, if Rome would not summon a Council or would not ratify its decisions when it had met, the only way out for those who would not recognize Rome's authority was to appeal to the Emperor.

The possibility of this appeal was the one radically new factor in ecclesiastical procedure since the Peace of Constantine. From Constantine onwards, nearly all the Emperors professed some form of Christianity. Some, like Constantius II (337–361), were heretics or supporters of heretics ; others like Gratian (375–383)

[1] J. R. Palanque, in Fliche and Martin, III, p. 479 : " Les pontifes romains . . . exercent en dehors de l'Italie une authorité régulière et traditionelle qui prend à cette époque des formes nouvelles, plus précises que par le passé ".

and Theodosius I (379-395) were sincere Catholics ; during the reign of Theodosius I the whole Empire became legally Catholic ; but almost every Emperor during our period was at one time or another asked to intervene in doctrinal disputes and proved willing to intervene. The very profession of Christianity, that should logically have caused him to leave their decision to the Church, had in the existing circumstances the opposite effect. Even the Catholic protagonists in the arguments, rashly seeking quick remedies against heresy triumphant, resorted on occasions (ever afterwards regretted) to the Emperor as to a Court of Appeal ; and even Catholic Emperors would respond. As for those who wished to avoid an appeal to Rome, this resort and response became their regular procedure.

The reason is not far to seek. For hundreds of years the Emperor had been at the head of the state's religion and the tradition was far too strong to cease with the cessation of the worship of the Emperor as a god. The language of the Court continued to be reminiscent of a religious cult and a succession of six professedly Christian Emperors in the West retained the old pagan title of *pontifex maximus* or " high priest ". Even after the young Gratian had refused the title, the Emperors continued to exercise without question the prerogative of deciding what the religion of the Empire should be ; and the universal acceptance of their legal absolutism inevitably gave to their decisions a personal rather than what we should call a constitutional character.

From this it was, in the circumstances, a short though a fatal step to claiming to decide what variety of Christianity the legally established Church should teach and to use the material might of the Empire to further the doctrines that appealed to the Emperor rather than those that the Church defined—a practice that, incidentally, favoured theologians accommodating enough to set the Emperor's political preoccupations above theology and skilled in devising ambiguous and comprehensive formulas that would find acceptance among the greatest possible number of his subjects. The see of Rome, then as always, was constantly blamed for being too rigid in its outlook.

In the East, where the power and the legal traditions of the

Empire were more and more coming to be concentrated during
our period, and where there were several great sees eager to find
a means of evading the appeal to Rome, these tendencies were
overwhelmingly strong and had a profound and enduring effect
upon the ultimate status of the Church there ; but that lies outside
the scope of this volume. In the West the most notable episodes
in the relation between Church and State which took place during
our period and are recorded in these Lives were those in which
the Church, in the person of St. Ambrose, successfully asserted
her authority in spiritual matters over the Emperors. But even in
the West the tendencies in question could be dangerous and we
read, not only of imperial support of heretics against Catholics,
but of St. Martin's anguish and St. Augustine's embarrassments
in connection with different forms of imperial action against
heretics and in favour of Catholics. For the distinction that St.
Ambrose and St. Augustine were perhaps the first to draw clearly,
between the State's enforcement of the judgements of the teaching
Church and the State's claim to judge of the teaching of the
Church and enforce its own judgement, had little meaning as yet
to the heirs of the imperial tradition.

II

THE MONASTIC MOVEMENT

EVERY one of the five subjects of these Lives played a part in
furthering the contemporary monastic movement. Three of them
were monastic founders who themselves lived the monastic life,
so far as their circumstances allowed, and the two others founded
or supervised monasteries and convents in their dioceses and
acted as directors of individual ascetics. But, indeed, it would be
hard to find any group of five outstanding figures in the religious
life of that time of whom the same could not be said. Monasticism,
using the term in its wider sense to cover both the solitary and
the conventual life and women as well as men, was as characteristic of the pursuit of Christian perfection in the two hundred

and fifty years after the Peace of Constantine as martyrdom had been in the two hundred and fifty years preceding it, and for much the same reason; it was the form imposed by the circumstances of the time upon the renunciation of all things to follow Christ.

Christ Himself had made it very plain that there was a degree of renunciation not imposed upon all believers but open to those who wished to be in the fullest sense His disciples. It was a renunciation, not only of sin (which every convert renounced at baptism), but of family, position and possessions, things in themselves entirely legitimate and capable of Christian use. We find in these Lives the word *conversio*, which we now apply to the renunciation of error and the entry into the Church, used for this further renunciation.

During the centuries of persecution the two kinds of *conversio* amounted in most cases to very much the same thing. Though active persecution was by no means continuous, nor ubiquitous even when it was active, Christianity was nearly all the time a proscribed religion and anyone who practised it was liable at any time to be betrayed to a magistrate by an informer or to be hounded out of whatever position or employment he held. The Christian's life, even during the lulls in persecution, was in most places a continuous exercise in the renunciation of most of the good things the world had to give and, chief among them, security; and uncounted thousands were confronted with, and accepted, the demand to renounce also their lives.

With the Peace of Constantine came wholly different conditions. For the greater part of our period, so far from conversion to the faith involving abandonment of prosperity in this world, it might become a passport to promotion in it. Then it was that the renunciation of the world, instead of being involved almost automatically in the profession of the faith, had to be actively pursued by means specially devised to facilitate it; and the devising and utilising of these means became the chief preoccupation of the more fervent Christians during the fourth and fifth centuries and is one of the chief themes of these biographies.

The ascetic movement had had, of course, its pioneers even in the centuries of persecution and, indeed, can trace a continuous descent from the first generations of Christians and the teaching of the Apostles. The methods of these pioneers require some notice here because they survived into our period and many of the new developments in the religious life were built upon them.

First among the renunciations was always voluntary and consecrated celibacy or virginity, with which must be grouped the voluntary and consecrated perpetuation of widowhood of which St. Paul speaks. It was a free and deliberate renunciation, not only of the evil of fornication, but of the good of marriage, made for the purpose of following Christ more singlemindedly. And apart from its place in the spiritual development of those who practised it, it provided the appallingly sensual pagan world with a standing testimony to the power of the spirit to overcome the flesh.

In the first centuries, these *continentes*, as they were called, usually lived in their parents' households ; and they did so in many cases until well into our period, as these Lives show us. The Church, however, when in the person of the bishop she gave her blessing to the entry of a Christian upon such a life, endeavoured to regulate it to some extent by imposing, upon those she consecrated to it, certain restrictions on their way of living, their diet, their clothing and so forth. She also combated by her admonitions the temptations to self-righteousness to which a life lived on this austere level in the midst of ordinary Christians inevitably gave rise.

Sooner or later institutions were bound to come into existence to meet the special needs of this kind of life. There are traditions of communities going back to Apostolic times. It is certain that towards the end of the third century there were to be found houses, especially in Egypt, where consecrated virgins could live together. It was in the same period that the eremitical or hermit life began among men dedicated to religious celibacy who sought greater solitude than could be found in their family circle and went farther and farther away from the towns to obtain it. The great pioneer St. Antony (whose life covered approximately the hundred years before our period begins) began to draw to himself many imitators and disciples.

All these beginnings had been made before the Peace of Constantine ; but the beginnings of monasticism as a recognized institution for men coincided with considerable precision with the cessation of the last great Roman persecution in A.D. 311. The movement was indeed a flight from the world, but from its spiritual, not from its physical dangers.

Egypt, and then Palestine and Syria, were the scenes of these first developments ; and the first decade of the movement, the years from 305 to 315, saw, in Egypt, the divergence of the two main types of monasticism, though neither of them at this stage took precisely the form in which it was destined to be perpetuated. The first type is known after St. Antony as the Antonian type, the colony of hermits. Its members were drawn together by a common desire to benefit by the teaching of some spiritual master, but each pursued his own way of life in his own hut or shelter, bound by no vow of obedience, setting himself his own standard of asceticism, and joining with the other hermits only in the weekly celebration of the Eucharistic rites. The second type was the Pachomian, named after the Egyptian St. Pakhom (Latinized as Pachomius). It was coenobitic or conventual, that is to say, it was an institution for the common life.

The first Pachomian monasteries were practically villages or small towns, with hundreds or even thousands of monks distributed among a number of houses having each its own meal-times and daily programme of work, though the whole community met in the church for liturgical worship several times a day. These colonies were hives of activity. Their occupations included the reading and memorizing of Scripture as well as handicrafts of all kinds, carried on for the support of the community but also as an essential factor in the religious life. All was under the absolute rule of the Abbot and obedience was held to be the first of the monastic virtues.

At the same time there continued to be hermits, or anchorites as they were sometimes called, who sought to live in remote spots completely separated from their fellows. Their importance in the picture was out of all proportion to their numbers, because it was at first taken for granted that the completely solitary existence was the highest form of all forms of the religious life.

Nevertheless it was not long before there were signs of a healthy tendency to bring even the eremitical life under spiritual direction and also to discourage its adoption by untried beginners. Both the Pachomian and the Antonian monasteries, working as it were from opposite ends, made their contribution to this process. It became an accepted practice in the former for the Abbot to permit those whom he deemed ripe for it to make themselves hermitages outside the monastery, where they lived alone but still under his authority. About the same time in Palestine and Syria, where the individualistic hermit life was beginning to manifest the oriental extravagances that long continued to characterize it there, Antonian monasticism underwent a deeply significant modification. The monks, though they continued to inhabit separate huts or cells scattered over a considerable area, lived their lives in the manner prescribed for each by the Abbot. In this way there came into existence the form that still persists in the East under the name of the *laura* or " enclosure ".

Then, about the year 360, a very important development of coenobitic monasticism took place in Cappadocia, in the heart of Asia Minor. It was the work of St. Basil the Great, who had studied monasticism in Syria and Egypt. He modified the Pachomian pattern, partly by greatly reducing the size of the community and bringing it together under one roof, and still more by insisting on the spiritual value of community life as such. He even went so far as to put forward what was then the revolutionary idea that the coenobitic life was actually superior to the eremitical. Almost as revolutionary and equally salutary was his discouragement of that spirit of emulation in asceticism which was the bane of Egyptian monachism.

With these various forms of monasticism in mind, it will be easier to follow the successive stages of its introduction into the West, in which nearly all of our five Western Fathers played leading parts.

The first propagandist of monasticism in the West appears to have been St. Athanasius, Bishop of Alexandria and Primate of Egypt from 328 to 373.[1]. Soon after his election as bishop, when

[1] The year 328 is the one accepted by Bardy in Fliche and Martin, III, 101. The remaining dates in this paragraph are taken from the table in de Labriolle's chapter on the beginnings of monasticism in the same volume (pp. 322 sqq.).

still a comparatively young man, he had paid his first visit to the great monastic centres of Upper (that is to say, southern) Egypt ; and it was soon after this that he suffered his first exile for his championship of Catholic orthodoxy against Arianism. This brought him to Trier (Trèves) in northern Gaul in November, 335. In 341 he was banished again and this time he resided for a while in Rome. On each occasion he spread the new ideas ; and sixteen years later, in the year following St. Antony's death, he wrote (in Greek) the great monk's life, the first biography of its kind, which was almost immediately translated into Latin and made a great sensation.

These enforced visits of St. Athanasius to the West undoubtedly gave a great impulse to the ascetic movement there and were directly responsible for what was probably the first Western experiment in the religious life in community, made by Eusebius, Bishop of Vercelli (not far from Milan), with his clergy, about 345. Little, however, is known of the progress of monasticism in Italy in the generation immediately following this. A tract written in Italy about the year 360[1] distinguishes various grades of ascetics living the celibate life but makes no mention of communities of them. But St. Ambrose, on becoming Bishop of Milan (in 373 or 374), did much, both directly and through his sister, to promote religious communities for both men and women.

Meanwhile, a great pioneer had appeared in Gaul. St. Hilary of Poitiers had been among those exiled by Constantius for his resistance to Arianism. His place of exile had been Phrygia, in Asia Minor, where he had been forced to live from early in 356 until late in 359. Those were the years when St. Basil was studying monasticism in the countries of its origin but they were also the years when monastic ideals were being propagated in Asia Minor in a somewhat extravagantly ascetic form by an Armenian named Eustathius of Sebaste ; and the topic was being discussed everywhere in the East.

He returned to Gaul in A.D. 360 and was at once supplied with an instrument for putting into execution what he had learnt in Asia. This instrument was his young disciple Martin, who during

[1] *Consultationes Zacchaei et Apollonii* ; see de Labriolle, loc. cit., p. 349.

his exile had been experimenting in the eremitical life in Italy
but rejoined him in Poitiers immediately upon his return. There,
under Hilary's direction, Martin established his first monastic
community. He founded a second community two miles outside
Tours when he became bishop of that city. The plan of it seems
to have been that of the *laura*, to judge by the description given
of it by Martin's biographer, who saw it first two or three years
before Martin's death in 397.

By that time there were great numbers of convents both for
men and for women in Gaul, many of them founded by men
who had been taken from St. Martin's monastery to become
bishops elsewhere. We read, in what is apparently the account
of an eye-witness, of two thousand monks and many nuns
attending Martin's funeral at Tours. Celibates living alone, both
men and women, also abounded; but their lives, lived too often
under no adequate supervision, aroused much criticism.

By this time St. Jerome was a great figure in the ascetic and
monastic movement in the West, as a spiritual director of consecrated virgins, a caustic critic of those who obeyed no direction,
and the superior of a monastery of his own at Bethlehem, from
which a continuous stream of letters and pamphlets in Latin
flowed westward. He had begun his career as an ascetic by
experimenting with the eremitical life in Syria; then at the
bidding of Pope Damasus he had resided in Rome from 382 to
385. There he had become the spiritual director of a group of
wealthy Roman ladies who were living a semi-conventual life on
the Aventine. Many of them had followed him to Palestine and
it was to one of them that he addressed the letter or tract on the
life of consecrated virgins that figures in the *Dialogues* of
Sulpicius Severus.

St. Augustine was another pioneer whose course was in some
degree (in his case, in a pre-eminent degree) shaped by a stay in
Italy. He was at Milan from 384 to 387. He tells us in his
Confessions (VIII, vi) of the impression made upon him when
he was told of the lives of the hermits, and of Ambrose's
monastery outside the walls of Milan—it all came as news to
him. When he returned to Africa shortly after his baptism he at

once formed a religious community for himself and his friends ; but his permanent work as a founder followed, rather, the model of Eusebius of Vercelli, in that it provided community life under a Rule for his cathedral clergy, after he became Bishop of Hippo in 396. This community, like Martin's, became a nursery for bishops, who spread the institution all over North Africa.

This was the decade when the " literary millionaire "[1] afterwards known as St. Paulinus of Nola retired from his great estates in Aquitaine and Spain to a semi-monastic life near Naples ; and his friend and fellow Aquitanian Sulpicius Severus, the biographer of St. Martin, retired to a similar seclusion at the same time. But these men were, in a sense, amateurs in the movement. The next great Western founder, whose retirement from the world must closely have followed theirs, was, like St. Martin, still a young man when he made his renunciation and he devoted all his powers to his vocation. This was St. Honoratus, born on a great estate in northern Gaul, whose Life is in this volume. The monastery that he founded at Lérins (an island off Cannes) in the first years of the fifth century became, not only another great nursery of bishops, but perhaps the greatest centre of Catholic thought and spirituality in fifth-century Gaul.

It seems to have been, during the lifetime of Honoratus, a closely knit community of monks living under the Abbot's personal and paternal supervision. (It is of some interest to note that St. Patrick was in all probability trained under this regime after his escape from slavery, and St. Vincent of Lérins after leaving the army). No Rule, however, survives that can be traced back to the founder and, though there is a suggestion of the Basilian community in the description of the Lérins of Honoratus, and again in the Rule inspired by Lérins, written towards the end of the fifth century by St. Caesarius of Arles,[2] there are no tangible grounds for surmising that a knowledge of Basilian monasticism had reached him, even though in his early travels he had made a forced sojourn on the coast of Greece. So far as is known, St. Basil's far-reaching innovations were first introduced into the

---

[1] Dudden's description of him.
[2] Note the insistence on life under a single roof (rule 3).

West by St. Benedict of Nursia, who blended them with his own psychological insight, his sense of what was practicable and his Roman sense of law to form an essentially new and essentially stable type of monasticism that eventually proved to be what the West was waiting for.

All that, however, was long after our period and meanwhile the stamp of Egypt was upon all Western monasticism, both in Italy and Gaul and in Ireland, where it took root during the life-time of St. Patrick. An essentially Egyptian spirituality, seen at its best, is presented in the famous treatises of John Cassian, who, after spending many years in Egypt, founded a monastery at Marseilles at much the same time as Honoratus was establishing his own monastery on the same coast ; and nowhere is the mark of Egypt more conspicuous than in the first *Dialogue* of Sulpicius Severus, which had quite phenomenal success in popularizing monastic ideas among Western readers.

III

The Cultus and Lives of the Saints

Throughout our period and for very many centuries afterwards the Bible held the first place in the devotional reading of the faithful. The writers of these Lives quoted Scripture with the utmost freedom and familiarity ; and the references given in the footnotes to the translations only partially indicate the extent to which the diction of most of the originals is saturated with biblical phraseology.

At the beginning of our period, the Acts or Deeds of the Martyrs provided almost the only supplementary devotional reading. But the interest in these writings was associated with an intense and growing devotion to the actual bodily relics of the martyrs, which ordinarily consisted of their bones. The memory of the martyrs and their fearful sufferings was still fresh and vivid in the Church's consciousness and all Christians regarded with deep veneration these fragments of their broken bodies in which the Holy Spirit had dwelt, inspiring and sustaining them in their agonies.[1]

There existed, moreover, a lively conviction that the divine power that had manifested itself, while the martyrs were alive, in feats of supernatural heroism and endurance, would continue to manifest itself in actions of supernatural potency through the relics of the bodies that had thus endured, or even through objects that had been in the possession of the martyrs or had come into contact with the relics. There are frequent allusions in these Lives to such beliefs, and to the eagerness with which the discovery of relics was hailed and the relics were transported to a fitting resting-place.

But it was just at the beginning of our period that the veneration of Christians for the heroes of the faith found a new object. It was the period, it will be remembered, when the quest for Christian perfection was finding new channels, now that the call to die for the faith was no longer a possibility ever-present to the mind. It was natural enough, therefore, that, without relinquishing the cultus of the martyrs, Christian hero-worship should find new objects in those who renounced the world to carry on the Christian's warfare in the desert against the powers of darkness. In due course their exploits came to be recounted and read with the same avidity as those of the martyrs had been.

Very significant also was the fact that, as in the case of the cultus of the martyrs, so in this new devotion, an intensely vivid realization of the action of the Holy Spirit, in the Christian hero, to animate and sustain him in the combat against human or diabolical enemies of the soul, created an expectation that in the course of the combat the same divine power would manifest itself in visible dominion over irrational nature. It was universally believed that the same potency that nerved the martyr to endure while in the body the scourge and the rack, operated through his body, when his spirit was in glory, to heal the diseases of those whom his body touched. Who, then, would deny that one and the same Spirit sometimes enabled the hermit to endure tremendous fasts or put the demons to flight and sometimes caused bread

[1] See de Labriolle's chapter on " Morale et Spiritualité " in Fliche and Martin, III, p. 375.

for his meal to appear without human agency or constrained the beasts to do him service? The martyr or ascetic whose heroism was such that he drew upon that divine power in the one field might draw upon it in the other. No boundary line could exist for the Spirit of God; there could be none for His servants, and none in the mind of the devotee.

One word was in fact used where our modern world needs two. The Latin word *virtutes* (the equivalent of the Greek *dynameis*) is used throughout these Lives, sometimes in the sense of moral virtues, sometimes in the sense of miracles or miraculous powers. In one of the *Dialogues* of Sulpicius Severus (I, 17) we read that in the monasteries of Egypt the primary *virtus* is obedience;[1] a few pages further on (I, 21), *virtutis signa* means " manifestations of miraculous power ". Sometimes the translator, thinking in terms of these alternatives, is left uncertain as to which meaning is intended. Clearly he is guilty of an anachronism in thinking in terms of alternatives so sharply contrasted. Frequently it has seemed best to have recourse to the ambiguous term " spiritual powers."

But much more is involved than a technical problem for the twentieth-century translator. It is not easy to exaggerate the psychological importance of these linguistic facts. On the one hand, there is no doubt that the use of the same word to cover spiritual power manifested in physical miracles and spiritual power manifested in heroic virtue was rooted in the same sound conviction that inspired St. Paul to write to the Corinthians (I Cor. xii, 4–11) that one and the same Spirit was operating in all the ministrations of the Church—wise preaching, sacred science, faith, the gift of healing, the working of miracles[2] and so forth. On the other hand, the usage, when embodied in popular hagiography, was capable of creating a demand for stories of physical miracles which, even if it could be satisfied without sacrificing the truth, almost inevitably involved the sacrifice of the rightful emphasis on character and the moral virtues in the portraiture of the saint.

[1] " virtus prima est oboedientia ".
[2] The word here is in the Greek *dynameis* and in the Latin *virtutes*.

There is, indeed, an exceedingly interesting passage in one of the Lives in this volume[1] in which the author, a very holy bishop, makes what is in part an apology for disappointing these expectations and in part a remonstrance with the point of view that they imply (and displays, incidentally, great dexterity in picking his way between the terminological pitfalls of his theme). Nor was he alone, in our period, in trying to allay the expectations in question. In the East, two Doctors of the Church, St. Gregory Nazianzen (who died in 390) and St. John Chrysostom (who died in 407) wrote on this topic, the former to explain that miracles of feeding, as contrasted with human organisation of relief, were for the benefit of unbelievers rather than of believers ; and the latter to say that miracles were no longer needed for the conversion of the pagans now that the Church was no longer in her cradle.[2] In the West St. Augustine argued in his *Retractations* (1, 12, 9) that, if physical miracles were allowed to continue, men's minds would continue to be fixed on things visible and grow cold from their repetition.

Nevertheless, Augustine himself wrote in his *Confessions* and elsewhere of the miracles worked through relics that he witnessed at Milan ; and there were many to take the view that miracles were still to be expected, for " the hand of the Lord is not shortened ". Sulpicius, indeed, with notable lack of logic, carried this point of view to the length of arguing that anyone who refused to believe his stories of St. Martin's miracles was thereby casting doubt on the Gospel story, since Christ promised that miracles should be worked by all believers.[3]

Both points of view are represented in the Lives in this volume. I am not suggesting, of course, that any of the writers doubted the possibility of miracles occurring in their time or denied that their heroes had worked any. What is in question is the varying extent to which the biographers severally encouraged the expectation of physical miracles and made a special effort to meet it—but the reader will discover all this for himself.

---

[1] The *Discourse* of St. Hilary of Arles on St. Honoratus, § 37 ; see the footnote there.
[2] See Delehaye, S. J. in *Analecta Bollandiana*, t. 38 (1920), p. 75, where the references are given.
[3] *Dialogues*, I, XXVI.

It will probably be helpful to conclude with a word on the literary antecedents of these Lives[1]. Mention was made, in connection with the spread of monasticism in the West, of the publication in A.D. 357 of the *Life of St. Antony* by St. Athanasius.[2] The life had an even greater place in the Christian literature of the period, for it created a new *genre* and largely determined the lines of its development. It was the first work to meet the new demand for stories of the heroes of asceticism to set beside the Acts of the Martyrs. It had much to say of encounters with demons in the desert and also of the way in which Antony attained to likeness to God through divine illuminations.

Though it made an immense impression, it had the field to itself for a generation, except for a Life of St. Paul, the first hermit, written by St. Jerome in the seventies of the century. (A Life of St. Pachomius in Greek was probably written soon after the Life of St. Antony but does not seem to have got into general circulation at that time). Then suddenly, with the closing years of the fourth century and the first years of the fifth, came something like a rush of writings concerning the monks and hermits. In the early nineties St. Jerome published a Life of the Palestinian monk Hilarion. There followed the Life of St. Martin that is in this volume, written in Gaul very shortly before Martin's death in November, 397; and within the next three or four years Sulpicius followed it up by his so-called Letters on St. Martin and his two Dialogues, the first of which purports to be in part an account of a journey among the monks of Egypt.

There is some doubt as to whether it was written before or after the publication of another work that also takes the form of a travel document and tells stories of the Egyptian monks. This was *The Story of the Monks of Egypt*, written originally in Greek. The journey is supposed to have taken place in the years 394 and 395. The recital contains much the same medley of heroic pieties, stupendous austerities and physical miracles as the work of Sulpicius. In addition, there are stories of strange beasts and

---

[1] Here I follow in the main de Labriolle in Fliche and Martin, III, 306–320.
[2] The date is disputed; some make it a few years later. I am following the table of dates in Fliche and Martin, III, 322 sqq.

demonic manifestations in comparison with which the narrative in Sulpicius is timid and restrained.

It has been suggested that the book was written as a romance, and it may well have been. After all, there is nothing wrong in writing a novel. It was only a few years earlier that St. Jerome had written a short novel about a hermit who went back to the world.[1] Indeed, I do not see why it should be considered an outrage to suggest that the first part of the First Dialogue of Sulpicius has something of that blend of fact and fiction that we find and approve of in an historical novel. But it can hardly have been imitated from the Greek work, for the latter was almost certainly not translated into Latin until after the Dialogues were written.

The so-called *Lausiac History* by Bishop Palladius of Bithynia is definitely a recital of facts concerning the monks of Egypt, written in the firm belief that, in the supernaturalized atmosphere of that land of " God's friends," miracles abounded. It was published about the year 420. (That was probably the year of the publication of the first of Cassian's books on Egyptian monasticism, but in them the biographical and descriptive element is almost wholly subordinated to the exposition of the spiritual doctrine of the " Fathers of the Desert ".)

By this time, however, the Egyptian tradition in hagiography had no need in the West of further reinforcement from Egypt, for it had taken firm hold in the immense vogue of the Martinian writings of Sulpicius Severus, which continued to be widely read for more than a thousand years. Certain special problems which they present are discussed in the Introductory Note to the Life of St. Martin.

As for the remaining Lives in the volume, they show the influence of the Sulpician model in very varying degrees. They really constitute, for all their differences, the beginning of a separate and distinctively Western biographical tradition, with its Western types of holiness and its Western approach to them. But, if their setting has been indicated, the editor's task is done, for they are in this volume to be read.

[1] *Vita Malchi.*

THE LIFE OF ST. MARTIN OF TOURS

BY SULPICIUS SEVERUS

SULPICIUS SEVERUS (sometimes erroneously called Saint Sulpicius by confusion with Saint Sulpicius of Bourges, who died in 591) was born about A.D. 363 of a noble family in Aquitaine (south-western Gaul). He received a good education, made a happy marriage and achieved a great reputation at the bar. When he was approaching thirty, his wife died and he soon afterwards retired from the world, about the same time as his friend and compatriot, St. Paulinus of Nola. Henceforward he lived a life of semi-seclusion under the direction of St. Martin, whom he visited several times in his monastery. He seems at some period to have been ordained priest. Shortly after Martin's death (almost certainly in November, 397) he was living at Primuliacum, generally supposed to be a village between Toulouse and Narbonne, in a house belonging to his mother-in-law Bassula to whom one of his so-called "letters" on St. Martin is addressed. He is thought to have died about A.D. 420. He was attacked by St. Jerome for Millenarianism and there is a story of his having been led astray by Pelagianism in his old age and doing penance for this, and for his proneness to loquacity, by keeping silence for the rest of his life. It seems unlikely that he was ever a wilful heretic but his writings show that he was temperamentally prone to unbalanced views.

His career as a writer is closely bound up with St. Martin, for whom he had the deepest veneration. He wrote and completed his Life of him before the saint's death. He wrote the Letters and Dialogues relating to St. Martin during the years immediately following it. During the same period he wrote a history of the Church (generally known as the *Chronicles*) from the Creation to A.D. 400. By these writings he won a great and well-deserved literary reputation in his own life-time, and they were still popular at the time of the Renaissance. They played a great part in promoting the devotion to St. Martin all over France and contributed not a little to the popularization of monasticism also. They are the ultimate source of all Lives of the saint.

Their effectiveness was due in part to the extraordinary story they tell and in part to their own vividness and admirable style, described by Gibbon, a fastidious critic and no friend of hagiographers, as " a style not unworthy of the Augustan age ". His chief writings have, moreover, impressed most of his editors and translators—even some entirely hostile to their religious standpoint—with the sincerity of Sulpicius as a writer and particularly as a biographer. But it is precisely this appearance of sincerity, taken in conjunction with his other qualifications as a biographer—his intimacy with his subject, his legal training and his literary skill—that creates what many have felt to be the riddle of this biography. No biographer of his period was better qualified to write a truthful life of a contemporary saint and no biographer of his period—we may almost say, of any period—has written a Life more full of astounding prodigies. A Protestant translator (the reference is given below) has stated the problem fairly and forcefully from the point of view of one to whom the truth of the miraculous element is barely admissible :

> The writer so frequently and solemnly assures us of his good faith, and there is such a verisimilitude about the style, that it appears impossible to accept the theory of wilful deception on the part of the writer. And then, he was so intimately acquainted with the subject of his narrative, that he could hardly have accepted fictions for facts, or failed in his estimate of the friend he so much admired and loved. Altogether, this *Life of St. Martin* seems to bring before us one of the puzzles of history.

It has, however, been suggested that the very fact that Sulpicius possessed considerably literary skill makes it possible to suppose what would be absurd in the case of most of the writers in this volume, namely that the whole story is an artificial literary concoction, largely a patchwork of extracts from the Lives of other saints, having a very meagre historical foundation in a comparatively insignificant and ineffective historical Martin. An attack on these lines was published in France in 1912 (*St. Martin de Tours* by E. Ch. Babut). But, brilliant though it was and effective up to a certain point, it was marred by many extravagances on Babut's part. These were dealt with faithfully in a classical essay on the subject in the *Analecta Bollandiana* (vol. 38, for the year 1920), by H. Delehaye, S.J., who admitted, however, that Sulpicius had a strong tendency to exaggerate as well as a good deal of malice towards the contemporary clergy.

Even to summarize the arguments of the two protagonists would take up altogether disproportionate space here. (There are some excellent pages on the topic in P. de Labriolle's *Histoire de la Littérature Latine Chrétienne*, 1920, of which there is an English translation by H. Wilson, 1924). Moreover, it is in general the intention of this series to leave the contemporary biographies as far as possible to speak for themselves.

Nevertheless the case of Sulpicius is exceptional and may reasonably be held to require exceptional treatment. Moreover, a translator, if he tries to reproduce something of the manner and literary effect of the original, has a better opportunity than most of forming an opinion as to what rings true and what does not ring true after the necessary allowance has been made for the requirements of an artificial literary form. I have therefore set down, for what it may be worth, the impression that was left on my mind after I had completed the translation of all the Sulpician writings on St. Martin and (for comparison) all the other biographies in this volume (for Sulpicius is not the only one of our biographers to use an artificial literary form). In doing this, I have kept in mind all the time the fact that what we really want to know about the matter is, not what sort of man and writer Sulpicius was, but how far we can form a true picture of Martin through his writings. For the sake of brevity I will omit the " perhaps's " and " probably's ".

First, then, Sulpicius did not, as Babut suggests, " create " St. Martin, though he certainly exploited him. There was an immense popular devotion to St. Martin before Sulpicius had published a line about him, and this was founded in part on his simple holiness and in part on an almost universal belief in his powers as a miracle-worker. Sulpicius found all this in existence when he first made the acquaintance of the saint in his monastery a few years before Martin's death. He found also in Martin himself a personality that completely captivated him, and moved him to become a disciple of Martin to the extent of renouncing his more secular activities.

It was in this first phase that he composed the first and most important of his Martinian writings, namely the Life. The nucleus of this was based on authentic traditions of the monastery and the countryside, interpreted in the light of the personal impression that Martin had made on Sulpicius. He put into the telling of the story considerable literary skill—some of the anecdotes are told with quite remarkable vividness—but that is by no means the same thing as saying that it is told insincerely. Frequently he introduces touches, such as the effect of the fluttering of the white cloths at the pagan funeral and the simile of the top in describing the fall of the sacred tree, that can only have come from an eye-witness. Here and there he seems to have an uneasy conscience, marked by overmuch protesting that he is telling the truth; but that is not the case with the Life taken as a whole.

When all reservations have been made, there can be perceived through the narrative in the Life, sometimes dimly but at moments quite clearly, a great child of God moving serenely through his many tasks with his thoughts all the time on heaven and possessed of that utter simplicity of faith that can almost be said to force God to work miracles. The impression given by the narrative is borne out by some of the phrases in the concluding word-picture of the saint in his old age. The simile of the blacksmith relaxing by letting an occasional blow fall on the anvil, used to illustrate the continuity of Martin's life of prayer, could never have occurred to Sulpicius unless he had been drawing from life, for we must remember that he had no tradition of saint-portraiture behind him such as a modern writer would have, and nothing in his writings leads us to suppose that he had deep experience of contemplative prayer himself.

It is true that we get an impression that it was not altogether without reason that Martin was unpopular with his fellow bishops, before as well as after his breach with them over the affair of Priscillian. A somewhat uncouth figure, ill-educated, not always on happy terms even with his own clergy and always too much either the monk or the apostle of the countryside to take kindly to the administrative work of his diocese or to collaboration in the Provincial synod—such a character must have been exasperating to many of his colleagues, and all the more because he was universally reputed among the common people to be a saint on the Apostolic level. To this extent Babut had the truth on his side ; but it is hardly fair to accuse Sulpicius of having distorted the truth here, seeing that this is the picture that shows through his Martinian writings.

It is probably also true that there was in Martin a streak of peasant superstition. The more fantastic details in the stories of demons are probably to be attributed to the biographer's incessant striving after dramatic effect but, even allowing for this, it seems likely that Martin himself was fanciful in this regard and possibly also in one or two of his theological speculations. But as a preacher of the God-man Christ Jesus to the simple he can have had few equals, for faith and power, in the Church's history. Furthermore, seeing that the popular acclamation of him as a miracle-worker certainly preceded the literary reputation given him by Sulpicius and that such acclamation is by no means given indiscriminately to everyone who is popularly deemed holy, we may well deem it possible that God, who at long intervals in the history of His Church has, for special purposes of His own, raised up a pre-eminent wonder-worker, did this in St. Martin of Tours who would thus stand near the head of the series that includes St. Bernard of Clairvaux and St. Vincent Ferrer. If, further, we care to speculate on God's purpose in this particular case, it would not be difficult to connect the spread of the faith through Martin's miracles with the part that Gaul, which when he began his career was mainly pagan, was presently to play under the Franks as the corner-stone of Catholic Christendom during its formative period.

So much can be read, partly in the pages of the Life, and partly *through* them. All the greater was the shock to me when I came to translate the Letters and certain passages in the Dialogues. I had to keep reminding myself that artificiality does not necessarily mean insincerity; that the Letter which is no letter is perhaps the most difficult of all literary forms and one which writers of a much less decadent literary generation than that of Sulpicius have failed to use naturally; and, again, that the literary devices of the dialogue-form are perfectly legitimate, provided that they are accepted as literary devices and nothing more—and, to do poor Sulpicius justice, he is honest enough about that before the end!

By constantly reminding myself of these things, I enabled myself in the end to view the contents of these documents reasonably dispassionately. Even so, I was left with certain very painful impressions. First, the great success of the Life seemed to have turned the author's head and to have brought out in him in full measure the literary vanity latent in all of us who write for publication. It had converted him, moreover, into a literary log-roller of the most blatant type. That in itself, however, would have mattered little to anyone besides himself. What really mattered was that, in setting out to exploit his success (as any author would do), he committed the grave offence of exploiting Martin. He was like a novelist who has made a hit with a hero and exploits the character by writing a long series of further novels about him—with the enormous difference, in the case of Sulpicius, that his hero was not, originally at any rate, a character in fiction.

Not that I would say for a moment that *all* the stories about Martin in the Letters and the Dialogues are fictitious; but it seems to me very clear that in these later writings Sulpicius scraped together, by hook or by crook, any current story about Martin that could be made to suit his purpose and raised all of them to a monotonously high pitch of marvellousness in order to maintain at all costs the level that he had achieved, for the most part quite naturally, through the greater part of the Life.

Unfortunately, owing to the not very exacting literary standards of his age, he achieved a second success. I say " unfortunately " because the result was to create for St. Martin a second and very vulnerable reputation by superimposing upon popular devotion a literary vogue. Worse still, Sulpicius fixed for centuries a hagiographical tradition that rates the anecdotes of wonder-working above spiritual portraiture, to the great detriment of our understanding of both the natural psychology and the supernatural spirituality of the saints. Not that we can see nothing of St. Martin in the writings in question—here and there we get delightful glimpses of a real person and occasionally, surely, of a real wonder-worker; but all the time we have to be making allowances for literary requirements and poses, which is not restful.

But I will not intrude further between Sulpicius and his modern reader except to say that the strongest confirmation of my impression of the artificiality of much of these later writings comes when we suddenly run into a sober and convincing piece of historical writing such as might have come straight out of his *Chronicles*. The style unconsciously changes, becomes prosaic and workmanlike, with the minimum of straining after literary effect. The writer's historical training has reasserted itself and he has forgotten for the moment that he has a certain literary reputation to keep up.

To turn to less controversial matters, the literary merits of the writings of Sulpicius on St. Martin and the popularity of their subject have attracted a number of translators in various languages. I have unearthed three versions in English, ranging in date from 1844 to 1928 ; and there may be others.

The earliest of these is printed in the first volume (1844, pages 632–669) of an American theological monthly of the day entitled *Bibliotheca Sacra and Theological Review*. It covers only the Life and the Letters. It formed part of a series entitled "The Early History of Monasticism from the Original Sources ". As a rendering into a now rather old-fashioned English it is not without its merits, especially in the earlier sections, but it suffers from a certain lack of sympathy with its subject, as was only to be expected in view of the avowed purpose of the series which was " to warn the whole church . . . of the fatal rocks [of monkery] on which the early church was dashed " (p. 669). And the mention of " merits " evoked from the translator the following comment : " This was the death in the pottage which had now been two centuries in the seething ; and by partaking whereof, the maddened church had been cast into her delirious ravings for holy pilgrimages and the ascetic life " (p. 331). The translator, indeed, shows considerable self-restraint in keeping these lively emotions mainly to the footnotes.

The second translation is by the Rev. Alexander Roberts, D.D., of St. Andrew's University and was published in vol. XI of the *Select Library of Nicene and Post-Nicene Fathers*, 1894. It comprises all the works of Sulpicius Severus. As a translation it is frequently ponderous but gets more into the spirit of the original in the Dialogues where I have been glad upon occasion to borrow a happily turned phrase.

Finally, there is a frequently lively translation of all the Martinian writings of Sulpicius by Mary Caroline Watt (Sands and Co., 1928). Unfortunately it is made, not from the Latin, but from a French version ; and, as the French tradition of translation is to sit somewhat loosely to the original, by the time the English is reached the connection with the Latin is somewhat irregular. The French translator is

Paul Monceaux and his Introduction, which is also translated, is of considerable value.

The present translation, which is quite independent of the foregoing except for a very occasional phrase, has been made from the text of Karl Halm printed in vol. I of the *Corpus Scriptorum Ecclesiasticorum Latinorum* (the " Vienna Corpus "). This was published as long ago as 1866 but, though defective in many respects, appears not to have been superseded. The very rare departures from it are noted and explained where they occur.

THE LIFE OF ST. MARTIN, BISHOP OF TOURS
BY SULPICIUS SEVERUS

DEDICATION

SEVERUS TO HIS MOST DEAR BROTHER DESIDERIUS

YES, brother and second self, I have written a little book on the life of our holy Martin, but I had decided to keep it uncopied and within the walls of my house. For I am the weakest of creatures and was loath to submit it to the world's judgement, for fear that an all too unpolished diction should prove displeasing to the reader (as indeed I think it will) and that I should be deemed the proper object of general reprobation for having had the effrontery to annex a subject that should have been reserved for writers of competence. But when it is you who ask, and ask so often, I cannot say no. For what could I refuse to your affection, whatever the injury to my self-respect? Besides, I have let the book go to you with some confidence because I cannot think that you will betray it to anyone else, since that is what you have promised.

Nevertheless I have a fear that you may prove to be a gateway for it and that, if it once passes through, it can never be recalled. If that should happen, and you see it being read by others, will you, in your kindly indulgence, ask the readers to attend to the matter rather than to the language and not to take it too much to heart if a faulty locution should impinge upon their ears ; for the Kingdom of God comes not by eloquence but rests upon faith. Let them remember also that salvation was not preached to the world by orators (though Our Lord could assuredly have arranged for that too, if it would have served His purpose), but by simple fishermen.

For my part, indeed, from the day that I set myself to write (thinking it a sin that the miracles of so great a man should remain unknown), I made up my mind to feel no shame for solecisms.

For I had never attained to any great knowledge of these matters ; and, if I had ever gleaned anything from the study of them, I had lost it all by long disuse. Spare me, however, the necessity for these painful excuses by letting the book be published, if you are agreeable, with the name suppressed. To make this possible, please erase it from the title-page, so that the silenced page announces (and what more is wanted ?) the book's subject and does not announce the author.

I

Preface

MANY mortals, in the empty quest of earthly glory, have looked to win what they thought would be enduring remembrance for their own names by penning the lives of men of eminence. By so doing, they certainly gathered in, if nothing enduring, at least a little of the fruit for which they hoped, for they perpetuated their own memory, however uselessly ; and their readers, too, were stirred to no little emulation by the pictures of great men thus set before them.

But none of this anxiety of theirs was for the blessed and eternal life beyond ; and how do they profit if their writings win a glory that must perish with this world ? And what does posterity gain by reading of Hector fighting or Socrates philosophizing, seeing that it is not only folly to imitate them but madness to do less than wage strenuous war against them ? For by valuing human life for its present activities only, they committed their hopes to romances, their souls to the tomb. Yes, they trusted for their immortality solely to the memories of men, whereas it is the duty of man to seek enduring life rather than enduring remembrance and to seek it, not by writing or fighting or philosophizing, but by a life of devotion, holiness and piety.

This common error, when perpetuated in literature, has had sufficient influence to send many questing after empty philosophy or that silly valour. For this reason I think it worth my while to write the life of a very holy man, to serve hereafter as an example

to others and to rouse in the reader a desire for true wisdom, for
the heavenly warfare and for a valour inspired by God. And I
reckon that I too shall be the gainer by the work, in being able to
look, not to a futile remembering by men, but to an eternal reward
from God. For though I have not myself so lived that I can be
an example to others, I have at least taken pains to ensure that
one who really should be imitated does not remain unknown.

I shall proceed, then, to write the life of the holy man, Martin,
as he lived it, first before he was a bishop and then during his
episcopate, in spite of having been quite unable to ascertain all the
facts. Thus, the things to which he himself was the only witness
are not known at all, for he did not look for praise from men and,
if it had rested with him, all his mighty works would have remained unknown. For matter of that, even of what I have ascertained I have omitted much, deeming it sufficient to record only
what is outstanding. There was the reader also to be considered,
who might be wearied by the accumulated mass of material. But
I do ask those who are intending to read to give credence to what
is said and not think that I have written anything not duly ascertained and tested. Rather than utter falsehoods, I would have
chosen to say nothing at all.

II

Martin, then, was born at the town of Sabaria, in Pannonia,[1]
but was brought up in Italy, at Pavia.[2] His parents were somewhat above the lowest grade in worldly dignity, but were pagans.
His father had begun life as a common soldier and rose to be a
military tribune.[3] Martin himself in his youth served in the

[1] The administrative Province of Pannonia was roughly equivalent to as
much of modern Hungary as lies south and west of the Danube, that is to say,
within the frontiers of the Roman Empire in Martin's day. It had not then been
occupied by Magyars, though other Mongol peoples may have begun to infil-
trate into it. It had a very mixed population. Since it had come under Roman
rule, Teutons had entered it in force. Sabaria or Savaria is the modern Stein-
an-Anger or, in Hungarian, Szombat-Hély. The year of Martin's birth seems
to have been A.D. 330. Dates as far apart as 316 and 336 have been proposed.

[2] Latin, Ticinum. It was Charlemagne who gave it the name Papia, which
became Pavia. Martin's father's legion was presumably moved there from
Sabaria.

[3] Very roughly, a battalion commander. There were six tribunes in a legion,
which had originally contained from 4,200 to 6,000 men, though at their time its
numbers were falling rapidly to less than half those figures.

soldiery that uses earthly weapons, in the cavalry of the Imperial Guard under the Emperor[4] Constantius, and afterwards under the Caesar Julian.[5] But it was not voluntary service, for, from almost the earliest years of his hallowed childhood, this remarkable boy aspired to the service of God.

At the age of ten, against the wish of his parents, he took himself off to a church and asked to be made a catechumen. He was soon in the most wonderful way wholly taken up with the work of God and at the age of twelve longed for the desert.[6] His tender age prevented him from fulfilling his desire, but his mind, ever fixed on hermitages and the Church, continued to dream, even in these boyhood years, of the life to which he was afterwards consecrated.

But the Emperors had issued an edict that the sons of veterans were to be registered for military service and his father, who grudged him his auspicious occupations, betrayed him to the authorities. Thus at the age of fifteen, as a prisoner in chains, he bound himself by the military oath.[7] He was content with only one servant to attend on him and even then, topsy-turvy fashion, it was the master who performed the services, often to the extent of taking off the servant's boots himself and cleaning them. They took their meals together and it was generally the master who waited.

He was in the army nearly three years before his baptism but kept himself free from the vices in which men in that position[8]

---

[4] Latin, " rex ", which Severus uses almost consistently for the correct terms *imperator* and *Augustus*. For students of the constitutional history of the Empire, the distinctions between these terms are of considerable importance but, as nothing in this Life or any other Life in this volume seems to turn on these distinctions, all three terms have been rendered " Emperor " indiscriminately throughout, whenever they refer to one of the reigning sovereigns, in accordance with common usage.

[5] Constantius II became Emperor in the East on the death of his father, Constantine the Great, in A.D. 337, and sole Emperor in 350, dying in 361. Julian, afterwards known as the Apostate, was his nephew and was made by him Caesar or junior Emperor in November, 355, when he was sent to take over the command of the army in Gaul. But it was almost certainly not Julian under whom Martin served.

[6] i.e., for the life of a hermit in the desert.

[7] In spite of the telescoping of events by Sulpicius, it is not likely that Martin's actual service in the army began at this age. These conscripts were not, as a rule, actually taken into the army until they were eighteen.

[8] Latin, " illud hominum genus ". It seems probable, both from the form of this sentence and from what follows, that the reference is not to the vices of the soldier but to the vices of the unbaptized. It was a common practice at that

are apt to indulge. Great was his kindness towards his fellow-soldiers, and wonderful his charity, while his patience and humility were more than human. As for abstemiousness, it is superfluous to praise it in him. He practised it to such an extent that even at that time he was regarded as a monk rather than as a soldier.

In these ways he so won the hearts of all those serving with him that they felt for him a quite extraordinary affection, amounting to veneration. Though not yet reborn in Christ, he acted as one already robed in the good works of baptism—caring for the suffering, succouring the unfortunate, feeding the needy, clothing the naked, keeping nothing for himself out of his army pay beyond his daily food. For even then he was no deaf hearer of the Gospel, and he took no thought for the morrow.

III

So it came about that one day when he had nothing on him but his weapons and his uniform, in the middle of a winter which had been fearfully hard beyond the ordinary, so that many were dying of the intense cold, he met at the city gate of Amiens a coatless beggar. This beggar had been asking the passers-by to take pity on him but all had gone past the unfortunate creature. Then the God-filled man understood, from the fact that no one else had had pity, that this beggar had been reserved for him. But what was he to do? He had nothing with him but the cape[1] he had on, for he had already used up what else he had, in similar good works. So he took the sword he was wearing and cut the cape in two and gave one half to the beggar, putting on the rest himself again.

---

period to put off baptism until middle age or the approach of death, in accordance with a popular though theologically erroneous belief of the day that certain grave sins, if committed after baptism, could be forgiven once only, if at all, and then only with great difficulty ; whereas it did not much matter what sins one committed before baptism, which wiped out all the past. Compare St. Augustine's reference in the *Confessions* (I, xi) to hearing people say on every side : " Let him do what he wants ; he is not yet baptized." See the Introduction, section I.

[1] Latin, " chlamys ", really a Greek word, used for the shorter forms (worn by officers) of the cape or cloak that, in different lengths for different ranks and worn over the tunic, formed part of the military uniform of the day (see Trench, *Synonyms of the New Testament*, section 50). The *sagulum* that appears in the Life of St. Germanus in this volume was a form of it (see, e.g., section IV, with footnote 2 there).

This raised a laugh from some of the bystanders, for he looked grotesque in the mutilated garment ; but many had more sense, and sighed to think that they had not done something of the kind ; indeed, having more to give, they could have clothed the beggar without stripping themselves. And that night, in his sleep, Martin saw Christ wearing the half of his cape with which he had clothed the beggar. He was told to look carefully at Our Lord and take note that it was the garment he had given away. Then he heard Jesus say aloud to the throng of angels that surrounded Him : " Martin is still only a catechumen but he has clothed Me with this garment."

But Our Lord Himself had once said : " In doing it to one of these least regarded ones, you were doing it to Me ",[2] and He was only acting on His own words when He declared that He had been clothed in the person of the beggar and reinforced His testimony to so good a deed by graciously showing Himself in the very garment that the beggar had received. But this most blessed man was not puffed up with vainglory by the vision but saw God's goodness in his own good deed. And being then twenty-two years old[3], he flew to be baptized. But he did not immediately abandon the military life, for he was overborne by the entreaties of his tribune, on whose personal staff he was serving and who promised him that when his term as tribune was over he would abandon the world. Buoyed up by this hope, Martin remained a soldier, though only in name, for nearly two years after his baptism.

IV

Meanwhile the barbarians were making incursions into Gaul and the Caesar Julian concentrated his army at Worms.[1] There

[2] Matt. xxv. 40.
[3] Halm has *duo de viginti* (" eighteen ") but the oldest MSS. support " twenty-two ".
[1] Latin, " Vangionum civitas ", which could, however, refer to some settlement of the Vangiones other than their chief town, Worms, the name of which at this period was Barbetomagus. But the point is immaterial, since *all* the settlements of the Vangiones were in the hands of the barbarians at the time when Julian concentrated his army, which he did at Rheims, the date being July, 356 ; and in any case it is practically certain that Sulpicius has got hold of the wrong expedition as the setting for Martin's discharge.

he began to distribute a bonus to the soldiers. They were called up one by one in the usual way until Martin's turn came. But he thought it would be a suitable time for applying for his discharge, for he did not think that it would be honest for him to take the bonus if he was not going to fight. So he said to the Caesar : " I have been your soldier up to now. Let me now be God's. Let someone who is going to fight have your bonus. I am Christ's soldier ; I am not allowed to fight." [2]

These words put the tyrant in a rage and he said that it was from fear of the battle that was to be fought the next day that he wanted to quit the service, not from religious motives. But Martin was undaunted ; in fact he stood all the firmer when they tried to frighten him.

" If it is put down to cowardice," he said, " and not to faith, I will stand unarmed in front of the battle-line tomorrow and I will go unscathed through the enemy's columns in the name of the Lord Jesus, protected by the sign of the Cross instead of by shield and helmet."

So he was ordered to be removed into custody so that he could prove his words and face the barbarians unarmed. The next day the enemy sent envoys to ask for peace, surrendering themselves and all they had. Who can doubt in these circumstances that this victory was due to this man of blessings and was granted to him so that he should not be sent unarmed into the battle ? The good Lord could have kept His soldier safe even among the swords and javelins of the enemy but, to spare those hallowed eyes the sight of other men's deaths, He made a battle unnecessary. For Christ could not rightly have granted any other victory for the benefit of His own soldier than one in which the enemy were beaten bloodlessly and no man had to die.

---

[2] It seems clear from the whole tenor of the Life up to now that Martin regarded himself as, in intention at least, a religious and as having been made eligible for religious vows by baptism.

V

After leaving the army he sought out the holy Hilary, Bishop of Poitiers,[1] a man well known at that time for his proved fidelity in the things of God. He stayed with him for a while and Hilary tried to attach him more closely to himself and to bind him to the sacred ministry by conferring the diaconate upon him. But he refused again and again, vehemently protesting his unworthiness, until this deeply understanding man saw that there was only one way of keeping a hold on him and that was by conferring on him an office which could be taken as a slight on him. He therefore told him that he must be an exorcist, and Martin did not resist ordination to this office for fear that it might look as if he regarded it as beneath him.[2]

Not long after this he was prompted in a dream to pay a visit, in the cause of religion, to his native land and to his parents, who were still in the bondage of paganism. The holy Hilary gave his consent but by his many tearful entreaties laid him under an obligation to return. So he set off; but it is said that he felt depressed as he entered upon this journey, and called the brethren to witness that he would meet with many misfortunes, which did in fact come about.

First, he lost his way in the Alps and fell among brigands. One of them lifted his axe and poised it for a blow at his head but the other one checked his hand as he was striking. Eventually his hands were tied behind his back and he was handed over to the first as his prisoner, to be plundered. The brigand took him to a more secluded spot and began questioning him as to who he was. He replied that he was a Christian. Was he not afraid?

---

[1] Latin, " Pictava ". St. Hilary, Doctor of the Church, became Bishop of Poitiers in one of the years from about 350 to 353. Since it seems clear from the narrative that he was already a bishop, and able to ordain, when Martin joined him, and that Martin went to him straight from the army, this is one of the crucial dates for settling the chronology of Martin's life.

[2] The office of exorcist, the second of the minor orders, was in Martin's day more than merely a step towards the major orders. See, for example, the Life of St. Ambrose in this volume, section XXI, with footnote 2 there. See also the Introduction, Section I.

asked the other. But he declared with the greatest firmness that he had never felt safer, since he knew that the Lord's compassion is never closer than when the trial comes; in fact, he was much more sorry for the other man, who was disqualifying himself for Christ's compassion by a life of brigandage.

Thus embarked upon a discussion of the Christian religion, he preached to the brigand the Word of God. But why make a long story of it? The brigand became a believer, escorted Martin back and put him on his way again, asking him to pray to Our Lord for him. He was seen afterwards leading a pious life; indeed, the story I have just related is told as it came from him.

VI

So Martin went on his way. He had passed Milan, when the devil, taking human form, met him on the road and asked him his destination. Martin replied that his destination was where God was calling him.

" Then wherever you go," said he, " and whatever you attempt, you will have the devil against you."

To which Martin answered in the words of the Prophet: " The Lord is my helper; I shall not be afraid of what men may do to me." [1] And at once the enemy of souls vanished. Thus he carried out his purpose and plan and liberated his mother from the errors of paganism, though his father persisted in its evil ways. Moreover, he brought many to salvation by his example.

Now, the Arian heresy had been making headway all over the world and particularly in Illyricum,[2] and presently Martin was

---

[1] Ps. cxvii (cxviii) 6.

[2] The Arian heresy was named after a priest of Alexandria, called Arius, who, in his turn, was indebted to the theories of a Syrian priest named Lucan. It was essentially an attempt to rationalize the Incarnation. Drawing on the terminology of Platonism, in the form in which it had come down to the Christian era, it identified the *Logos* or Word of St. John with the *logos* of Plato and declared that, since the *Logos* was distinct from God the Father, He could not be God, God being one. On the contrary, the Son was not of the same *ousia* or substance as God, but was created, like other creatures, out of nothing, and became the man Jesus. The doctrine was condemned at the Council of Nicæa, but, chiefly owing to the skilled championship of Eusebius, Bishop of Nicomedia, was kept alive as a major issue in the Councils of the Church and the

contending most strenuously, almost single-handed, against infidelity in the episcopate. He suffered severely for this, for he was publicly flogged and in the end forced to leave the city. Returning to Italy, he learnt that the Church in Gaul was in a disturbed state also, with the departure of the holy Hilary, whom the heretics had forcibly driven into exile.[3] He therefore made himself a hermitage at Milan. But there too he became the object of the harshest persecution, at the hands of Auxentius, the fountain-head and leader of Arianism there,[4] who, after inflicting on him much ill-treatment, drove him from the city.

He now judged it best to accept the situation and retired to an island named Gallinaria,[5] with a priest of many virtues as his companion. Here he lived for some time on roots, and during this period he made a meal of hellebore, a plant which they say is poisonous. But when he felt the strength of the poison working in him, and death was imminent, he met the threatening danger with prayer and at once all the pain vanished.

Not long after this he learnt that the Emperor had repented,

---

politics of the Empire for half a century afterwards. It was also largely through Eusebius and his missionary bishop Ulfilas that the Goths, and in consequence the Vandals, were converted to Arianism, so that when the heresy had at last largely died out within the confines of the Empire, its inhabitants were suddenly confronted with it again as the belief of their barbarian oppressors.

The name Illyricum covered the greater part of what is now Yugoslavia, together with Pannonia (see note 1 to section II above). The strength of Arianism there is further illustrated in the Life of St. Ambrose in this volume (see especially section XI and footnote 1 there).

[3] The Emperor Constantius II (see note 5 to section II) was very much under the influence of Arian bishops at the Court and had ordered the exile of the leading Western bishops who had refused to sign the condemnation of St. Athanasius promulgated by the predominantly Arian Council held at Milan in November, 355. St. Hilary went into exile (to Phrygia, in Asia Minor) some time during A.D. 356 ; but his fellow-bishops refused to allow anyone else to be intruded into his see and his priests continued to administer his diocese in his name in accordance with orders that they from time to time received from him.

[4] Auxentius was a native of Asia Minor and a bitter anti-Catholic who in A.D. 355 had been forced upon the see of Milan by Constantius II after the Catholic bishop, St. Dionysius of Milan, had been sent into exile in the general " purge " of Catholic bishops that followed the Council of Milan (see previous note). He managed to hold his position as bishop until his death, which was the occasion of the forcible elevation of St. Ambrose to the episcopate (see the Life of the latter, section VI).

[5] Now Gallinare, originally named (it seems) from the half-wild poultry that abounded on it. It is a small uninhabited island off the Italian Riviera, not far from the modern town of Albenga (then Albingaunum).

and had granted the holy Hilary leave to return. He therefore
set out for Rome in the hope of meeting him there.[6]

VII

Hilary, however, had already passed through the City, so
Martin followed in his track. He was given a very warm welcome
by him and made himself a hermitage not far from the town.[1]

It was during this period that a certain catechumen joined
him, who wished to be trained by this most holy man. After a
few days he fell ill and lay racked by a high fever. Martin
happened to be away at the time and when he returned on the

---

[6] Severus himself in his Chronicles (II, 45) gives a fuller and more accurate
account of this affair. There was no repentance on the part of Constantius,
whose action was taken at the request of the Arians themselves. For the Arians
in the Eastern part of the Empire were finding St. Hilary as great a nuisance,
from their point of view, as those in the West had done and, like them, wanted
to be rid of him. Constantius, therefore, early in A.D. 360 ordered him back to
Gaul ; and although he did not revoke the sentence of banishment from his see,
there is good reason to think, in spite of conflicting evidence, that St. Hilary did
in fact regain possession of it, and was rejoined by Martin there, in the summer
of 360 while Constantius was still alive.

[1] The word rendered " hermitage " here and in the last section is " monasterium ", which does, of course, by derivation mean a dwelling for a solitary,
though eventually both " monasterium " and the related word " monachus "
came to be more or less confined to their original opposites, i.e., to establishments in which the religious life is lived communally and to the members of
these establishments. In this Life, " monasterium " is used both for a hermitage
and for a community of hermits living under the direction of one superior—
the first form of monasticism in the West (see the Introduction, section II).
After all, the events related took place more than 150 years before the Rule of
St. Benedict was published, and when the vocabulary of monasticism, like the
institution itself, was in a fluid state in the West. It is of interest to note that
in the first of the Dialogues that follow the Life, which Severus wrote a little
later and in which he is not incorporating stories of the early life of Martin
but dealing with monks and hermits of the East, where several different types
of the religious life were already well defined, he uses " monasterium " consistently for the community, as distinct from the hermit's cell or hut. But, so
far as the Life is concerned, a translator seems to have no alternative but to
render the word sometimes " hermitage ", sometimes " monastery ", according
to the context.

Thus, in this section and the next, the word relates to Martin's first foundation
in Gaul, at the place now known as Ligugé (about 5 miles from Poitiers), which
seems to have begun as a hermitage proper, and ended with a considerable
number of disciples clustered around Martin. In section X, however, we pass
abruptly in the middle of the section to a description of a deliberately organised
community of hermits of the type described above, for which " monastery "
seems the only practicable rendering in a translation such as the present. But
" Laura " might be technically a more accurate term (see the Introduction), and
certainly the later monasteries of Ligugé and Marmoutier, both of which
claimed descent from St. Martin, were very different from any " monastery "
conceived by him.

third day he found a corpse ; death had come so suddenly that he had departed this life without baptism.

The body had been laid out and was surrounded by sorrowing brethren, who were performing the sad rites, when Martin came hurrying up, weeping and uttering lamentations. But, with his whole soul possessed by the Holy Spirit, he ordered the others out of the cell where the body lay, fastened the door, and stretched himself out over the lifeless limbs of the dead brother. For some time he gave his whole self to prayer. Then, made aware by the Spirit of God that divine power was present, he raised himself a little, fixed his eyes on the dead man, and awaited without misgiving the outcome of his prayer and of the Lord's mercy. Hardly two hours had gone by before he saw the dead man stir slightly in all his limbs, then blink, as his eyes opened again to see. Then indeed he turned to the Lord with shouts of gratitude and filled the cell with the sound of them. The brethren standing outside the door heard and at once ran in. And what a marvellous sight ! The man they had left dead, they saw alive.

Thus restored to life, he at once received baptism and lived for many years afterwards. He was the first among us to be the subject of Martin's miracle-working and to bear witness to it. He was in the habit of relating how, when he was out of the body, he had been brought before the tribunal of the Judge and had heard the dismal sentence of consignment to a place of gloom among the generality of men.[2] Then two angels had represented to the Judge that he was the man for whom Martin was praying. He was therefore ordered to be taken back by these same angels and to be restored to Martin and to his former life.

The immense renown of this man of blessings dates from this time. He was already regarded by everybody as a saint ; now he was looked upon as a man of power and in very truth an apostle.

[2] The reference is presumably to the Limbo of the unbaptized.

VIII

Not long after this he was passing by the farm of a man of good position by this world's reckoning, named Lupicinus, when his attention was caught by the cries and wailings of a crowd of mourners. Much concerned, he stopped and enquired the reason for this weeping. He was told that a young serf belonging to the household had hanged himself. Hearing this, he went into the hut where the body lay, shut everybody out, laid himself upon the body and prayed for a while. Presently the dead man's features showed signs of life and his faded eyes looked into Martin's face. He made a long slow effort to raise himself, then took the hand of the man of blessings and stood upright on his feet. In this way, with all the crowd looking on, he walked with him up to the front of the house.

IX

It was somewhere about this time that Martin was wanted as Bishop of Tours.[1] But it was difficult to get him to leave his hermitage, so a citizen of Tours named Rusticus came and knelt at his knees and got him to come out by pretending that his wife was ill. A number of the townsmen had previously been posted along the road, and it was practically as a prisoner that he reached the city.

Incredible numbers had assembled in the most extraordinary way, not only of the people of Tours but also from neighbouring towns, to give their votes.[2] There was but one purpose among them ; all had the same desire and the same opinion, which was that Martin was the fittest to be bishop and that the Church would be fortunate to get such a priest. There were a few, however, including some of the bishops who had been summoned to consecrate the new prelate, who were so abandoned as to oppose. They said, if you please, that Martin was a despicable individual

---

[1] Almost certainly in A.D. 372.
[2] The ultimate choice lay in the hands of the bishops of the Province ; see the Introduction, section I.

and quite unfit to be a bishop, what with his insignificant appearance, his sordid garments and his disgraceful hair. But the folly of these men, who in their very efforts to vilify this remarkable man were singing his praises, was laughed at by the people, whose judgement was sounder than theirs. Nor were they permitted to do anything contrary to what the people, by God's will, were purposing.

Nevertheless particularly strong resistance was offered, it is said, by one of the bishops present, named Defender.[3] It was much remarked, therefore, that he received unpleasant mention in the reading from the Prophets on that occasion.[4] For it so happened that the Lector whose turn it was to read had been held up by the crowd and was not in his place and, in the confusion among the ministers during the wait for the absentee, one of the bystanders picked up a psalter and plunged into the first verse he saw. It was : " Out of the mouths of babes and sucklings thou hast brought praise to perfection, to destroy the enemy and defender." [5] When these words were read, the congregation raised a shout and the opposition was put to shame ; and it was generally thought that God had prompted the reading of this particular psalm in order that Defender should hear its condemnation of his proceedings. For while the praise of the Lord had been brought to perfection out of the mouths of babes and sucklings in the person of Martin, he himself had been exposed as an enemy and destroyed at the same time.

X

What Martin was like, and his greatness, after entering the episcopate, it is beyond my powers to describe. For with unswerving constancy he remained the same man as before. There was the same humble heart and the same poverty-stricken clothing ; and, amply endowed with authority and tact, he fully

---

[3] Latin, " Defensor ", as also in the quotation below from the Psalm, see note 5. Defensor was Bishop of Angers (Duchesne, *Fastes Episcopaux*, II, 352).
[4] i.e., at the solemn Mass.
[5] Ps. viii. 3 (2), in the older Latin Psalter (known as the " Roman "). The Psalter now in use has *ultorem* (" avenger ").

sustained the dignity of the episcopate without forsaking the life
or the virtues of the monk.

For a time he occupied a cell next to the cathedral. Then,
when he could no longer endure the disturbance from his many
visitors, he made himself a hermitage about two miles from the
city.[1] The place was so secluded and remote that it had all the
solitude of the desert. On one side it was walled in by the rock-
face of a high mountain, and the level ground that remained was
enclosed by a gentle bend of the River Loire. There was only
one approach to it, and that a very narrow one.

His own cell was built of wood, as were those of many of the
brethren ; but most of them had hollowed out shelters for themselves in the rock of the overhanging mountain.[2] There were
about eighty disciples there, being trained in the pattern of their
most blessed master. No one possessed anything of his own ;
everything was put into the common stock. The buying and
selling which is customary with most hermits was forbidden
them.[3] No craft was practised there except that of the copyist,
and that was assigned to the younger men. The older ones were
left free for prayer.

It was seldom that anyone left his cell except when they
assembled at the place of worship. All received their food
together after the fast was ended. No one touched wine unless
ill-health forced him to do so. Most of them wore clothes of
camel's hair ; softer clothing was looked upon as an offence there.
This must be regarded as all the more wonderful because there
were many among them of noble rank, who had been brought up
to something quite different before forcing themselves to this

[1] At what was afterwards known as Marmoutier, a corruption of " major
monasterium ".
[2] The author has jumped some 20 years and is describing the community
that he saw when he first visited St. Martin (see section XXV). For the bearing
of this on the renderings of the word " monasterium ", see note 1 to section VII.
[3] " Hermits " here renders " monachi " ; see note 1 to section VII. It was a
common practice of the Egyptian hermits, even when their cells were grouped
around a single Abbot, to support themselves by selling the products of some
handicraft, e.g. basket-making ; and Severus is emphasising the fact that the
disciples whose cells were grouped around St. Martin differed from their
Egyptian counterparts in living in obedience to the authority of their master
and in practising a religious communism under his direction. See the Introduction, section II.

lowliness and endurance. Many of them we have since seen as bishops. For what kind of city or Church would it be that did not covet a bishop from Martin's monastery?

XI

But I must come to his other miracles, performed during his episcopate.

Not far from the town, and near the monastery, there was a place to which sanctity had been mistakenly attributed with the idea that martyrs were buried there. There was even an altar there, erected by previous bishops. But Martin did not lightly give credence to uncertainties, and made constant efforts to get from the older priests and clerics the name of the martyr and the occasion when he suffered. He explained that he felt grave doubts of conscience, seeing that no certain and settled tradition had come down to them.

For some time, therefore, he kept away from the place, not condemning the cultus, since he was not sure of his ground, but at the same time not lending his authority to popular opinion, in case he should be strengthening a superstition. Then one day he took with him a few of the brethren and went to the place. Standing on the grave itself, he prayed to Our Lord to make it known who was buried there and what his character had been. Then, turning to the left, he saw a ghost standing close by, foul and grim. He ordered him to give his name and character. He gave his name and confessed to a guilty past. He had been a robber, and had been executed for his crimes, but had become an object of devotion through a mistake of the common people. In reality he had nothing in common with martyrs ; glory was their portion, punishment his.

The others who were present had heard a voice speaking in an inexplicable manner but had seen no one. Martin now described what he had seen and gave orders for the altar which had stood there to be removed. Thus he rid the population of a false and superstitious belief.

XII

Some time after this he happened, when on a journey, to en-counter the corpse of a pagan being carried to its grave with superstitious rites. He had seen the approaching crowd from a distance and stopped for a little, not knowing what it was, for there was nearly half a mile between them and it was difficult to distinguish what he saw. He made out, however, a band of rustics, and linen cloths (that had been spread over the body) fluttering in the wind. He supposed, therefore, that unhallowed sacrificial rites were being performed, for it was the custom of the Gallic rustics, in their lamentable infatuation, to carry round their fields the images of the demons covered with white veils. With uplifted hand, therefore, he made the sign of the Cross before the ap-proaching crowd and ordered them not to move from where they were and to put down what they were carrying.

Then indeed there was a wonderful sight to be seen. First the unfortunate creatures turned as rigid as rocks. Then they tried with all their might to advance but, being quite unable to move forward, they kept turning round in the most ridiculous whirligigs. Finally, completely beaten, they put down the body they were carrying and, looking at one another in their bewilderment, silently speculated as to what had happened to them. However, when the man of blessings found that the assemblage was a funeral pro-cession and not for sacrifices, he raised his hand again and set them free to pick up the body and go on. Thus, when he wished, he made them halt and when he chose he let them go.

XIII

Again, in a certain village he had demolished a very ancient temple and was proceeding to cut down a pine-tree which was close to the shrine, when the priest of the place and all his pagan following came up to stop him. These same people had been quiet enough, at Our Lord's command, while the temple was being thrown down but they were not prepared to see the tree felled.

He painstakingly explained to them that there was nothing sacred about a tree trunk and that they had much better be followers of the God he himself served. As for the tree, it ought to be cut down because it was dedicated to a demon.

Then one of them, more audacious than the rest, said to him : " If you have confidence in the God you say you worship, stand where the tree will fall, and we will cut it down ourselves ; and if your Lord, as you call Him, is with you, you will not be harmed."

Martin, with dauntless trust in God, undertook to do this. Thereupon all the assembled pagans agreed to the bargain, reckoning the loss of their tree a small matter if, in its downfall, it crushed the enemy of their religion. And as the pine leant to one side, so that there was no doubt on which side it would fall when cut through, Martin was bound and made to stand on the spot chosen by the rustics, where they were all quite sure that the tree would come down. Then they began to cut down the tree themselves with great joy and delight. A wondering crowd stood at a little distance.

Gradually the pine began nodding and a disastrous fall seemed imminent. Standing at a distance, the monks grew pale ; and, so frightened were they as the danger drew near, that they lost all hope and courage, and could only await the death of Martin. He, however, waited undaunted, relying on the Lord. The tottering pine had already given a crack, it was actually falling, it was just coming down on him, when he lifted his hand and met it with the sign of salvation.

At that—and you would have thought it had been whipped like a top—the tree plunged in another direction, almost crushing some rustics who had ensconced themselves in a safe place. Then indeed a shout went up to heaven as the pagans gasped at the miracle, the monks wept for joy, and all with one accord acclaimed the name of Christ ; and you may be sure that on that day salvation came to that region. Indeed, there was hardly anyone in that vast multitude of pagans who did not ask for the imposition of hands,[1]

---

[1] The reference would appear to be their admission as catechumens, which is described in almost the same terms in the account of a very similar scene at the end of section 2 (IV) of the Dialogue *Postumianus* below (p. 10). See also the Introduction, section I.

abandoning his heathenish errors and making profession of faith in the Lord Jesus.

It is certainly a fact that before Martin's time very few, in fact hardly anyone, in those parts acknowledged Christ but now His Name, thanks to Martin's miracles and example, has gained such a hold that there is no district there not filled with crowded churches or with monasteries. For he immediately built a church or a monastery in every place where he destroyed a pagan shrine.

XIV

It was somewhere about this time that in the course of this work he performed another miracle at least as great. He had set on fire a very ancient and much frequented shrine in a certain village and the flames were being driven by the wind against a neighbouring, in fact adjacent, house. When Martin noticed this, he climbed speedily to the roof of the house and placed himself in front of the oncoming flames. Then you might have seen an amazing sight— the flames bending back against the force of the wind till it looked like a battle between warring elements. Such were his powers that the fire destroyed only where it was bidden.

In a village named Levroux,[1] however, when he wished to demolish in the same way a temple which had been made very rich by its superstitious cult, he met with resistance from a crowd of pagans and was driven off with some injuries to himself. He withdrew, therefore, to a place in the neighbourhood where for three days in sackcloth and ashes, continuously fasting and praying, he besought Our Lord that the temple which human hands had failed to demolish might be destroyed by divine power.

Then suddenly two angels stood before him, looking like heavenly warriors, with spears and shields. They said that the Lord had sent them to rout the rustic host and give Martin protection, so that no one should hinder the destruction of the temple. He was to go back, therefore, and carry out faithfully the work he had undertaken. So he returned to the village and, while crowds

---

[1] Latin, " Leprosum ".

of pagans watched in silence, the heathen sanctuary was razed to its foundations and all its altars and images reduced to powder.

The sight convinced the rustics that it was by divine decree that they had been stupefied and overcome with dread, so as to offer no resistance to the bishop ; and nearly all of them made profession of faith in the Lord Jesus, proclaiming with shouts before all that Martin's God should be worshipped and the idols ignored, which could neither save themselves nor anyone else.

XV

I will also relate what happened in the country of the Aedui.[1] He was demolishing a temple there also, when a frenzied mob of rustic pagans made a rush at him and one of them, more audacious than the rest, drew his sword and went for him. Throwing back his cloak, Martin offered his bare neck to the stroke. Nor was the pagan slow to strike but, when his hand was well above his head, he fell flat on his back. Stricken with the fear of God, he asked for pardon.

Nor was the following incident dissimilar. Once, when he was destroying some idols, someone planned to stab him with a large knife. But in the very act of striking, the weapon was struck from his hand and disappeared. More often, however, when the rustics were protesting against the destruction of their shrines, he so subdued their pagan hearts by his holy preaching that the light of the truth penetrated to them and they themselves threw down their own temples.

XVI

He had the gift of healing in such a degree that a sick man hardly ever came to him without at once being cured, as may easily be seen from the following example. There was a girl at Trier who was suffering from such acute paralysis that for a long time she had been altogether without the use of her body. She was as good as dead in every part of her and drew only a fluttering breath. Her grieving relatives surrounded her, only awaiting her death.

[1] This district centred round Augustodunum, the modern Autun, a very long way from Tours.

Suddenly it was announced that Martin had come to the city. When the girl's father heard the news, he ran breathlessly to plead for his daughter. It happened that Martin had already entered the cathedral. There, with the congregation looking on and many other bishops present, the old man with loud lamentations clasped his knees.

" My daughter ", he said, " is dying of a disease of the most pitiable kind and—worse than death—is alive only in her breathing; her body is already a corpse. Please come to her and bless her. I am sure that you are the one to make a cure."

Dumbfounded and embarrassed by such language, Martin tried to refuse. He protested that the matter was not in his province ; the old man was mistaken about him and he was quite unworthy to be used by Our Lord for such a manifestation of power. But the weeping father continued to insist passionately and to beg him to come and see the lifeless body. In the end he was overborne by the bishops standing by, and went with him to the girl's home.

A huge crowd was waiting at the street door to see what the servant of God would do. First he resorted to his usual weapons in cases of this kind and prostrated himself on the ground in prayer. Then, after looking at the sick girl, he asked to be given some oil. This he blessed, then poured the hallowed liquid, now a powerful remedy, into the girl's mouth. At once her voice came back to her. Then, at his touch, little by little each of her limbs began to recover its life. Finally, in the sight of all, she rose and stood firmly on her feet.

XVII

On this same occasion,[1] a serf of a man of proconsular rank[2] named Tetradius, having been entered by a demon, was dying pitiably in agonies. Martin was therefore asked to lay his hands on him. He ordered the man to be brought to him, but it proved impossible to get the wicked spirit out of the hut where he was,

---

[1] i.e. during this visit to Trier, as in the next two episodes.
[2] The rank attaching to the governorship of certain Provinces.

such frenzied attacks did he make with his teeth on anyone who approached.[3]

Tetradius then came and knelt at the knees of the man of blessings and begged him to come himself to the house where the demoniac lived. Martin, however, protested that he could not go to the unhallowed house of a pagan. For Tetradius at that time was still held fast in the errors of paganism. He therefore promised that, if the demon were expelled from the boy, he would become a Christian. Martin then laid his hands on the boy and drove the evil spirit out of him. Tetradius, on seeing this, made profession of faith in the Lord Jesus. He became a catechumen at once and was baptized not long afterwards. He always cherished an extraordinary affection for Martin as the instrument of his salvation.

At this same time and in the same town he was entering the house of a certain householder when he stopped on the threshold, saying that he saw a frightful demon in the hall. When he ordered it to go, it took possession of the master of the house, who was waiting for Martin in the interior of the house. The unhappy man began to gnash his teeth and to maul everyone who approached him.

The house was thrown into disorder, the slaves were all confused and there was a rush to get out of the way. Martin placed himself before the frenzied man and began by ordering him to stand still. But he still kept gnashing his teeth and opening his mouth to bite. Martin then put his fingers into the gaping mouth, saying : " If you have any power at all, devour these." At this the man drew his jaws back wide apart, as if he had a red-hot iron between them, trying to avoid touching the fingers

[3] Here and in the next two episodes and, indeed, in most of the accounts of exorcisms in this volume, neither the grammar of the original nor the context allows of any consistent distinction being made, either in the subjects of the verbs or in the reference of the pronouns, between the demon and the possessed man ; for the temporary identity between the two is too vividly present to the narrator's imagination. (The same feature appears in some of the Gospel narratives, e.g. Mark v. 2 sqq.) In these circumstances the attempt to distinguish in the translation between the demoniac and the demon by such devices as passing from " he " to " it " must generally be arbitrary ; and the results are often odder than the use of the same pronoun throughout. As a rule, therefore, the attempt has not been made unless there has been a special reason for it in a particular case.

of the man of blessings. Eventually he was forced by penalties and torments to abandon the body he occupied and, not being allowed to go out through the mouth, was discharged in the excrement, leaving filth behind him.[4]

XVIII

Meanwhile the city had been alarmed by a sudden rumour of a movement and inroad of the barbarians,[1] so Martin ordered one of the demoniacs to be brought to him and told him to say whether the report was true. He admitted that there had been ten demons besides himself who had spread this rumour through the population, in the hope that by the ensuing panic, if by nothing else, Martin might be driven from the town ; there was nothing further from the minds of the barbarians than an invasion. This admission was made by the evil spirit before everybody in the cathedral and freed the city from the disquieting fears that had been overhanging it.

Then again, at Paris he was passing through the city gates accompanied by a great crowd when, to everybody's horror, he kissed the pitiable face of a leper and gave him his blessing. The man was at once cleansed from all trace of his affliction, and coming to the cathedral the next day with a clear skin he gave thanks for his recovered health. And I must not omit to mention the frequent miracles which threads pulled from Martin's clothing or hairshirt worked on the sick. When tied round a finger or hung round the neck of the patient, they often banished his malady.

XIX

Arborius was a man of Prefectorial rank [1] and of conspicuous holiness and strong faith. He had a daughter who was wasting away from the acute fevers of a quartan ague. A letter from

[4] Compare the account of an exorcism by St. Germanus in this volume, section IX. Modern accounts of exorcisms in heathen countries tell of similar phenomena. For the apparent confusion of pronouns, see the preceding note.
[1] Trier (or Trevès) was a military base some sixty miles from the frontier.
[1] i.e., he had been the Governor of a Province.

Martin happened to be brought to him and he placed it in her bosom at the very moment when her temperature was rising and at once the fever left her. This made such an impression on Arborius that he immediately made an offering of his daughter to God and dedicated her to perpetual virginity. He then set off to visit Martin and presented the girl to him as concrete evidence of the extent of his powers, seeing that she had been cured by him from a distance; nor would he allow the ceremony of her clothing and consecration as a virgin to be performed by anyone but Martin.

A man named Paulinus, who was afterwards to be an example to all, had begun to suffer from acute pain in one eye and a fairly thick film had by now grown over the pupil. Martin, by touching the eye with a fine paintbrush, restored it to its former state and at the same time banished all the pain.[2]

Martin himself once by some accident fell from an upstairs landing and rolled down a rough uneven staircase, receiving many injuries. As he lay half-dead in his cell in extreme pain, an angel appeared to him during the night and washed his wounds and dressed his bruises with a healing ointment. By the next day he was so sound and well that you would have thought he had not been injured at all.

But it would be tedious to go through all the instances; and these few out of a great number must suffice. Let it be enough if in things so surpassing I have told the whole truth, and among so many have never been wearisome.

XX

In the midst of these great matters I must insert some lesser ones—though, in truth (such is the general depravity and corruption of our times) it must be reckoned a sufficiently

[2] This Paulinus, who reappears in section XXV and in the Dialogues that follow, is identified by Halm in his index with St. Paulinus of Trier, who was one of the bishops exiled by Constantius II after the Council of Milan (see note 3 to section VI); but this is practically impossible on chronological and other grounds. It becomes quite clear in section XXV that the reference is to the author's friend St. Paulinus of Nola, on whom see footnote 1 to that section.

remarkable occurrence when the firmness of the churchman does not give place to the fawning of the courtier.

Many bishops, then, from various parts of the world had assembled to meet the Emperor Maximus, a man ferocious by nature and, moreover, elated by his victory in a civil war.[1] The foul fawning of all of them upon the sovereign was much remarked, and the dignity of the priesthood with unworthy weakness lowered itself to win imperial patronage. Martin alone retained Apostolic authority. For even when he had to petition the Emperor on somebody's behalf, he commanded rather than requested and, though frequently invited to his banquets, he kept away, saying that he could not sit at table with a man who had robbed one Emperor of his throne and another of his life.[2]

Maximus, however, maintained that he had not become Emperor of his own accord but had simply been defending by the sword the burden of rule that had been thrust upon him by the soldiers at God's prompting. And God's will could hardly be against a man who, by such an unbelievable turn of events, had ended victorious. He added that none of his opponents had fallen except in battle. In the end Martin was so far overcome by his arguments and entreaties as to attend a banquet, to the enormous delight of the Emperor at having gained his point.

Invitations were sent out as if for a great festival and among the guests were men of the very highest rank, including Evodius,

[1] Maximus was a Spaniard in command of the imperial forces in Britain and was acclaimed Emperor by them. At their head he crossed the Channel and overthrew the forces of Gratian, the senior Emperor in the West, who was himself murdered (A.D. 383). He then established himself at Gratian's northern capital, namely Trier, and claimed to rule over Gaul, Britain and Spain. He appears again in the Life of St. Ambrose, where further details will be found in section XIX and the footnotes there. His dealings with the episcopate, and with Martin in particular, during his short reign were concerned chiefly with the proceedings against the heretic Priscillian and his followers. Maximus himself was a Catholic; see Dialogue I, (2, VI). No reference is made to these proceedings in this Life; but some sections of the Dialogues (II, (III), 11-13) are devoted to St. Martin's part in them and explanatory footnotes will be found there. In view of the strained relations that arose between St. Martin and Maximus in connection with these proceedings, the intercourse between the two described in this section must belong to the early days of Maximus' usurpation.

[2] Gratian after his defeat and capture was murdered, but it was never proved that it was by the orders of Maximus, who always denied it. His half-brother Valentinian II should have succeeded him in the rule of the portion of the Empire that Maximus had seized.

who was Prefect, and Consul also,[3] and one of the most upright men that ever lived, and two Counts[4] wielding immense authority, the brother and the uncle of the Emperor. Between these sat one of Martin's priests, Martin himself occupying a stool placed next to the Emperor. Towards the middle of the meal a servant, in accordance with custom, brought a goblet to the Emperor. He ordered it to be given instead to our most holy Bishop and waited expectantly to receive it from the Bishop's own hands. But Martin, after drinking himself, passed the goblet to his priest, holding that no one had a better right to drink immediately after himself and that it would not be honest of him to give precedence over the priest either to the Emperor or to those who ranked next to him.

The Emperor and all who were present were so struck by this action that the very gesture by which they had been humiliated became for them a source of pleasure. And the news went all round the palace that Martin had done at the Emperor's table what no other bishop would have done even when dining with the least of his magistrates.

He also foretold, long beforehand, to this same Maximus that if he made an expedition into Italy, where he was wanting to go, in order to make war on the Emperor Valentinian, he could count on being victorious at the first onset but also on utter destruction a little later. And this we saw come to pass. For at his first approach Valentinian fled ; then, less than a year later, on taking up arms again, he captured and killed Maximus within the walls of Aquileia.[5]

[3] " Prefect " was at this time a common term for the Governor of a Province. The ancient Roman office of Consul, though now merely honorary and no longer elective but bestowed by the Emperor, was a much coveted dignity. Evodius was Consul in A.D. 386, but the Latin (" praefectus idemque Consul Evodius ") does not necessarily imply that this banquet took place in the year of his consulship.

[4] Latin, " comites ", a term which at this period was attached to a number of offices or might mean simply " courtiers ", but when used without qualification and in a context like the present may be taken to denote one of the highest grades in the military hierarchy, the *comes* in this sense being the commander-in-chief of all the troops in a large group of Provinces.

[5] This was A.D. 388. The share of the young Valentinian II in this victory was entirely nominal, the real victor being Theodosius I, then the Emperor in the East, to whose protection Valentinian had fled. The episode is treated more fully in the Life of St. Ambrose in this volume ; see section XIX and the foot-notes there.

XXI

It is certain that Martin actually saw angels very often, even to the extent of engaging in continuous conversation with them. As for the devil, it was so fully within his power to see him that he recognized him under any form, whether he kept to his own character or changed himself into any of the various shapes of " spiritual wickedness ".[1]

When the devil found that he could not avoid recognition, then, since stratagems failed to deceive, he frequently assailed him with violent abuse. Once he burst into his cell with a tremendous clatter, holding in his hand a blood-stained ox-horn. Fresh from committing crime, he displayed his right hand covered with blood. " Martin," he said gleefully, " where is your power? I have just killed one of your people." Martin thereupon called the brethren together and told them what the devil had revealed and ordered them to go carefully through all the cells to see who had been the victim of the tragedy. They reported that none of the monks was missing but that a rustic hired to cart wood was gone into the forest. He told some of them, therefore, to go and meet him. Thus he was found not far from the monastery, already almost lifeless. But, though at his last gasp, he made it plain to the brethren how he came by his mortal wound. He was tightening up some thongs that had got loose on his team of oxen when an ox had tossed its head and dug a horn into his groin. And before long he was dead.

You must judge for yourself of God's reasons for permitting the devil to wield such power. As regards Martin, the marvel lay in the fact that, in the instance just related and also in many others of the same kind, no matter how often they happened, he foresaw the event far in advance or else was given news of it and announced it to the brethren.

[1] Eph. vi. 12.

XXII

Quite often, however, the devil, resorting to a thousand malicious tricks to score off the holy man, would thrust his visible presence upon him under forms of the utmost diversity. Sometimes he presented himself with features disguised to resemble Jupiter, very frequently Mercury, often even Venus or Minerva. Against him, Martin, undaunted always, would protect himself with the sign of the Cross and the power of prayer. Very frequently, violent scolding could be heard, when a crowd of demons were abusing him in impudent language ; but Martin, knowing that it was all false and baseless, remained unmoved by their accusations.

Some of the brethren used even to tell how they had heard a demon in impudent language wanting to know why Martin had admitted into the monastery after their repentance certain brethren who had lost the grace of baptism by various misdeeds—and he specified the crimes of each. Martin had defended himself against the devil most firmly, saying that former offences could be wiped out by leading a better life and that the Lord in His mercy had ordained that absolution from their sins was to be given to those who had left off sinning. To this the devil had retorted that there was no pardon for the guilty and it was impossible for the Lord to extend His mercy to those who had once fallen away.[1]

At this Martin exclaimed (so it is said) : " If you yourself, wretched being, would cease to prey upon mankind and would even now repent of your misdeeds, now that the Day of Judgement is at hand, I have such trust in the Lord Jesus Christ that I would promise you mercy."

What a holy boldness, so to presume on the loving-kindness of Our Lord ! For even though he could quote no authority for this, he showed where his feelings lay.[2]

And, as we are on the subject of the devil and his wiles, it would seem not out of place, though not strictly relevant, to relate the

[1] See note 8 to section II ; also the Introduction, section I.
[2] This topic recurs in the Dialogue *Postumianus*, section VII ; see note 2 there.

following incident, partly because Martin's miraculous powers do to some extent appear in it and partly because a situation that was deemed worthy of a miracle may well be put on record, to serve as a warning should anything of the kind occur anywhere again.

XXIII

There was a young man of most noble birth named Clarus, who afterwards became a priest and is now entitled by his happy end to be numbered among the blest.[1] He had left all and gone to join Martin and very soon was a shining example of the highest degree of faith and of all the virtues. He had established himself in a hut not far from the Bishop's monastery and had many brethren living round him. Thus there came to him a youth named Anatolius, who used the monastic way of life to make a false display of humility and innocence, and for a time shared the common life with the others.

Then, as time went on, he began to speak of angels that were in the habit of conversing with him. As nobody would credit this, he produced certain manifestations that did induce a number to believe. Eventually he reached the point of asserting that angelic messengers passed between himself and God ; and it was now his ambition to be regarded as one of the Prophets.

But nothing could persuade Clarus to believe in him. Anatolius began threatening him with the wrath of God and immediate chastisement for not believing in a saint. He is said to have burst out finally into this speech :

" I tell you, this very night God will give me a shining robe from out of heaven and I will make my abode among you clad in it, and it shall be a sign to you that in me dwells the Power of God, who has presented me with His garment."

This declaration roused everybody to the highest pitch of expectation. And indeed, about midnight, the heavy thudding of dancing feet seemed to shake the ground under every hermitage

---

[1] The Roman Martyrology for November 8th mentions a St. Clarus who was a priest at Tours and died a few days before his master, St. Martin. See Butler's *Lives* (Thurston-Attwater) for November, under November 4th (p. 56).

in the place. You could see, too, the cell which housed this young man ablaze with a mass of lights ; and there was heard the thudding of feet running about in it, and what might have been the murmur of many voices.

Then came silence and he emerged and called one of the brethren, named Sabatius, and showed him the tunic he was wearing. The brother in amazement called the rest to come, and even Clarus came hurrying up. A light was brought and all carefully inspected the garment. It was exceedingly soft, with a surpassing lustre, and of a brilliant scarlet, but it was impossible to tell the nature of the material. At the same time, under the most exact scrutiny of eyes and fingers it seemed to be a garment and nothing else.[1]

Meawnhile Clarus had been urging the brethren to pray their hardest to be shown by the Lord what it was. The rest of the night, therefore, was spent in singing hymns and psalms. At daybreak he took Anatolius by the hand with the intention of taking him to Martin, being well aware that Martin could not be taken in by a trick of the devil. At this, the wretched man began to resist and protest loudly, saying that he had been forbidden to show himself to Martin. And when he was being forced to go against his will, between the hands of those who were dragging him the garment disappeared. Who, then, can doubt that Martin had this power also, that the devil was unable to keep up his illusions or conceal their nature when they were to be submitted to Martin's eyes ?

XXIV

It was remarked, however, about this same time that a youth in Spain acquired some authority by a number of manifestations and this so turned his head that he gave himself out to be Elijah. When many were so rash as to believe this, he went further and said that he was Christ. Even then he took some people in, and a

---

[1] It may be suggested that silk might have served the purposes of this impostor much as cheese-cloth serves those of his modern representatives. It was a great rarity in the West at this period. Sidonius Apollinaris, Bishop of Clermont, who died in 479, speaks of a garment of silk as one of the splendours of a young prince (Ep. iv. 20)—but it was well known in the eastern part of the Empire and Anatolius is a Greek name.

bishop named Rufus adored him as God, for which we afterwards saw him deposed from his office.

Again, many of the brethren have told me that at the same period there was someone in the East who boasted that he was John. We can infer from this that, with false prophets of this kind about, the coming of Antichrist is at hand; for in them he is already active, as the Mystery of Iniquity.[1]

Nor do I think I should pass over a very skilful ruse that the devil tried on Martin about this period. One day, announcing himself by a salutation,[2] he came and stood before Martin as he was praying in his cell. He was enveloped in a bright red light, thinking to deceive more easily if he shone with borrowed splendour. He wore, too, a royal robe and was crowned with a diadem of gems and gold, and gold gleamed upon his shoes. His face was serene and his expression joyful, so that he should be thought anything rather than the devil.[3]

At the first sight of him, Martin was staggered and for a long time there was complete silence between them. The devil spoke first.

" Martin," he said, " you see me. Acknowledge me. I am Christ. I am about to come down upon the earth and I wished first to manifest myself to you."

Martin received this in silence and made no kind of response, and the devil had the audacity to repeat his daring claim.

" Martin," he said, " why so slow to believe, now that you see? I am Christ."

Then, enlightened by the Holy Spirit, Martin knew that it was the devil and not Our Lord.

" The Lord Jesus ", said he, " did not say that he would come in purple robe and glittering diadem. I will only believe in a Christ who comes in the garments and the lineaments of His Passion, who comes bearing upon Him the wounds of the Cross."

[1] 2 Thess. ii. 7.

[2] It is difficult to give any other meaning in the present context to Halm's reading : " praemissa prece ".

[3] What follows will be better understood if it is borne in mind that Millenarian opinions were widely prevalent in the Church at this time and were favoured by Severus himself. They interpreted the thousand years' reign of Apocalypse xx. 1–6 as referring to a visible sojourn of Christ on earth, to reign as King with His saints ; and it was supposed that this was to come speedily.

At these words the devil immediately vanished like smoke, filling the cell with such a stench as to put it beyond doubt that it was the devil indeed. And should anyone think that I am romancing, I had the story, just as I have told it, from Martin's own lips.

XXV

You must understand that I had previously heard accounts of his faith, his life and his powers and burned with the desire to know the man himself. I therefore undertook as a labour of love a pilgrimage to see him. At the same time I was all on fire to write his life and I collected part of my information from him, so far as it was possible to question him, and learnt the rest from those who had first-hand knowledge.

You would never credit the humility and kindness with which he received me on that occasion. He congratulated himself and praised the Lord because I had thought so highly of him that I had undertaken a long journey especially to see him. And poor me!—I hardly dare say it—when he condescended to let me sit at his sacred board, it was he who fetched the water for me to wash my hands and, in the evening, it was he who washed my feet. Nor had I the courage to remonstrate or resist. I was so overborne by his authority that I would have felt it impious to do anything but acquiesce.

But all his talk while I was there was of the necessity of renouncing the allurements of the world and the burdens of secular life in order to follow the Lord Jesus freely and unimpeded. He quoted as an outstanding example in our own day the case of his Excellency Paulinus, whom I mentioned earlier.[1] He had abandoned immense wealth to follow Christ and was almost alone in

---

[1] " His Excellency " here, as in other Lives in this volume, renders " vir illustris ", which was a title confined to the very highest rank in the imperial service. It is possible, however, that it is not used here in its technical sense, in which case it might be rendered " that most distinguished man " or (as in section XX) " a man of the very highest rank." (Compare Dialogue II (III), 17 and note 2 there.)

St. Paulinus of Nola has already appeared in section XIX (see note 2 there). He was born about A.D. 354. He and the author were fellow members of the Aquitainian nobility, and personal friends. He inherited vast wealth, which was increased by his marriage, and was a man of wide culture and considerable literary gifts. He held also many public offices. He was not baptized, though he seems

our times in fulfilling the evangelical counsels. " There," Martin
kept exclaiming, " there is someone for you to follow. There ",
he cried, " is someone to imitate." He held that our generation
was blessed in possessing such an example of faith and virtue.
For a rich man with great possessions, by selling all and giving to
the poor, had illustrated Our Lord's saying, that what is impossible
to do is in fact a possibility.[2]

But what seriousness there was, what dignity, in Martin's words
and conversation ! And how eager he was, and forceful, and how
promptly and easily he solved scriptural problems. I know that
many are sceptical on this last point ; indeed, I have seen some
still incredulous even when it was I myself who told them. I
therefore call Jesus to witness, and the hope we all hold in common,
that never from any other lips have I heard so much knowledge,
so much natural talent and such purity of diction. It is little
enough praise when we remember Martin's miracles, but it may
surely rank as a wonder that not even this gift was lacking in a
quite uneducated man.

XXVI

But my book is asking to be ended, my story must be brought to
a close, not because there is no more to be said about Martin, but
because I, like an indolent craftsman, growing careless as his task
is ending, have abandoned the effort, beaten by the weight of the
material. For although it was possible to depict his outward
actions in words (after a fashion), no language at all—none, I can
say with truth—could ever depict his interior life, his everyday
behaviour and his mind ever fixed upon heaven. I say again, not
even Homer, if, as the saying goes, he returned from Hades, could
do justice to his perseverance and self-discipline in abstinence and
fasting ; to his capacity for night vigils and prayer ; to the nights,

---

to have had leanings towards Christianity. Before the age of 40, however, soon
after A.D. 390, he had retired from public life, accepted baptism and given away
most of his wealth. He was then ordained a priest at Barcelona, being practically
forced to it by popular clamour (A.D. 394 or 395) and in the year following settled
down to a semi-monastic life at Nola, in Italy. All this took place during the
life-time of St. Martin and before Severus had completed this biography of
him. Paulinus subsequently became Bishop of Nola and died A.D. 431. His
Feast is on June 22nd.

[2] Matt. xix. 26.

and days also, spent by him without any time taken from the work
of God for indulgence either in recreation or in business, or even
in sleep or food except in so far as nature insisted—it was all so
much greater in Martin than words can express.

Not an hour, not a moment passed without his either giving
himself to prayer or applying himself to reading. But in truth,
even during his reading or anything else he happened to be
doing, he never let his mind relax from prayer. Blacksmiths have
a way of striking on their anvils while working, as a kind of relief
from the strain ; that was precisely how Martin, when he seemed
to be doing something else, was praying all the time. A truly
blessed man, " in whom there was no guile "—judging no man,
condemning no man, never returning evil for evil. Indeed, he
had armed himself with such patience in the face of every injury
that, although he was a prelate, he could be wronged with
impunity by the lowest of his clergy. He never dismissed them
from their posts for such offences nor, so far as it lay with him,
did he exclude them from his charity.

XXVII

No one ever saw him angered, no one saw him excited, none
saw him grieving, none saw him laughing. He was always just
the same, with a kind of celestial joy shining in his face, so that
he seemed more than human. There was never anything on his
lips but Christ, nor anything in his heart but kindness, peace and
mercy. He was constantly weeping, too, for the sins of those
whom he believed to be his calumniators—men who, with
poisoned tongues and the bite of adders, used to pick him to
pieces in his retired and peaceful life.

Indeed, I have come across some who were so envious of his
spiritual powers and his life as actually to hate in him what they
missed in themselves but had not the strength to imitate. And—
oh, grievous and lamentable scandal !—nearly all his calumniators
—there were not a great many—nearly all his calumniators were
bishops. There is no need to mention names, though several of
them are barking now at me. It will serve the same purpose if

any of them who reads this and recognizes himself is made to blush. For his anger will be an admission that it applies to him, though I might, in fact, have had someone else in mind.

Besides, if such people exist, I have no objection to being hated by them in the company of such a man as Martin. I can be quite sure that this little work will give pleasure to all good Christians. I will only add that if anyone reads it sceptically he will be sinning. I am clear in my own conscience that my motives for writing were the certainty of the facts and the love of Christ and that I have only related what is well known, only said what is true. As for the reward prepared (as I hope) by God, not he who reads, but " he who believes " [1] shall have it.

[1] Mark xvi. 16.

THREE LETTERS OF SULPICIUS SEVERUS
ON ST. MARTIN OF TOURS

THESE so-called letters (if a translator's impressions are any guide), though perhaps something of a literary *tour de force*, in other respects show Sulpicius at his worst. They were written to supplement the biography of St. Martin he had just completed but convey the minimum of information with the maximum of over-elaboration and literary affectation—so much so that, if we had nothing else to go by, I for one would find it very difficult to give him much credit for sincerity. As it is, while accepting the fact that in these shorter pieces he surrendered himself almost unrestrainedly to his literary foibles and vanities (not unparalleled in our own eighteenth-century literature) we should keep in mind at the same time the fact that he was also the author of the Life. If we do this, we may reasonably draw the inference that some very strong influence intervened to enable the literary poseur of the Letters to sustain almost throughout the longer work (apart from the conventional insincerities and flourishes of the Dedication and Preface) a comparative simplicity and restraint. That " something " can only have been a deep affection and reverence for his master in the spiritual life and the living presence of the saint in his own monastery, which together brought out in Sulpicius a genuinely religious nature and a regard for truth which existed under the character of " the literary man " to which he all too easily reverted in his own home.

THREE LETTERS OF SULPICIUS SEVERUS

LETTER I

TO THE PRIEST EUSEBIUS[1]

YESTERDAY a number of monks came to see me, and there was continual story-telling and prolonged conversation. In the course of it, mention was made of a little book I have published on the life of that saintly man Martin and I was very pleased to hear that it is being eagerly and widely read. At the same time I was informed of a remark made by someone prompted by a malicious demon : how was it (he had asked) that Martin, who had raised the dead and averted flames from houses, was liable himself to dangerous accidents and had recently been badly burnt in a fire.

What a miserable wretch, whoever he is ! In his words we see again the unbelief of the Jews and hear their words as they reviled Our Lord as He hung upon the Cross : " He saved others; He cannot save Himself." Obviously whoever the man is, he should have been born in those days and then he would have had no difficulty in using those words against Our Lord Himself. Certainly the will to disbelieve would not have been lacking in one who uttered similar blasphemies against one of Our Lord's saints.[2]

And what of it, anyhow, whoever you are ? Has Martin no powers, has Martin no holiness, because he was in danger from a fire ? That man so blessed ! and in all things like the Apostles, even in being thus insulted. We are told that the heathen had the same thoughts about Paul when the viper bit him : " This man ", they said, " must be a murderer. Though he has been saved from

---

[1] See the Dialogues, *Postumianus* (2, IX).
[2] The last two sentences render the text as expanded by Babut's incorporation of several words from the text in the Book of Armagh. The Latin as he reconstructs it runs : " Vere plane iste quicumque est si illis temporibus natus esset utique in Dominum hanc vocem emittere potuisset. Profecto nequaquam ei voluntas ad perfidiam defuisset, qui simili sanctum Domini blasphemat exemplo." See the Introductory Note to the Dialogues.

the sea, the fates will not let him live." But he shook the viper off into the fire and suffered no harm. They expected to see him fall down suddenly and quickly die but, when they saw that no harm befell him, they changed their minds and said that he was a god.

Why, even from that example, most unhappily inspired of mortals, you should have been able to have convicted yourself of lack of faith, seeing that, if you found a difficulty in the fact that Martin seems to have been touched by the flames, you should on second thoughts have seen his virtues and power in the very fact that he was touched ; since, though surrounded by flames, he did not perish.

And think of this, wretched man, think of this (what you seem not to know), that almost all the saints were more remarkable for the dangers they incurred than for their miracles. I can, indeed, see Peter, strong in faith, walking on the sea in defiance of nature and treading the shifting waters with feet of flesh and blood. But the preacher to the Gentiles does not seem to me a lesser man because the waves swallowed him up and the waters restored him as he ascended from the depths after three days and as many nights.[3] In fact, I almost think that it was a greater thing to have lived in the depths of the sea than to have walked above them.

But I do not suppose you had read these things, foolish man, or, if you had, you did not attend to them. For it was part of a divine plan (and not merely to instruct the human mind as to the dangers from shipwrecks and snakes !) that the blessed Evangelist should have set down such an occurrence in his sacred writings ; and the Apostle, who gloried in nakedness and hunger and perils from robbers, shows us that to suffer from all these things is the common lot of the saints, but tnat tne especial virtue of the righteous has always been to endure them and overcome them and that, patient and ever unconquered through all their trials, they are the greater in victory the more they had to bear.[4]

This incident, therefore, which has been cited as a proof of

---

[3] Based on a misreading of 2 Cor. xi. 25.
[4] This translation of this long sentence approaches paraphrase in parts, and necessarily so, since the author's Latin, like his scriptural lore, is here somewhat confused—perhaps the nemesis of overmuch elaboration of his theme

Martin's frailty, really redounds to his credit and glory, seeing
that, when tried by a most dangerous situation, he came out
victorious. As for its omission by me from the little book I wrote
on his life, that is nothing to wonder at. I state in the book itself
that I do not include all his doings—if I had tried to recount
everything, I should have presented my readers with an enormous
volume. It is not as if Martin had done so little that the inclusion
of everything was practicable. However, as a question has arisen
over this particular incident, I will not let it remain untold. I will
relate the whole episode as it took place, in case I should be suspected of deliberately omitting what could have been used to
discredit this man of blessings.

Towards the middle of one winter, Martin had come to a certain
parish on one of his periodical visits such as bishops are in the
habit of paying to churches in their dioceses. The clergy had got
the sacristy of the church ready for him to sleep in. They had
made up a big fire under the crumbling and excessively thin
concrete flooring[5] and had built a bed for him with a great
quantity of straw. When Martin had settled down on it, he was
horrified at the unaccustomed softness of this all too enticing
couch, for it was his habit to lie on the bare earth with nothing
but a piece of sackcloth over him. He felt as though someone had
done him an injury, and threw all the bedding away. In removing
it, he happened to pile some of the straw immediately over the
furnace. Then, tired out by his journey, he laid himself down to
rest as usual on the bare ground.

Towards midnight the heat of the fire, drawn up through the
flooring, in which (as I have said) there were cracks, set the dry
straw on fire. Martin was roused from his sleep and, being thrown
off his guard by the unexpectedness of the event, by the extremity
of the danger and, most of all (as he used to relate), by the devil
himself lying in wait and assailing him, resorted less promptly
than he should have done to the power of prayer. For in seeking
to break out of the room, he struggled long and laboriously with
the bolt with which he had fastened the door, until he found the

---

[5] The ordinary Roman method of heating buildings was by a system of flues
under the floor, carrying hot air from a furnace in the basement.

conflagration becoming so intense around him that the fire was actually destroying the garment he was wearing.

Then at last he came to his senses and realized that safety lay, not in flight, but in the Lord. Thereupon, taking the prayer of faith for his shield and fixing his mind upon the Lord entirely, he lay down upon the flames. Then, sure enough, the fire by divine ordinance drew back and he continued to pray within a circle of flames that could now do him no harm. But the monks, who were now outside the folding doors and could hear the crackling and the raging of the conflagration, burst the bolts that held the doors and, thrusting aside the burning material, took Martin out from among the flames, though one would have supposed that by now he would have been burnt to ashes by a conflagration that had lasted so long.

I will only add—and I call Our Lord to witness to my words—that Martin himself told me, and confessed it with sighs, that on this occasion he had been caught by the devil's wiles. That was why, when startled out of his sleep, he had not had the sense to think of meeting the danger with the prayer of faith. And so long as he tried, with mind distraught, to break out through the door, the fire was fierce all round him. But as soon as he had once more taken the Cross for his standard and prayer for his weapon, the flames in the centre had fallen back and he had felt them now as dew upon him, after they had been giving him the most cruel burns.

Therefore " let every reader understand "[6] that Martin was certainly tested by that danger but in truth was not found wanting.

Letter II

To The Deacon Aurelius

After you had left me in the morning, when I was sitting alone in my cell, I fell into a train of thought that often occupies my mind—hopes for the future, disgust with the present, fear of the

[6] Matt. xxiv. 15.

Judgement, and dread of its penalties. From that I was brought
to what had, indeed, been the starting point of the whole meditation—the remembrance of my sins ; and it saddened and exhausted
me. My limbs were fatigued by the anguish of my mind and,
when finally I stretched them on my bed, sleep stole upon me,
as is so often the effect of grief.

But sleep is always rather light and uncertain in the morning
hours, and hovers over one's limbs in an undecided fashion, so
that one is just awake enough to know that one is sleeping, which
never happens in any other kind of slumber. It was then that
I suddenly seemed to see our holy Bishop Martin, dressed in a
white robe, his face ablaze, his eyes like stars, his hair glowing
red. He appeared to me in the same bodily form and features
that I knew so well, but in such a way that—a thing not too easy
for me to put into words—he could be recognized by them without its being possible actually to look at them.

Smiling a little, he held out to me the book I had written on
his life. I embraced his sacred knees and begged his blessing, as
my custom was ; and I felt the caressing touch of his hand upon
my head as, among the formal words of the blessing, he repeated
the Name of the Crucified, so familiar on his lips. But presently,
while my eyes were still fixed upon him (for I could not have
enough of the sight of his countenance) he was suddenly taken
from me, snatched up on high. He traversed the immense
spaces of the upper air and I was able, gazing intently, to
follow him as he was swiftly borne upwards on a cloud ; but,
when the heavens had opened and received him, he could no
longer be seen.

Soon afterwards I saw the holy priest Clarus, who had lately
died, ascend in the same way as his master.[1] I had the imperti-
nence to want to follow him but, while I toiled and struggled to
take the steep steps heavenwards, I woke up. I shook off my sleep
and had just begun to congratulate myself on the vision, when a
boy of the household entered, looking unusually sad, and speaking
and sobbing in the same breath.

" What are you trying to tell me with such a sad face ? " said I.

[1] See the Life, section XXIII, and the footnote there.

" Two monks ", he replied, " have just arrived from Tours. They have brought news that my lord Martin is dead."

I admit I broke down. Bursting into tears I wept unrestrainedly. Even now, while I write this to you, my brother, the tears are flowing, and I refuse to be comforted in such unbearable sorrow. But you who were my partner in affection for him—when the news came I wanted you to share my grief. Come, then, to me at once, that together we may mourn over him whom together we love.

Yes, I know that there should be no mourning for such a man, who, after overcoming the world and passing triumphantly through this earthly life, has now received the crown of righteousness. But my grief will not cease at my orders. An advocate, truly, has gone on before me, but my solace in this life is lost.

And yet, if sorrow could listen to arguments, I ought to be rejoicing. For he is now mingling with the Apostles and Prophets and, with due respect to all the saints, is second to none in that assemblage of the righteous. And his particular place, I hope, I believe, I trust, is in the company of those who have washed their robes in blood, where, cleansed from every stain, he walks in the throng whose leader is the Lamb.

For although the character of our times has been such as not to afford him the opportunity of martyrdom, he none the less will share the martyr's glory. If it had been given to him to have a part in those struggles that were waged in the days of Nero and Decius,[2] then (I call the God of heaven and earth to witness) he would have mounted of his own free will upon the rack or he would have flung himself spontaneously into the fire and, even in the midst of the furnace, would have sung a hymn to the Lord among the sheets of flame, peer of the Hebrew youths.

If the persecutor had chosen for him the torture inflicted on Isaias, he would have given his limbs to the teeth and blades of the saws as fearlessly as the Prophet. If impious fury had preferred to hurl this man of happy destiny from the rock's edge upon the mountain's face—I bear unhesitating witness to the

[2] Reckoned, in St. Augustine's enumeration, as the first and seventh persecutions respectively, the latter being less than 150 years distant from the date at which Severus was writing.

truth—of his own free will would he have fallen. Or if he had fared as the Teacher of the Gentiles and been assigned to the sword and, as so often happened, had been led to execution with other victims, he would have prevailed upon the executioner and been the first to win the blood-stained palm.

But indeed there is not one of those pains and penalties before which so often frail humanity gives way which he would not have met unyieldingly, so little deterred from witnessing to Our Lord that, happy in his wounds, rejoicing in his agonies, he would have smiled under any torments.

He did not have to endure these things; nevertheless he achieved martyrdom though he shed no blood. For of what human sorrows did he not, for the hope of eternity, endure the pain—in hunger, in night watchings, in nakedness, in fasting, in the insults of the envious, in the persecutions of the wicked, in care for the sick, in anxiety for those in peril? Who was in sorrow and Martin did not sorrow too? Whose fall was not his shame? Who perished and he did not sigh? And all this in addition to his daily and varied warfare against the forces of human and spiritual wickedness.[3] But though he was assailed by every kind of trial, his will to conquer, his patience in waiting, his serenity in enduring, always gave him the victory.

Truly a man whose kindness, mercy and charity exceeded all words. Daily, even among holy men, charity grows colder in our cold generation, but in him it went on increasing day by day to the very end. For myself, I benefited in a special degree from this quality of his, for he had a special place in his heart for me, all unworthy and undeserving as I am.

And now the tears are flowing again and a sigh wells up from the very depths of my breast. Where is the man in whom, after this, I shall find such rest for my soul and by whose charity I shall be comforted? What a wretched, what an unhappy fate is mine! Shall I ever be able, as long as I live, to cease to grieve that I survived Martin? Will life for the future have any pleasure for me? Will there be a day or an hour without tears? And in your company, my very dear brother, shall I be able to speak of him

---

[3] This passage is modelled on, and in part quoted from, 2 Cor. xi. 27–29.

without weeping? But shall I ever be able to talk to you without speaking of him?

But why do I provoke you to tears and lamentations? Listen; though I cannot console myself, I want you to be consoled.

Believe me, he will never be far from us, never. He will be amongst us when we talk of him; he will stand by us when we pray. He will often bestow on us the sight that he has already been pleased to grant today, of himself in glory; and he will protect us by constantly renewing the blessing that he gave a little while ago. He has shown us, furthermore, by the pattern of the vision, that heaven stands open for his followers and has instructed us whither to follow him. He has taught us where our hopes should be placed and on what our minds should be fixed.

But how will it all end, my brother? For I know myself too well to think that I can climb that steep path and pass within, burdened as I am with such a grievous load, which is dragging me down in my wretchedness to the horrors of hell, with the weight of my sins upon me and the stars above denied to me. But there is still a hope, just one, just one last hope, that, what I cannot obtain myself, I may be reckoned to have earned through Martin's prayers.

But why, brother mine, am I keeping you so long with a letter so garrulous that I delay your own coming? And now the page is full and will hold no more! Yet I had a reason for writing at some considerable length. This letter was bringing bad news and I wanted the same sheet to bring you consolation in the form of something like a chat together.

LETTER III

SULPICIUS SEVERUS GREETS BASSULA, HIS REVERED PARENT[1]

IF it could be right to bring an action against a parent, I should obviously take you into the praetor's court in righteous indignation

---

[1] His mother-in-law. The opening paragraphs must be understood, not as a serious remonstrance, but as somewhat heavy jocularity superimposed on the author's habitual affectation of reluctance to have his writings published.

on charges of robbery and theft. For why should I not complain
of the injury you have done me? You have left me without a
scrap of writing in the house, not a book, not a letter—to such an
extent do you rob me of everything and pass them all on! If I
write an intimate letter to a friend, if perhaps I dictate something
to amuse myself but with the intention of keeping it out of sight,
it all gets to you almost before it is written or dictated. I think
that you must have my shorthand writers pledged to you and that
it is they who are responsible for the publication of my futilities.

But I cannot be angry with them, if it is you they are obeying.
If they are under my orders, it is mainly through your generosity,
and they still regard themselves as yours as much as mine. You
alone are the culprit, you alone are to blame. For me you lay
traps, and them you outwit with your wiles, with the result that
things written for intimates or carelessly thrown off are handed
over to you without any selection, in their first rough draft and
quite unpolished.

And, to say nothing of the rest, how comes it that the letter I
recently wrote to the deacon Aurelius reached you so quickly?
I was at Toulouse[2] and you were at Trier, drawn all that way
from your native land by anxiety on behalf of your son. What
opportunity had you for stealing that private letter? And yet I
have received a letter from you in which you say that " in the
letter in which I speak of the death of our holy Martin " I should
have described the manner of his passing. As if I had sent out
that letter to be read by anyone except the one to whom it was
supposed to go! Or as if I were destined for a work of such
magnitude as making known through my own writings all that
ought to be known about Martin!

So if there is anything you want to hear about the death of the
holy Bishop, address your enquiries for preference to those who
were present. As for me, I have made up my mind to write
nothing for you, for fear you publish it everywhere. However, if
you will give me your promise that you will read it to nobody, I
will do what you ask in a few words and give you the benefit of
as much as I know myself.

[2] Latin, " Tolosa ".

Martin, then, foresaw his own death long in advance and told the brethren that the time was at hand for his body to be dissolved. In the meantime occasion arose for him to pay a visit to the parish of Candes.[3] The clergy of the Church there were quarrelling among themselves and he wished to restore peace and, though well aware of his approaching end, would not refuse to go, with a reason of that kind for going. He thought that it would be a fitting end to his mighty works if he left to this Church a legacy of peace restored.

He set out, therefore, with the numerous and holy company of disciples with which he always travelled. He noticed on the river some water-fowl diving for fish and gorging their voracious crops with continual captures. " There ", he said, " you have a picture of the demons. They lie in wait for the unwary, catch them before they know, devour them when they have caught them, and are never satisfied with those they have devoured." Then, exercising over those birds the same authority with which he used to put the demons to flight, he ordered them with words of power to leave the stream in which they were swimming and betake themselves to waterless and unfrequented regions.

At this, all the wild-fowl formed themselves into a flock and, flying in one body, left the river and made for the mountains and forests. There were many witnesses and it caused them no little astonishment to see in Martin powers so great that he could even order birds about.

He stayed for some time at the village and church he had gone to. Then, when peace had been re-established among the clergy and he was thinking of returning to his monastery, suddenly his bodily powers began to fail him. He called the brethren together and informed them that the end had come. Then indeed did sorrow and grief fall upon all, and they wailed as with one voice :

" Father, why are you deserting us ? To whose care are you leaving us when we are orphaned ? Ravening wolves will attack your flock and, with the shepherd struck down, who will save us from their bites ? We know that you long to be with Christ, but

[3] Latin, " Condate ". There were several towns in Gaul with this name, but the identification with Candes seems to be now undisputed. Candes is, like Tours, a town on the Loire, but is over 30 miles further down the river.

you are sure of your reward and the delay will not make it less. Have pity on us instead of deserting us."

Martin was touched by these tears (he was always united to Our Lord in the abundance of his compassion) and he is reported to have wept; and his only reply to the mourners were the words with which he addressed Our Lord: " Lord, if I am still necessary to Thy people, I do not refuse the toil; Thy will be done."

And in truth, with a choice between hope fulfilled and sorrow prolonged, he hardly knew which of the two he wanted, for he neither wished to desert his flock nor to be kept any longer from Christ. To his own desires, however, he attached no weight and to his own will he left nothing. He surrendered himself entirely to the judgement and disposal of Our Lord, and this was his prayer :[4]

" Lord, this warfare in the body is a heavy burden and to have fought until now is enough. But if it is Thine order that I toil on still, mounting guard over the camp of Thy people, I do not refuse, nor plead the feebleness of age. I will consecrate myself to the fulfilment of the duties Thou dost lay upon me; I will fight on under Thy banners, so long as it is Thy command. Sweet to an old man is release after labour, but the will can triumph over length of life and knows no yielding to old age. But shouldst Thou now be indulgent to my years, it is Thy will, O Lord, and it is good. As for these for whom I fear, Thou Thyself wilt be their guardian."

Yes, a man no words can describe! unconquered by toil, unconquerable by death, who had no preference for either alternative, neither fearing to die nor refusing to live.

By now he had been subject for some days to a high fever, but he never relinquished the Work of God. Spending his nights in prayers and vigils, he compelled his worn-out limbs to obey his spirit. He lay on that noble bed of his—ashes and sack-cloth—and, when his disciples begged him to let them at least lay some

---

[4] The Latinity and rhetoric of the elaborate composition that follows strikingly resemble those of Severus himself. We were told, indeed, three sentences back, that Martin's only reply to his petitioners was the short and simple prayer there quoted. To that, the rest adds virtually nothing.

common straw under him, he replied : " It is not fitting that a Christian should die except upon ashes. If I leave you any different example, I shall have sinned."

But he never ceased to direct his eyes and hands towards heaven and, unconquered in spirit, never relaxed from prayer. The priests who by this time had gathered round him asked that they might ease his poor body by turning him onto one side. " Let me," said he, " let me, my brethren, keep my eyes on heaven rather than on earth, so that my spirit may be set now in the right direction for the journey to the Lord it is about to take." As he said this, he saw the devil standing near him.

" Why are you standing here, blood-thirsty beast," said he ; " you will find nothing for yourself in me, you dismal creature. Abraham's bosom is awaiting me."

With these words, he yielded up his spirit. Those who were present have declared to me that his face looked like the face of an angel, while his limbs were found to be as white as snow. " Who would have thought ", said those who saw it, " that he had been covered with sackcloth and lain in ashes ? " For he already looked as he will appear with transfigured body in the glory of the resurrection to come.

No one could believe what a vast multitude gathered for the funeral. The whole city poured out to meet the body.[5] Everyone from the farms and the villages was there, and many even from the surrounding towns. Great, indeed, was the grief of all ; great, especially, the lamentations of the sorrowing monks. It is said that nearly two thousand of them were assembled on that day—Martin's especial glory ; for it was his example that had caused this plant so to multiply and bear fruit for the Lord's service. In truth the shepherd was driving his flocks before him —the pale hosts, the hooded ranks of that holy throng, some old men with their labours ended, some recruits newly sworn to Christ's service.

Then came the consecrated virgin choir, abstaining from the unseemliness of weeping and concealing their grief under a holy

[5] The city in question is Tours, to which Martin's body was brought for its interment, which, according to the undoubted tradition of the Church at Tours, took place on November 11th. The year was almost certainly A.D. 397.

joy. But though the strength of their faith might forbid them to weep, their feelings forced a sigh. And right and proper was this sadness at his death, and no less holy was their gladness at his glory. You could pardon their weeping; you could join in their rejoicing. For every man owed it to himself to weep, and to Martin to rejoice.

Thus this multitude, chanting the hymns of heaven, accompanied the body of the man of blessings to the place of burial. Compare it, if you like, with a worldly pageant—and I will take a triumphal procession, not a funeral. What can you find in that to rival Martin's obsequies? Let others drive before their chariots captives with hands bound behind their backs; Martin's body was followed by those who, with him for their leader, have overcome the world. Let others have the honour of the disordered clappings of a frenzied populace. Martin was applauded with sacred psalmody; Martin was honoured by celestial songs. The others, when their triumphs are over, shall be thrust into hell's fury; Martin enters rejoicing into Abraham's bosom. Martin, the poor man, the lowly, goes rich into heaven. And from there, I hope, he looks down upon us and protects us both, me as I write and you as you read.

THE DIALOGUES OF SULPICIUS SEVERUS

THESE Dialogues come last, chronologically speaking, among the writings of Sulpicius about St. Martin, as their references to the other writings would of themselves be sufficient to show. If we regard as historical fact the journey which one of their characters is supposed to have made and combine the "three years ago" of section III of Dialogue I with the references to the circulation of the Life in Italy and elsewhere contained in section XXII, we obtain for the Dialogues a date just before A.D. 400. We are probably safe in accepting this as the date of the Dialogues even if we regard the journey of Postumianus as a dramatic fiction.

It is fairly evident that they were not written with the same unity of purpose as inspired the Life. It is not until we are half way through the first, and by far the longer, of the two Dialogues that we reach the glories of St. Martin to which the whole of the Life is devoted. The earlier half is taken up with an enthusiastic account of Egyptian monasticism.

This is not to say that this first part of the Dialogues is without interest for the modern reader or, for that matter, for the modern student of the life of St. Martin. It is of interest for the stories it tells and, from the historical point of view, as one of the first and certainly one of the most successful pieces of literary propaganda for what was, at any rate in the West, the still very modern institution of monasticism, of which Martin was the outstanding pioneer there. In this respect it ranks high among the makers of public opinion in the incipient Christendom of the fifth century.

It is probably true also to say, as Babut has done (see the references given below), that as propaganda it is directed particularly against the attack made by a former disciple of Sulpicius upon the monastic movement in general and the ascetic theories of St. Jerome in particular. This renegade disciple was a certain Vigilantius, who in A.D. 396 travelled to the East and visited St. Jerome at Bethlehem with an introduction from Sulpicius' friend, St. Paulinus of Nola. On leaving Bethlehem he charged St. Jerome with being associated with the alleged heresies of Origen of Alexandria (see section VII of this Dialogue and the notes there) and this drew an angry reply from St. Jerome (Ep. 61). Then, on returning to Aquitaine, Vigilantius published a general attack on St. Jerome, concentrating particularly on his teachings concerning the ascetic life.

This attack was eventually answered by St. Jerome in a violent pamphlet entitled *Adversus Vigilantium*. In the meantime, however,

63

(so Babut suggests) Sulpicius had been much distressed by his former disciple's attack on asceticism in general and St. Jerome in particular and had sent Postumianus (after whom this first Dialogue is named) to the East, partly in order to check the charges made by Vigilantius by first-hand information. Consequently the first part of this Dialogue may be regarded as his own reply to Vigilantius in this war of pamphlets. (See " Sur Trois Lignes Inédites de Sulpice Sévère ", *Moyen Age*, 2ᵉ Série, t.x ; also *The Book of Armagh*, ed. Gwynn, 1913, pp. cclxxvi–cclxxviii.)

This is a sufficiently probable conclusion, but a reservation must be made regarding the phrase about " sending Postumianus ", which assumes that Postumianus existed in real life and not merely as a character in the Dialogues. That is an assumption that is commonly made but is by no means necessary, as we shall see in a moment.

Besides these objects in writing the Dialogues, it would appear that Sulpicius had two others, considerably less praiseworthy. One was to " boost " the Life he had written and the other was to vent his spleen against Martin's successor in the see of Tours and the whole very powerful anti-Martin party associated with him. These purposes are only too painfully evident at several points.

To give effect to all these purposes he chose a literary form doubly suited to them, namely the dialogue. It enabled him, first, to give variety and liveliness to his treatment of his material and secondly to put into the mouths of other characters sentiments that would hardly be seemly in his own. This second advantage was enhanced by his putting himself into the Dialogues as one of the characters but giving himself a very small speaking part. The other, or literary, gain from the dialogue form is frankly avowed by the author towards the end (II (III) 5).

Nor, indeed, is there the slightest reason why it should not be avowed, for there is nothing to be ashamed of in making use of the dialogue's literary appeal. Furthermore, it would be entirely wrong and unfair to accuse an author of untruthfulness or insincerity because he introduced into his dialogues fictitious characters making fictitious journeys and the like. Such devices have been employed by some of the greatest writers of the world without detriment to the essential truths they were setting out to convey.

Whether in actual fact the use of the dialogue form has caused this particular writer to distort the essential truth in any particular statement is, of course, another question, to be considered on its merits in this as in any other case. Sulpicius himself, in the very passage in which he avows his use of a literary fiction, insists that it has not caused him to depart from what to him was the essential truth he was intending to convey, namely the real facts about Martin's miracles.

Every reader is entitled to judge for himself whether the author's claim is justified but at least he should approach the question unprejudiced by the possibility that the setting of these narratives is to some extent at least fictitious.

Even if he regards the very existence of most of the characters as a literary fiction, precisely the same rule should in fairness be applied. If, for example, he concludes (as he may well do) that neither Postumianus nor his journey ever existed outside the Dialogues, he may possibly be led by other considerations to the further conclusion that the author, having once employed fiction as a literary device for the setting of his stories, was unable to resist the temptation to blend fiction even with the essential stories within the setting; but he has no right to reach this conclusion on the sole ground that the author employed fiction for the setting, particularly as he makes no secret of the fact.

Setting this question aside, we may perhaps add that, even if the author had not avowed the fictitious character of the setting, any attentive reader might well have deduced it. For although these dialogues are, with the exception of a few passages, very well written, considered as a piece of Latinity, they are by no means well handled considered as a literary fiction. The author's inexperience in this rather difficult literary form has caused his unintentional lapses from realism to be numerous and sometimes ludicrous. Detective-minded readers with a bent for such pastimes could find some amusement in compiling a list of them—it would be far too long for insertion here. However, these blunders in dramatic technique scarcely impair the freshness and liveliness of the composition as a whole.

This brings us to the question of the numbering of the dialogues. It is now generally agreed that there were originally only two dialogues, divided as in the translation that follows. It is almost equally certain that they originally had the separate titles used here. The early MS. incorporated in the *Book of Armagh*, and made from a copy made (according to Babut) within fifty years of the original publication of the Dialogues, shows these divisions and titles unmistakably. (See the *Book of Armagh, Liber Ardmachanus*, ed. J. Gwynn, Dublin, 1913; and, on this question, Babut's communication to it, pp. cclxvii–cclxxv). On how the division into three dialogues came about, opinions differ; Babut's (for example) is questioned by Fr. Delehaye, S.J. (*Analecta Bollandiana*, t. 38 (1920), pp. 12, 13). Happily it need not delay us and we may rest content with the author's own division based on his representation of the two conversations as taking place respectively on two consecutive days.

Two other large changes were made in the text, quite early in its history, in the shape of the deliberate omission from many copies of two quite lengthy passages. The first of these passages consists of the greater part of the last section of the *Postumianus* (section XIV of the miscalled " second " dialogue ; this traditional numbering is preserved in brackets throughout this translation to facilitate reference to the older editions). The reason for the omission was that the teaching concerning Anti-Christ and the Second Coming attributed in it to St. Martin was regarded by many as heretical and had been expressly condemned by St. Jerome. Indeed, it caused the whole book of Dialogues to be put on a kind of Index of Prohibited Books drawn up in Gaul about A.D. 470 and erroneously called the Gelasian Decree (see Babut, loc. cit., pp. cclxix, cclxx) ; and the omission seems to have been made from most, if not all, of the copies made in Gaul about that time.

The other omission was of a passage in the *Gallus*, namely of sections XV and XVI. These sections contain a most violent and unpleasant attack on Bishop Brictio or Brice, St. Martin's successor in the see of Tours and actually the reigning bishop when the attack was published. This bishop was undoubtedly very hostile to St. Martin and he was moreover driven out of the see, after reigning more than thirty years, by grave charges against him. He thereupon retired to Rome, where (according to St. Gregory of Tours, *Historia Francorum*, II, 1 ; X, 31) he repented of his hostility to St. Martin and lived for seven years, at the end of which he was sent back to his see by the Pope. There he reigned again as bishop for another seven years, built a small basilica over the tomb of St. Martin and lived and died in great sanctity. After his death in about 444, he began to be venerated as a saint and figures as such at some length in Butler's *Lives* under November 13th.

It seems to be clear from the evidence of the MSS. that someone in authority about the middle of the fifth century (Babut suggests Bishop Perpetuus, who succeeded to the see in A.D. 461) brought about the suppression of this attack on Bishop Brictio as a contribution to the termination of the long feud between the pro-Martin and the anti-Martin factions. Few readers of the passage will question the wisdom of this step ; but it may be added that not the least offensive feature of it is what would appear to be (in effect) a libel, not on Brictio, but on Martin himself, whom Sulpicius was intending to glorify. For the latter, in his inordinate desire to score off his bishop, puts into his hero's mouth the ingeniously two-edged remark with which the passage ends and in which spitefulness and piety are combined in a manner entirely characteristic of Sulpicius at his worst. Fortunately, as was said in the introductory note to the Life, we are not compelled to judge either Sulpicius or St. Martin by these later writings alone.

Both these passages were restored in later times and, of course, appear in the following translation. The text from which the translation has been made is that used for the Life and the Letters, namely Karl Halm's (vol. I in the Vienna *Corpus Scriptorum Ecclesiasticorum Latinorum : Sulpicii Severi, Libri qui supersunt*). This text, though constructed as long ago as 1865 and on a very incomplete collation of MSS., has not yet been superseded. I have departed from it in a few cases where Babut, with the aid of the MS. in the *Book of Armagh* (of which Halm knew nothing) was able to supply missing lines or phrases or to reconstruct sentences where Halm's text was, on his own admission, hopelessly corrupt (loc. cit., pp. cclxxi–cclxxv). These passages, four in all (one is in the *Letters*), are duly pointed out in the footnotes. Babut also suggested, on the same basis, a large number of minor verbal emendations ; but since, in all these cases, Halm's text is complete and gives a satisfactory sense, only a thoroughgoing textual recension would enable an intelligent choice to be made between Babut's readings and Halm's in any particular case ; and, short of that, it seemed best to follow Halm consistently.

Finally, as regards earlier translations, of the three translations of the Life mentioned in the introductory note to it, two are continued to include the Dialogues, namely those of Roberts and Watt. I need add nothing to my earlier remarks on them except to say that the lively Latin Dialogues seem to have galvanized Dr. Roberts into a certain liveliness of a kind in the earlier portions of it, so that I have been glad, on perhaps three or four occasions, to borrow a happily turned phrase.

THE DIALOGUES OF SULPICIUS SEVERUS

DIALOGUE I

POSTUMIANUS[1]

I

GALLUS and I were together one day; he is a very dear friend of mine, partly because he brings back Martin to me, having been one of his disciples, and partly on his own account.[2] In came my friend Postumianus who, three years before this, had left his native land to go to the East and had now returned from there to see me. I embraced this most affectionate of men and kissed his knees and his feet. For a moment or two we were overwhelmed; then we took a turn together, shedding tears of joy; finally we spread sacking on the ground and sat down.

Postumianus spoke first. Looking at me, he said:

" When I was in a remote part of Egypt, I took it into my head to go down to the sea. There I found a merchant-ship ready to set sail, with a cargo consigned to Narbonne. That night I dreamt that you stood by me and put your hand on me, to force me to go

---

[1] Comprising what are traditionally known as Dialogues I and II.

[2] The Latin " Gallus " could be either a proper name or else a general term for an inhabitant of Gaul, and one translator of Severus does in fact take it in the latter sense throughout the Dialogues. The general trend of the Dialogues, however, seems to indicate that it should be treated as a proper name, but was almost certainly chosen by the author for his character in the dialogue because he wished to make him a symbolic figure (see, for example, sections IV, V, VIII and XXVII. The Gauls were a Celtic people, speaking originally a language akin to Welsh, who constituted the bulk of the population of the greater part of what is now France and Belgium. The whole of this region had been fairly thoroughly Romanized since its conquest by Julius Caesar (58-50 B.C.), but a contrast is drawn in this first dialogue (section XXVII) between the comparatively rustic Gauls and the more urban and refined Aquitainians, i.e. the inhabitants of the south-west portion of Gaul—Gascony and the surrounding regions—to which Severus himself belonged and where probably he wrote the Dialogues. Indeed, throughout most of this Dialogue, both Severus and Postumianus make friendly fun of the Gauls as a people to which they do not themselves belong, though the roles of Postumianus and Gallus are practically reversed, through some confusion, in section 2, VIII.

and embark on that ship. Very early, as soon as it was light enough, I rose from where I had been sleeping and began to turn my dream over in my mind, and I was suddenly seized with such a strong desire to see you that I embarked without further delay. On the thirtieth day I was put on shore at Marseilles and from there got here in ten days—good travelling to match all that devotion! And now you, seeing that I have sailed across all those seas and crossed so much land to see you, must send everybody else away and let me take possession of you and enjoy you."

" But what have I been doing," I replied, " even while you were stopping in Egypt, but keeping you company in my heart and mind? And our friendship completely occupied my thoughts, which were with you day and night. So you needn't think that there is going to be a moment now when I am not feasting my eyes on you and hanging on your lips, listening to you, talking to you, with absolutely no one admitted to the privacy which this quite secluded little cell of mine makes possible. For I am sure you will not take it amiss if my friend Gallus is present. You can see that he is as much overjoyed at your arrival as I am."

" Right you are," said Postumianus ; " Gallus here shall be one of us. I certainly don't know much about him, but if he is such a very great friend of yours, it is impossible for him not to be a friend of mine, especially as he is a product of Martin's training. Nor shall I mind telling both of you my story if you want it, all at one sitting if you like. After all, I came here for that purpose, to give my Sulpicius here what he wants "—and here he grasped both my hands—" even if I have to be long-winded ! "

II

" Well," said I, " you have certainly shown what devoted affection can do, travelling for my sake over all those seas and all that land—all the way, so to speak, from the sunrise to the sunset. So come on, for we are quite private together and have nothing to do but to attend to you while you talk. I would like you to tell us in detail the whole story of your travels. How flourishing is the

Christian religion in the East? How far are the faithful left in peace? What of the monks and their ways? What sort of wonders and miracles does Christ work through His servants? For quite certainly in *this* country the conditions of life are such as to make life itself a burden to us. It would be very pleasant to hear from you that in the desert, at any rate, life is possible for Christians."

To all of which Postumianus replied :

" I will do what you evidently want. But may I first hear from you whether all the bishops who were here when I left are still as we knew them before I set off? "

" Best not ask those questions," was my reply. " Either you know as much as I do (which I think is the case) or, if you don't know, you are better without hearing it. I can't conceal the fact that those you are enquiring about are no better than when you knew them and that even the one man who once had an affection for me and enabled me to breathe when the others were persecuting me has been unkinder to me than he should have been. I don't want to say anything harsher than that about him, because he was once a friend of mine and because I had an affection for him even when he was supposed to be my enemy. At the same time, when I have been silently turning the situation over in my mind it has been a very sharp sorrow to me that I have almost completely lost the friendship of such a wise and pious man.

" But let us leave this very sad subject. We would much rather listen to what you just now promised to tell us."

" As you wish," said Postumianus, after which we fell silent for a little. Then he pulled the sacking he was sitting on nearer to me and began his story.

III

" Three years ago,[1] which was when I left here and said good-bye to you, Sulpicius, we set sail from Narbonne and four days

[1] If we are to take this journey as an historical fact and section XXIII of this Dialogue as something more than a piece of literary log-rolling on the part of Sulpicius, Postumianus would seem to have started on the journey in the year in which the Life of St. Martin was first published, which was just before the saint's death, almost certainly in 397.

later we put in at a port in Africa[2]—good sailing indeed, thanks
be to God! I was glad to be able to go to Carthage, to visit the
places connected with the saints and especially to kneel at the
tomb of the martyr Cyprian.[3]

" On the fifteenth day we were back in harbour and put out to
sea again. We were making for Alexandria, but, with a south wind
against us, we were nearly driven on to the Syrtis.[4] The sailors,
however, realized the danger and guarded against it by dropping
anchor and bringing the ship to a standstill.

" The mainland lay under our eyes and we went ashore in
dinghies. We could see no sign of human habitation and I went
on further in order to explore the locality more thoroughly. About
three miles from the shore I caught sight of a little hut among the
sand-dunes, with a roof, just as Sallust says, like the keel of a ship,
and touching the ground.[5] It had a good solid floor of timbers,
not because they are afraid of a violent cloud-burst—such a thing
as rain there has never been heard of—but because the wind rises
to such force there that if once the slightest breeze begins to blow,
even when the weather is comparatively calm, there will be more
wreckage in those lands than on any sea.

" No plants or any seeds spring up there, in such shifting soil,
with the dry sand drifting with every breath of wind. But where
certain promontories lying back from the sea break the force of
the wind, the soil is a little firmer and produces some scanty and
prickly grass—sufficient pasturage for sheep. The inhabitants live

[2] The term " Africa " at this period generally denoted the Roman administrative Province of Africa, roughly the modern Tunisia, with its capital at Carthage,
near the modern Tunis. It might be extended to cover the whole coastal strip
of North Africa, from Tunisia westward to Morocco and eastward to about
Benghazi, but not Cyrenaica and Egypt.

[3] St. Cyprian, Bishop of Carthage, martyred A.D. 258.

[4] There were two dangerous sand-banks of this name, the Syrtis Minor in
the Gulf of Gabes or Cabes, in the south-west corner of the Gulf of Tripoli,
and the Syrtis Major in the Gulf of Sindra, in the south-east corner. The
mention of Cyrenaica at the end of this section shows that the Syrtis Major
is meant here. It should be remembered that coastwise navigation was the
general rule at this period.

[5] " Oblong, with curved sides ", adds Sallust ; i.e. like a boat lying upside-
down on the shore, from which, indeed, according to Sallust, the form was
derived, for the first settlers on the coast of which he is speaking, having no
wood, did actually use the upturned hulls of their ships as huts to live in. The
coast however was not that of Cyrenaica, but that of Numidia (eastern Algeria)
(*Jugurtha* XVIII, 8). The historian Sallust, a contemporary of Julius Caesar,
was the writer on whom Severus principally modelled his style.

on milk ; but the more skilful and, if such a term is permissible, the richer of them, eat barley bread. That is the only crop reaped there. So rapid is its growth, thanks to the nature of the soil, that it generally escapes destruction by the savage winds. It is said to ripen by the thirtieth day after sowing.

" The only reason men have for settling there is that they are free from all taxes. It is the extreme edge of Cyrenaica, next to the desert which lies between Egypt and Africa, through which Cato once led an army when pursued by Caesar.[6]

IV

" To this hut, then, which I had seen from a distance, I directed my steps. I found there an old man in a garment of skins, turning a hand-mill. We greeted each other and he gave us a warm welcome. We explained that we had been driven onto this coast and were prevented by a heavy swell at sea from continuing our voyage for the present. We had come ashore and, as is the way of human nature, had wanted to learn something of the character of the locality and the ways of the inhabitants. I added that we were Christians and particularly wished to know whether there were any Christians in these solitudes.

" At that he burst into tears of joy and threw himself down at our knees. Kissing us again and yet again, he asked us to pray with him. Then he spread sheep-skins on the ground and made us sit down. He set before us a truly sumptuous lunch—half a loaf of barley bread! There were four of us, so with him there were five. He also brought a bunch of some herb whose name has slipped my memory. It was like mint, with an abundance of leaves, and tasted of honey. We found its exceedingly sweet taste delicious and had as much as we wanted of it."

I turned to our good Gallus with a smile. " What do you say to that, Gallus ? " said I. " Is a bunch of herbs and half a loaf for lunch among five men to your liking ? "

[6] That was in 47 B.C. For the sense in which the term " Africa " is used, see note 2 to this section. The Latin word represented here by Cyrenaica is (in Halm's text) " Cyrenorum ", which cannot come from any regular Latin term for either Cyrene, Cyrenaica or the Cyrenaeans, but the general sense is plain enough.

He is the shyest of men and coloured slightly, but took my chaff in good part.

" That's just your way, Sulpicius," he said, " never to let an opportunity go by of teasing us about our appetites. But it's most inhumane of you to try and force us Gauls to live in angels' fashion, though I suspect that even angels take pleasure in eating ! And as for that half loaf of barley bread, I should be afraid to start on it, even if I had it to myself. But by all means let that Cyrenaean be content with it, if it is his vocation to go hungry, either from necessity or by nature, and our friend's party as well, whom I strongly suspect of having been put off their food by a good tossing at sea. But we are a long way from the sea here and, as I have frequently pointed out to you, we are Gauls. But we had better let our friend get on with the story of his Cyrenaean."

V

" You may be sure," said Postumianus, " that after this I shall take good care not to praise anyone's abstemiousness for fear the difficulty of imitating it discourages our good Gauls altogether. As a matter of fact I had intended to describe the Cyrenaean's dinner party also and the other banquets that followed (for we were his guests for four days) but I will skip it or Gallus will think he is being made fun of.

" Well, the next day some of the population began to assemble, to get a look at us, and we discovered that our host was a priest, a fact he had most carefully concealed from us. Thereupon we set off with him to the church, which was about two miles away and cut off from our view by a mountain in between. It was made of interwoven branches of the commonest kind and was hardly more ambitious than our host's hut, in which it was impossible to stand upright.

" We made enquiries about the ways of the people and noted one remarkable fact, that they neither buy nor sell anything. Nor do they know the meaning of fraud or theft. As for gold and silver, to which the ordinary mortal gives pride of place, they neither possess them nor want to possess them. In fact, when I offered the priest ten gold pieces, he shrank back from them, protesting, with a deeper wisdom than mine, that gold could break a Church sooner than build it. So we made him a present of a little clothing.

VI

" This he accepted in the kindest way and, as the sailors were summoning us back to the sea, we took our departure. A prosperous run brought us to Alexandria within seven days.

" There we found a most unpleasant feud going on between the bishops and the monks. The origin and cause of this was the fact that the assembled bishops had several times in crowded synods apparently passed decrees forbidding anyone to read or possess the works of Origen.[1] He was regarded as a most skilful commentator on Holy Scripture but the bishops had cited some very doubtfully sound passages in his books. His supporters did not dare to defend these and took the line that they had been fraudulently inserted by heretics. Therefore, said they, because these passages had been deservedly censured it did not follow that all the rest should be condemned ; for the gift of faith would enable readers easily to distinguish between what was forged and must not be followed and what had received Catholic treatment and should be accepted. It was nothing to wonder at, they added, that the wily heretics had been at work on modern books

---

[1] Origen (born c. 185, died 254) was an Egyptian whose father had died for the faith. He was a pupil of Clement of Alexandria at the famous theological school there and succeeded him as the head of it, though he was later deprived of the position. By wide travel and reading he made himself the most learned Christian of his generation. He was the most prolific and, with the possible exception of Tertullian, the most brilliant writer of the early Church and the writer of its finest apologetic work, entitled *Against Celsus*. He was also its first systematic theologian, a great Biblical scholar, and a kind of universal consultant for Christians everywhere. He lived, moreover, an heroic Christian life and at the age of 65 was imprisoned and subjected to prolonged tortures in the Decian persecution. Unfortunately he indulged in a number of rash speculations concerning, for example, the Logos and His relations with the world of spirits, which had neo-Platonist and Gnostic tendencies and were of very doubtful orthodoxy. These made his writings for many centuries a storm-centre of theological controversies, the first of which had broken out A.D. 393, only a few years before Postumianus is supposed to have visited Alexandria. As regards the assertion, quoted by Postumianus, that some of the offending passages in his writings were interpolations by heretics, St. Vincent of Lérins, writing only a generation later (c. 434) said : " I do not deny it ; nay, I grant it readily. That such is the case has been handed down both orally and in writing, not only by Catholics but by heretics as well " (*Commonitorium*, ch. 17).

of recent date, seeing that in certain passages they had not been afraid to call in question the reliability of the Gospels themselves.

"Against these arguments the bishops were maintaining a stubborn front and, so far as their authority extended, were enforcing a ban on everything that was correct in these writings as well as on what was pernicious and on the author himself. In their view the books that the Church had approved up to now were sufficient and more than sufficient. The reading of this author would do more harm to the unwise than it would do good to the wise and should be avoided altogether.

" For my own part I had the curiosity to dip into these books and there was much that gave me great pleasure ; but I found a certain number of passages in which the author's ideas are undoubtedly pernicious and which his defenders maintain are forgeries. I certainly find it extraordinary that one and the same man could have differed so much from himself that, where he can be approved, he has no equal since the Apostles and, where he is rightly censured, no one has been convicted of more shocking errors.

VII

" For example, when a number of passages were being read that had been picked out by the bishops as demonstrably written against the Catholic faith, one in particular roused resentment. In this passage from a published work there was read the assertion that the Lord Jesus, who had come in the flesh to redeem mankind, and endured the Cross for man's salvation and tasted death to give man eternal life, would, by the same series of sufferings, redeem even the devil, since it would be in harmony with His goodness and loving-kindness if He not only restored ruined humanity but also delivered the fallen angel.

" When these and similar assertions were put in evidence by the bishops, the passions of the rival parties led to rioting. When the authority of the bishops failed to suppress this, a sinister precedent was set by calling in the civil governor to enforce discipline in the Church. The terror that he inspired dispersed the brethren. The monks were forced to flee in all directions ;

in fact, under the edicts that were published, they were not allowed to settle anywhere.

"A thing that disturbed me a good deal was the fact that Jerome, a thorough-going Catholic and a great expert in Holy Scripture, used to be regarded in former days as a follower of Origen and he was now going further than most in condemning all his writings.[1] Not, indeed, that I would dare to judge anyone hastily, but very eminent and learned men were reported to differ from him in this controversy. But anyhow, whether Origen's opinion was, as I myself think, only a mistake or whether it is a heresy, as it is supposed to be, not only was it not such as could be suppressed by any number of episcopal censures but it could never have spread so widely without the stimulus of controversy.[2]

" Such, then, were the disturbances that were agitating Alexandria when I arrived there. For my part, I was given a very kind reception by the bishop of the city, in fact a better one than I was expecting.[3] He even tried to get me to stop on there with him. But I was not at all inclined to settle in a place seething with bitterness after the calamities so recently inflicted on the brethren. For even though it can perhaps be said that they

[1] St. Jerome, Doctor of the Church and translator into Latin of the greater part of the Vulgate (c. 342–420), was drawn into this controversy through his former friend Rufinus and, as he was apt to do, expressed himself in somewhat violent language.

[2] I have tried to give a self-consistent rendering of this passage, in which the Latin is sufficiently ambiguous to allow different translators to take quite different views as to the nature of the impression made on Postumianus by St. Jerome's change of front. A complicating factor is the panegyric on St. Jerome in the next section ; but I do not think that there can be much doubt that Severus thought that, in this matter of Origen, Jerome had yielded unduly to the dominant opinion. But it must be remembered that Severus himself was in an embarrassing position with regard to Origen's opinion concerning the redeemability of the devil, since one of his stories in the Life (Section XXII) attributes the same opinion to Martin. Indeed, what with this difficulty, and his prejudice against bishops (except for Martin) pulling him in one direction and his desire not to compromise his own orthodoxy pulling him in the other direction, it is not surprising that throughout this section he manifests, in the person of Postumianus, a strong tendency to hedge, which no doubt partly accounts for the obscurities.

[3] The Bishop of Alexandria from A.D. 382–412 was Theophilus, described by Father Philip Hughes in his History of the Church (I, p. 231) as " a proud man, able and unscrupulous, a sinister figure indeed ". He was excommunicated not long after this by Pope St. Innocent I for the leading part he took in the persecution and banishment of St. John Chrysostom, Bishop of Constantinople, and died unreconciled.

ought to have obeyed the bishops, that was not a sufficient reason
for the infliction of such hardships, particularly by bishops, on
such a host of men living under the banner of Christ.

VIII

" I took my departure, therefore, and made my way to the
town of Bethlehem, which is six miles distant from Jerusalem
and sixteen days' journey from Alexandria. The priest Jerome is
in charge of the Church there, the diocese[1] being that of the
Bishop of Jerusalem. My previous acquaintance with Jerome,
made on my earlier journey, had left me with no doubt that there
was no one better worth seeking out. For, to say nothing of the
high quality of his faith and his wealth of virtues, he is a man so
learned, not only in Latin and Greek but also in Hebrew, that
no one would venture to compare himself with him in any
branch of knowledge. But I should be surprised if he is not
known to you, too, through his many books, for he is read all
over the world."

"As a matter of fact he is known to us only too well " said
Gallus. " For five years ago I read a little book of his in which
he most violently attacks and picks to pieces the whole tribe of
our monks.[2] For that reason our Belgic friends every now and
then get very angry because it says that we are in the habit of
stuffing ourselves till we are sick.[3] For my own part, I forgive
the man and I think that he must have been talking about the
monks of the East more than about those of the West, for a large
appetite amounts to gluttony in a Greek when it would be
natural in a Gaul."

" Gallus," I said, " you defend your nation like a proper

---

[1] Latin, " paroechia ". The rendering " diocese " in a text of this period
and a context such as the present gets decisive support from Fliche and Martin,
Histoire de l'Eglise, t. IV, p. 579.

[2] The reference is presumably to Ep. XXII *Ad Eustochium* (see the quotation
in the next section), which, however, treats of virginity in general and not
particularly of Gallic monks and nuns. Perhaps the cap was fitted on.

[3] Belgica (in full, Gallia Belgica), extending roughly from the Seine to the
Rhine, was part of Gaul. To render *Belgicus* here as " Belgian ", suggesting to
the modern reader a different nationality, would be historically misleading and
at the same time make nonsense of this passage.

lawyer. But tell me, is this the only vice that this book condemns in monks ? "

" No, indeed ! " said he. "He left out nothing whatever that he could carp at and rend and expose. He was particularly severe on avarice and equally on vanity. He had a lot to say about pride, and not a little about superstition ; and I will frankly admit that he seemed to me to have depicted the vices of a great many people.

IX

"And then, too, how faithfully and forcibly he dealt with intimacies between consecrated virgins and monks, and even with the clergy. It is said that for that reason he is not loved by certain people I would rather not name. For, just as our Belgic friend gets angry when we are remarked on for our excessive appetites, so these people are said to fume with rage when they read in that same little book : ' The consecrated virgin rejects her celibate blood-brother and looks for a brother not of her own blood.' " [1]

" Gallus, you are going too far ", said I at this. "Take care, or someone may overhear you who recognizes himself in it, and begin to love you no more than he loves Jerome. But as you are a bit of a scholar, I can suitably give you advice in a line from a writer of comedies :

' Flattery gets you friends and the truth gets you hated.' [2]

" But we had better be getting back, Postumianus, to what you began with, your tales of the East."

[1] Ep. XXII, *Ad Eustochium*, c. XIV. The words " a brother not of her own blood " represent the Latin *frater extraneus*, which had, in this sense, become practically a technical term in the ecclesiastical life of the period. St. Jerome is attacking what he calls the " agapetarum pestis ", which may perhaps be rendered " the soul-mate plague ". He is referring to the contemporary practice whereby a man and a woman, each consecrated to the religious life, would go about together and keep house together, while claiming to be keeping their vows. He says of them : " They occupy the same house, the same bedroom, often the same bed ; and when we form certain opinions they call us suspicious." But there is no specific reference to Gaul or Gallic monasticism in the letter ; and Eustochium, the nun to whom it was addressed, did not live in Gaul. Moreover, the letter (or treatise, as it might well be called) was written nearly twenty years before this Dialogue. Its introduction here seems highly artificial.

[2] Terence, *Andria*, I. 1, 41.

" Well, I was just going to tell you ", said he, " that I stayed
with Jerome for six months. His unceasing battles against evil-
doers, and unending controversies, have stirred up against him
all the hatreds of the damned. Heretics hate him because he
never ceases to attack them. The clergy hate him because he
denounces their lives and their crimes. But most certainly all
good men admire and love him; for those who think him a
heretic are just mad. I can say in all truth : the man's learning is
Catholic and his teaching sound. He is always wholly immersed
in reading, wholly in his books ; he rests neither night nor day ;
he is always either reading or writing something. If it had not
been for my fixed determination—in fact, my vow—to pay my
long-planned visit to the desert, I should never have wished to
leave the side of so great a man for a single moment.

"As it was, I handed over to him and placed in his charge all
my belongings and all the members of my household, who had
followed me much against my will and were a great tie to me ;
then, feeling as if I had shed a heavy burden and was completely
free, I returned to Alexandria. There I paid visits to the brethren
and from there I made my way to the Upper Thebaid, the
furthest point of Egypt.[3] For there, in the desert solitudes
stretching far and wide, a multitude of monks were said to live.
It would take too long if I tried to describe all the things I saw.
I will run through a few of them.

X

" Next to the Nile and not far from the desert there are a
number of monasteries, with usually a hundred monks in a
monastery. The first law of their lives is to live under the rule
of an Abbot, to do nothing by their own choice and to go by his
will and authority in everything. If one of them entertains the
idea of aiming higher and betaking himself to the desert to lead

[3] The Thebaid was the district named after Thebes, the ancient capital of
Upper (that is to say, southern) Egypt, now best known for the great ruins at
Karnak and Luxor. The whole region was then one of the chief theatres of
Egyptian monasticism, particularly in its Pachomian form, with a highly
organized communal life (see Introduction, section II).

a solitary life, he only leaves if he has the Abbot's permission. Obedience to the will of another is for them the first of virtues.

" When they have passed on into the desert, the Abbot arranges for bread and other food to be supplied to them. It so happened that, at the time of my visit there, one of them had recently retired to the desert and built his hut not more than six miles from the monastery, and the Abbot had sent him bread by two boys, the elder of whom was fifteen and the younger twelve. On their way back they met with an asp of extraordinary size. They were not in the least frightened and when it reached their feet it laid down its dark-blue neck as if a charmer's tune had cast a spell upon it.

" The younger of the boys picked it up and brought it along with him, wrapped in his cloak. Marching into the monastery like a conqueror, he found the brethren and, with everybody looking on, unfolded his cloak and set down the imprisoned animal with a distinctly boastful air. All but the Abbot were loud in their praises of the faith and spiritual power of such children but he, more wise than the rest, to check the growth of vanity at that early age, sobered them both with a beating, after scolding them well for making public what had been done through them by Our Lord. It was not their faith, said he, but the power of God that had brought this thing about and they must learn to serve God humbly and not to take a pride in wonders and miracles. They would do better to have a sense of their weakness than to be conceited about spiritual powers.

XI

" The monk in question heard about this, and how mere children had been in danger from an encounter with a snake and how, on the top of this, their victory over the snake had earned them a good thrashing. He therefore begged the Abbot not to send him bread or any food any more. Eight days then passed, at the end of which this servant of Christ had exposed himself to the danger of starvation. But though the fast was wasting his limbs, his mind was fixed on heaven and could not weaken. His

body was faint from lack of nourishment but his faith was as
strong as ever.

" Meanwhile the Abbot had been prompted by the Holy
Spirit to visit this disciple of his. He felt a paternal anxiety, and
a desire to know on what food this man of faith was supporting
life, seeing that he refused to be supplied with bread by human
agency. He set off himself, therefore, to seek him out. The
hermit saw from a distance the old man coming, went to meet
him, expressed his gratitude and took him to his cell.

" Entering it together, they saw a carrier made of palm-leaves,
filled with hot loaves, hanging on the door by the door-post. The
smell of hot bread was what they first noticed ; and when they
touched the bread it felt as if it had only lately been taken out of
the oven. On the other hand, they saw that the shape of the
loaves was not Egyptian. They were both of them astounded
and they acknowledged it to be a gift from heaven. The hermit
declared that it was to celebrate the Abbot's visit, while the
Abbot ascribed it to the faith and power of the hermit. And so
with great rejoicings both of them broke and ate the celestial
bread.

" When the old man got back to the monastery he told the
story to the brethren. It filled them all with such immense
fervour that each strove to be the first to enter the desert and its
holy solitudes, declaring that he would be miserable if he had to
remain behind in a large community where he would have to
endure the company of fellow men.

XII

" In the same monastery I saw two old men who were said to
have lived forty years there without leaving the place at all. I
don't think I should pass them over without mention because of
what I heard in praise of their spiritual powers both from the
Abbot himself and from all the brethren—how never a day
dawned that saw the first of them feasting or the other one angry."

Here Gallus looked hard at me. " Oh, I wish ", said he, " that
a certain friend of yours—I would rather not mention names—

were here now. I would so much like him to hear about that case, for we had all too much experience of his getting violently angry very often with a great many people. However, from what I hear, he has recently forgiven his enemies, so that, if he heard this story, the example it sets before us would only strengthen his conviction that not to give way to anger is a very fine virtue. Nor will I deny that he had good reasons for getting angry; but the harder the battle the more glorious is the victor's crown.

" For that reason I think that a certain person, if you know whom I mean, deserves high praise; because, although an ungrateful freedman has deserted him, he has had pity on him instead of reproaching him. He is not even angry with the man who seems to have taken him off." [1]

" If it had not been ", said I, " that Postumianus had quoted this example of overcoming anger, I should be feeling very angry with the fugitive; but, as it is not right to be angry, let us have no more references to these things which hurt me so much. It is you, Postumianus, it is you we want to listen to."

" I will do as you say, Sulpicius ", said he. " I can see you are both very anxious to hear more. But remember, I am not investing all this oratory in you without expecting interest. I'm glad to do what you ask, so long as the two of you do not refuse what I am going to ask a little later."

---

[1] This freedman of Severus is generally identified with the Pomponius whose burial on the coast of Syria is mentioned in the last section of the Dialogues, II (III), XVIII. Babut published an elaborate reconstruction (" Sur Trois Lignes Inédites de Sulp. Sévère ") (*Moyen Age*, 2° Série, t. x; see also *The Book of Armagh*, ed. by Gwynn, 1913, pp. cclxxvi–cclxxviii) in which he claimed to demonstrate that Pomponius had been induced to leave Sulpicius by a former disciple of Sulpicius named Vigilantius who took Pomponius with him when he visited the East A.D. 396. Pomponius is supposed to have died at sea and to have been buried at Ptolemais (afterwards Akka or Acre) but Vigilantius went on to Bethlehem to visit St. Jerome, with results that are briefly described in the introductory note to this Dialogue. It is true that Vigilantius seems to have had a retainer of Sulpicius with him when he visited St. Paulinus of Nola on his way out to the East in 396, and this retainer quite possibly might have been a fugitive and been named Pomponius and been buried at Ptolemais ; but that was eight years before the date assigned by Babut to these Dialogues, and the phrases and tenses Severus attributes to himself in the present passage and, still more, the remark that immediately follows here, connecting his forbearance with the story Postumianus has just told, would suggest that he is referring here to an abduction he has only just heard of. But, here again, the root of the trouble may well lie in treating as historical evidence the artifices of a highly artificial literary composition (see the author's own admission in the second Dialogue, section V).

" We have nothing ", said I, " with which we could repay you your loan, even without interest. However, ask whatever you have in mind, so long as you satisfy us now by going on with what you have begun. For we are finding your story very delightful."

" Not one wish shall I cheat you out of," said Postumianus ; " and since you have had an instance of miracle-working by one hermit, I will give you a few more instances out of very many.

XIII

" Well then, when I crossed the borders of the desert, about twelve miles from the Nile, I had with me as guide one of the brethren, who was familiar with the district. We came to where an aged monk was living at the foot of a mountain. At that spot there was a well, which is a very rare thing in those parts. The hermit had an ox whose whole work consisted of bringing up the water by turning the wheel of a machine, for the well was said to be a thousand or more feet deep.

" There was a garden there with an abundance of many different vegetables, which is most unnatural in the desert, where everything is so dry under the scorching heat of the sun that no seed can ever produce even the smallest root in it. The holy man obtained these results by the hard work he shared with the ox and by his own personal application. For it was constant watering that had given the sand the richness that caused the vegetables in the garden to flourish and ripen in the wonderful way we saw, so that the ox could live on them as well as his master.

" We, too, were given dinner by the holy man out of the same abundance. There I saw what you Gauls perhaps may not believe —the pot, with the vegetables in it that were being got ready for our dinner, boiling without a fire. The sun is so powerful that it will serve for any cooking you like, even for sauces for the Gauls !![1]

" After dinner, when evening was drawing on, he invited us to visit a palm-tree about two miles away, to which he sometimes

[1] This is one of the passages on which Babut (see the introductory note) based his contention that " Postumianus " had no first-hand knowledge of the Egyptian desert.

went for dates. For the desert possesses these trees, though no others, and these are scarce. Whether we owe them to the genius of the men of old or whether they are natural to the soil, I do not know. It may be that God, foreseeing that the desert would one day be inhabited by saints, made everything ready for His servants. For those who dwell in those remote places, where no other plants thrive, live for the most part on the fruit of these trees.

" Well, when we got to the tree to which our kindly host was taking us, we found a lion there. My guide and I shook with fear at the sight of it but the holy man went up to it without pausing for a moment and, alarmed though we were, we followed him. The wild beast, in obedience to a divine command (as you could see), discreetly drew back a little and stood motionless while our host picked some fruit within reach on the lower branches. Then, when he held out his hand full of dates, the beast ran up and took them as naturally as any domestic animal could have done and when it had eaten them it went away. We who were watching all this, still shaking with fear, had no difficulty in realizing how strong was the faith of the hermit and how weak was ours.

XIV

" We saw another equally remarkable man living in a hut that could only hold one person. It was told of him that a she-wolf was in the habit of standing by him while he ate his dinner. The beast seldom failed to be with him at the right time for the meal and would wait outside the door until he offered her the bread left over from his slender repast. Then she used to lick his hand and would thus take her departure with due ceremony and a mutual salutation.

" One day it so happened that the holy man was visited by one of the brethren and escorted him on his way back, so that he was away for a considerable time and only got back at dusk. Meanwhile the beast had arrived at the ordinary time for dinner. Finding her accustomed benefactor absent, she went into the empty cell and searched inquisitively for its owner. A palm-leaf basket happened to be hanging close by her with five loaves in it. Helping herself to one of them she devoured it. Then, with the crime accomplished, she went her way.

" When the hermit returned he saw that the carrier had been forced open and that a loaf was missing. He could see that the robber had been on familiar ground and he discovered near the threshold pieces of the stolen loaf. There could be no doubt as to the identity of the thief.

" For some days after this the beast failed to pay her usual visit ; she was evidently too conscious of her shameless deed to like to come to the man she had wronged. But the hermit sadly missed the distraction of his protegee's visit. In the end he got her back by his prayers and she was there at his dinner time in the old way after seven days' absence. But you could easily see the shame of a penitent in the way in which she did not venture to draw near but kept her eyes on the ground in deep abasement and was unmistakably asking in her own way to be forgiven.

" The hermit took pity on her confusion and told her to come closer and stroked the sad head with a soothing hand. Then he comforted his penitent with a double portion of bread. And so, with everything forgiven, she ceased to grieve and performed again the customary ceremony.

" Now, I ask you to consider the power that Christ manifested even in a case like this. In His service the brute creation displays intelligence and the savage beast grows meek. A wolf observes due ceremony, a wolf knows that theft is a crime, a wolf is troubled by a sense of shame. She comes when she is called, she offers her head to be stroked, and has a consciousness of pardon granted, as previously she showed remorse for wrong committed. This is Thy power, O Christ ! These are Thy wonders ! For all that Thy servants do in Thy name is Thine. And there is cause for us to sigh, when the wild beasts recognize Thy majesty and men revere Thee not.

XV

" But for fear that some may find this tale hard to believe, I will speak of still greater things. Christ is my witness that I am inventing nothing. I shall repeat no stories emanating from

uncertain sources; I shall tell only those I have learnt from
reliable men.

" Many live in the desert without even a hut. They are called
anchorites.[1] They live on the roots of plants and have no fixed
abode, as they want to avoid incessant visitors. Wherever night
overtakes them, there they remain. Now, there was a certain man
who had adopted this mode and rule of life, and two monks of
Nitria set out to find him.[2] For they had heard of his spiritual
powers and, though they had a long way to go, he had once lived
in the same monastery with them and been a dear and intimate
friend of theirs. The search for him was long and extensive but
at last, after more than six months, they found him far out in the
desert that borders on Memphis.[3] It was said that he had inhabited those solitudes for ten years.

" But though he shunned all human intercourse he did not repel
these old acquaintances and for three days gave himself entirely
to his well-loved friends. On the fourth day he was escorting them
back and had gone a little way with them when they saw a lioness
of extraordinary size coming towards them. She, although finding
three men together, showed no hesitation as to which to approach.
She crouched at the feet of the anchorite and, as she lay there,
manifested by a kind of sobbing and moaning the emotions of both
grief and entreaty. It touched them all and particularly the one
who knew that it was directed to him.

" She went ahead and they followed her, for by stopping and
looking back from time to time she made it very easy to understand
that she wanted the anchorite to follow where she led.[4] But why
so many words? They reached the beast's den, where the unfortunate mother was having to feed five cubs, which were now
full-grown but had remained permanently blind, with their eyes
closed just as they had come into the world. The mother brought

---

[1] " Anchorite " was the term used in medieval England (usually in the
spelling " anchoret ") for hermits in general. Its special meaning here is based
on its derivation from a Greek word meaning " retire " or " withdraw ".

[2] The Nitrian desert, another great centre of Egyptian monasticism, was in
Northern Egypt, west of the Delta.

[3] The capital of Egypt in the Pyramid Age. It was situated about fourteen
miles south of the modern Cairo, and therefore quite close to Nitria.

[4] The syntax of the original is in great confusion here, but there can be no
doubt what Severus is trying to say.

them out of the cave one by one to the anchorite's feet and showed them to him. Then at last the holy man could see what the animal was asking. Calling on the name of God, he touched the closed eyes of the cubs. They were immediately cured of their blindness, and their eyes opened to the light so long denied to them.

" Thus the brethren returned from their long-desired visit to the anchorite lavishly repaid for the toil it had cost them. For they had been permitted to witness a great miracle and had seen Christ glorified in the faith of a saint, to which they were themselves to bear testimony.

" But there is a further marvel to tell. Five days later the lioness returned to the benefactor who had done so much for her, bringing as a gift the skin of a rare wild animal. The holy man used often to wear it as a cape ; for he did not consider it beneath him to accept a gift brought to him by a dumb animal but regarded by him as coming from quite another donor.

XVI

" There was yet another anchorite in those parts who had a great reputation. He lived in that part of the desert that surrounds Syene.[1] When he first took to the desert it was his intention to live on the roots of the herbs which grow here and there in the sand and are most luscious and of an excellent flavour. But having no experience in choosing the right plants, he often picked unwholesome ones. Nor, indeed, was it easy to tell the effects of the roots from their taste, for they all tasted equally delicious but in many of them there lurked a hidden and deadly poison.

" The internal effect of eating these was torture. All his internal organs were racked by excruciating pains, and frequent vomitings accompanied by unendurable agonies exhausted his stomach and were undermining his whole system. In the end he was in terror of eating anything and after fasting nearly seven days he was almost at his last gasp.

[1] Syene is in the extreme south of Egypt, near the First Cataract and the modern Assouan Dam, and therefore by no means " in those parts " (" in illis regionibus "), if we mean, by that, the desert near Memphis.

"Just then a wild animal called an ibex approached, and came and stood near him. He offered it a bunch of plants that he had gathered on the previous day but dared not touch. The animal pushed aside with its muzzle what was poisonous and picked out what it knew to be harmless. Thus the holy man learnt from watching the ibex what he should eat and what he should reject and thereby averted the danger of starvation and at the same time escaped being poisoned by the plants.

"But it would take too long to repeat all that I found out for myself, or was told, about these dwellers in the desert. I was living in those solitudes myself for nearly a year and seven months, though more as an admirer of other people's virtues than as one capable of attempting himself such an arduous and difficult way of life. Most of the time I stayed with the old man who had the well and the ox.

XVII

"I visited two monasteries of the blessed Antony, which are still occupied by his disciples.[1] I also paid a visit to the place where the most blessed Paul, the first hermit, spent his life.[2] I saw the Red Sea and the ridge of Mount Sinai, of which the highest point almost touches the sky and is quite inaccessible. It was said that an anchorite lived somewhere within its recesses, but after a long and diligent search I failed to find him. For nearly fifty years he had been cut off from human society, wearing no clothes but covered with the bristles of his own body, but by a divine dispensation he was unaware of his own nakedness. When pious men tried to get near him, he would run to where he could not be followed and so escape human society.

[1] St. Antony of Egypt, the father of all monks, lived from A.D. 251 to 356. He spent many years as a hermit but, when he was nearly sixty, yielded to the requests of his disciples and founded his first monastery in the Fayum, in Middle Egypt, and other monasteries followed. They were not what we would now recognize as monasteries, being little more than groups of hermits' cells, the occupants of which lived each according to his own ideas and met only on Saturdays and Sundays for liturgical worship (see the Introduction, section II). A life of St. Antony was written by St. Athanasius.

[2] St. Paul, called the First Hermit, lived from about 228 to 342. He preceded St. Antony (unknown to the latter) by some years in the eremitical life, but was only discovered by him shortly before his death. The cave in which he lived was in the Thebaid (see note 3 to section IX). St. Jerome wrote a famous Life of him.

" One man only, according to report, had been allowed by him to meet him, and that was five years before this ; and I expect it was the strength of his faith that had earned this man this privilege. The story goes that when, in the course of some long talks, he enquired of the anchorite why he avoided men so assiduously, the latter replied that no one who lived much in the company of men could enjoy the company of angels. Many had not unreasonably concluded from this that the holy man received visits from the angels, and this was widely reported.

" However, I left Mount Sinai and returned to the River Nile. I travelled up and down its banks, both of which are crowded with monasteries. I saw that as a rule (as I said before) there would be a hundred monks to a monastery, but it was well known that there were cases of two or three thousand residing in the same community. Nor should you assume that the spiritual powers of those living together in great numbers are less than those which you have been hearing of in connection with men who have withdrawn from the company of their fellows.

" The virtue that ranks easily first in those places is, as I have already said, obedience. No new arrival at a monastery is admitted by the Abbot until he has been tested and has given proof that he will never refuse to obey any order of the Abbot, however arduous or difficult or intolerably humiliating it may be.

XVIII

" I will tell you of two great miracles of really incredible obedience. Others also come back to me, but people who are not roused to enthusiasm for a virtue by a few examples will gain nothing from a large number.

" There was a man, then, who had renounced the world and had presented himself at a certain very strictly conducted monastery and applied for admission. The Abbot proceeded to make many difficulties. The burden of discipline there, he said, was very heavy. His own orders were so harsh that even the most patient found them difficult to carry out ; the man had much better look for another monastery where he could live under an easier rule instead of trying to undertake what he could never carry through.

" But he could in no way be shaken by this alarming prospect. On the contrary, he continued to promise to obey in everything, even to the point of walking into the fire if the Abbot ordered it. When the Superior was challenged by that declaration, he lost no time in putting it to the test. There happened to be a hot oven near by, under which a large fire was being built for the purpose of baking bread. Flames were pouring out of the open side of the furnace and, in the hollow space inside, the fire was at full blast. The Superior ordered the new-comer to enter this, and he obeyed without hesitation. Without a moment's delay he stepped into the middle of the flames.

" Vanquished by such audacious faith, the flames at once gave way, as of old they had done before those Hebrew boys. Nature was beaten ; the fire fled ; the man himself, whom all expected to be ablaze, marvelled to find himself bathed as with a cooling dew. But, O Christ, why should it be accounted marvellous that the fire refrained from touching Thy recruit, so that the Abbot should have no need to regret his harsh command nor the disciple to repent of his obedience?

" Thus on the very day of his arrival, he was tested while as yet weak and emerged from the test perfected. And he deserved the happy outcome, he deserved the glory ; for he had won approbation by obedience and the glory by a martyrdom.

XIX

" What I am now going to tell you happened in the same monastery and (so it is said) quite recently. A man had come, just like the other one, to the same Abbot to ask for admission. Obedience had been set before him as the fundamental rule and he had promised to be unfailingly patient even under the most extreme demands.

" It so happened that the Abbot was holding in his hand a twig of storax that had long since dried up. He fixed it in the ground

and gave the stranger the task of watering the twig and continuing
to do so until, against all natural probability, the dry wood grew
green again in the arid soil. The newcomer submitted to the
harsh requirements of the order and began to bring daily on his
own shoulders water that had to be fetched from the River Nile
nearly two miles away.

"A whole year passed and there was as yet no end to the
labourer's toil, nor was it possible to hope that the work would
bring any result. Nevertheless, through all the labour, the virtue
of obedience held fast. The passing of a second year likewise
made a mockery of the futile efforts of the now exhausted brother.
The cycle of the third successive year was slipping by, and the
water-carrier was still at his task by night and by day—when the
stick flowered.

" I have myself seen the little tree that grew from that twig.
It is there to this day in the courtyard of the monastery, its
branches all green, as a witness to the worth of obedience and
the power of faith. But the day would be gone before I could
give a complete account of the many marvellous things I learnt
concerning the miraculous powers of these holy men.

XX

" I will give you just two other particularly striking instances.
One of them will be a notable warning against being inflated by
vanity, that most pitiable of vices ; the other provides an excellent
example of vice masquerading as virtue.

" There was once a holy man who was endowed with the most
incredible power of expelling demons from the bodies of their
victims, and day after day he would give unheard-of manifestations of it. He would effect cures, when he was present, by no
more than a word, and occasionally would do so even in his
absence, by sending threads from his hair-shirt or perhaps a
letter.

" Consequently he had an amazing number of visitors, for
people came to him from all over the world. To say nothing of
the lesser folk, there were frequently governors, counts and

judges of every grade among those laid at his door. Very holy
bishops, too, would lay aside their priestly authority and humbly
beg to be touched and blessed by him, believing with good
reason that they had been hallowed and visited by light from
above every time they had touched his hand or his clothing. It
was said of him that he abstained completely at all times from
drink of any kind and, as for food—Sulpicius, I will speak in
your ear, so as not to let Gallus hear this!—that he supported
life on no more than six dried figs.

" But in the course of time, just as his spiritual powers had
brought glory to the holy man, so, with the glory, vanity came
creeping in. When he first noticed this vice growing upon him,
he made great and prolonged efforts to shake it off, but he could
not altogether expel vain glory from at least his secret thoughts,
so long as his spiritual powers were undiminished. And everywhere the demons continued to acknowledge his authority and
he was quite unable to keep away the crowds that flocked to him.

" Thus all the time the hidden poison was working in him;
and he whose nod was enough to put demons to flight when
others were their victims was powerless to cast out this hidden
vanity from his own thoughts. So he turned to God with all his
heart and prayed (so it is said) that the devil might be granted
power over him for five months, so that he might become like
those he had cured.

" There is no need for many words. This man of surpassing
powers, famous all over the East for his manifestations and
miracles, to whose threshold the populace had flocked, at whose
doors the world's mightiest potentates had prostrated themselves,
was invaded by a demon and fastened up with chains. All that
demoniacs commonly suffer, this man suffered, until in the fifth
month he was purged at last, not only of the demon, but of what
it was even more important and desirable that he should be rid
of, the vice of vanity.

XXI

" But even while I am telling you this story, there comes to my mind the thought of the weakness and unhappy state of all of us. For is there one of us who, if he is greeted respectfully by even the most insignificant little man or if one woman flatters him with some silly compliment, is not immediately swollen with pride, instantly inflated with vanity ? He may be well aware that there is nothing saintly about him ; nevertheless he has only to be called a saint by some flattering or, perhaps, merely mistaken fools, to think himself a saint of the highest grade ! If after that he gets several presents made to him, he will claim that it is a special honour paid to him by a bountiful God, although his needs continue to be supplied when he is sleeping or relaxing ! And should he show even in a small degree some signs of miraculous power, why, he would think he was an angel !

" But let him only become one of the clergy, and then he will not wait to be eminent for either good works or spiritual powers before he broadens his fringes, takes delight in being saluted, swells with pride at all his visitors, and himself goes visiting everywhere. Whereas formerly he would go about on foot or on a donkey, now he rides grandly on foaming horses. Before this he was content with a common little cell ; now he builds lofty panelled ceilings and constructs numerous reception-rooms, with carved doors and painted cabinets. He will have no coarse clothing but wants the softest garments and demands as tribute from his dear friends among the widows and from his intimates among the virgins that one weaves him a good stiff cape and hood and another a flowing cloak.

" But let us leave this to be described more bitingly by that good man Jerome and get back to our subject."

" I don't know what you have left for Jerome to deal with," said my Gallus. " You have given us a short summary of all the habits of our people, and these few remarks of yours, if taken in the right spirit and pondered without resentment, should (I think) do them a lot of good and make it unnecessary after this for them to be kept straight by Jerome. But go on now with what you had begun to tell us and give us that example you promised us of vice masquerading as virtue. For I tell you frankly, none of the evils that plague us in Gaul is doing us more harm that that."

" I will do so," said Postumianus, " without keeping you on tenterhooks any longer."

XXII

" There was a young man who came from Asia, very rich and of a good family, with a wife and little boy. He had been in Egypt as a tribune[1] and in the course of frequent expeditions against the Blembi[2] had seen something of the desert and noticed the many dwellings of the holy hermits. He afterwards heard the message of salvation from the most blessed John[3] and lost no time in turning his back on the warfare that profits not, with its empty glory. He resolutely entered the desert and in a short time was a shining example of perfection in spiritual powers of every kind. He was a mighty faster, conspicuous for humility and strong in his faith ; and in his zeal for these things he easily rivalled the monks of old.

" In the midst of all this, the thought struck him (it was a suggestion from the devil) that he would do better to return to his own country and see to the welfare of his only son and all his household, including his wife. Surely this would be more pleasing to God than if he remained satisfied with having snatched himself from the world and neglected the religious duty of seeing to the salvation of his own family. All this had a delusive air of virtue that was too much for him. After four years as a hermit he abandoned his cell and the hermit's way of life.

" But when he reached the nearest monastery, which had a large community, and in reply to their questions acknowledged his reasons for quitting and his plans for the future, they all tried to dissuade him, and particularly the Abbot of the monastery.

---

[1] See the Life of St. Martin, note 3 to section II.
[2] Probably the Blemyes or Blemyi, inhabitants of what is now the Anglo-Egyptian Soudan.
[3] Presumably the then very famous hermit, John of Lycopolis, otherwise known as St. John of Egypt, who had recently died (A.D. 394) at the age of 90.

But he had a stubborn disposition and his opinions were fixed
and could not be uprooted. Fatally obstinate, he hastened on his
way, leaving all the brethren sorrowing at his departure.

" Hardly was he out of sight before a demon took possession
of him and, with a blood-stained froth dribbling from his mouth,
he began tearing at himself with his own teeth. Eventually he
was carried back to the same monastery on the shoulders of the
brethren. As the evil spirit could not be kept under control in
him, it became necessary to secure him with iron fetters and
fasten him hand and foot. Nor was it an unfitting punishment
for the fugitive, to be bound by chains, since he would not be
bound by his word.

" At last, after two years, he was delivered from the evil spirit
by the prayers of the holy man, and he was soon back in the desert
after that. He had had his lesson and was to be a warning to others
against being deceived by a delusive appearance of virtue and
against the disastrous fickleness with which an unreliable and un-
stable character will abandon what he has undertaken.

" But you must be satisfied with these examples of Our Lord's
mighty works, manifested in His servants to be a model or a
warning to us. I have done my part, in fact I have been perhaps
more long-winded than I ought to have been ; and now it's your
turn " (and here he addressed me) " to repay the debt with
interest by letting us listen to you telling lots of stories about
Martin in the old way. I have been looking forward eagerly to
this for a long time."

XXIII

" Oh, come ! " said I ; " isn't that book about my Martin
enough for you ? You know as well as anyone that I published
one about his life and miracles."

" I certainly know it," said Postumianus, " and your book is
never out of reach of my hand. Look, here it is ! Do you recognize it ? " And he displayed the book which had been concealed
in his dress. " It has been my companion ", he went on, " by
land and sea. In all my travels it has been my friend and com-
forter. And I must really tell you where that book has made its

way, and you will see there is practically no place in the world where the contents of this delightful story have not become public property.

" The first man to bring it to Rome was your great admirer Paulinus.[1] Then the whole city began fighting for it and I saw the booksellers in raptures. They looked upon it as a record profit-maker because nothing sold more quickly or fetched a better price.

" The book travelled well ahead of me and by the time I got to Africa it was being read all over Carthage. The only man who had not got it was that priest in Cyrenaica, and *he* made a copy of it when I lent it to him. And as for Alexandria, nearly everybody there knows it better than you do ! It has travelled all over Egypt, Nitria, the Thebaid and all the Memphite realms.[2] I saw it being read by an old man in the desert and, when I told him that I was a friend of yours, he and a number of other brethren commissioned me, if ever I got back to this country and found you safe and sound, to make you fill in the gaps which you said in your book you had left, with the blessed man's other miracles.

" So come on and let us hear all about the things you left out then (I imagine, in order to avoid boring your readers) and which many besides myself are asking for. For I am not asking to hear from you what I know well enough from the book."

XXIV

" It's true enough, Postumianus," said I, " that when I was listening just now with the greatest interest to what you were telling us about the miracles of those holy men, my mind kept going back to my Martin, though I said nothing ; and I could not help noticing that whereas each of your Egyptians performed one kind of miracle, this one man of ours did more than all they did between them. You certainly told us some very remarkable things but—if I may say so without offence to these holy men—there

---

[1] St. Paulinus of Nola. See Life of St. Martin, section XXV and note 1 there.
[2] Latin, " tota Memphitica regna ". The phrase, used A.D. 400, suggests sheer ignorance, but could conceivably be taken as rhetorically symbolizing all Egypt.

was absolutely nothing that I heard from you in which Martin was not their equal.

" Moreover, not only would I claim that there is not one of them whose powers can be compared with the graces given to Martin, but it ought to be borne in mind that, in comparison with the hermits, and still more with the anchorites, he was unfairly handicapped. For when they perform those undoubtedly marvellous feats we hear of, they are free from all entanglements and have only heaven and the angels looking on. Martin, on the other hand, moved among crowds and in the haunts of men, amidst quarrelling clergy and raging bishops, and harassed by almost daily scandals on every side. Nevertheless, he stood unmoved amid all these things upon a foundation of unshakeable spiritual power and worked wonders unequalled even by those dwellers in the desert, of our own or other days, of whom we have been hearing.

" And even if their achievements had been equal to his, would any judge be so unjust as not to see good reason for holding that Martin was the mightier? Think of him as a soldier fighting on unfavourable ground and yet coming out victorious, and compare the others also with soldiers, but with soldiers doing battle on equal or even advantageous terms. What follows? They may all alike win a victory, but the glory of it cannot be the same for all. And for matter of that, though you told us some remarkable things, you said nothing of anyone raising a dead man to life. That fact alone compels one to admit that no one can be compared with Martin.

XXV

" No doubt it is wonderful that the flames never touched that Egyptian, but fire quite often was subject to Martin also. You have given instances of wild beasts, with their ferocity subdued, obedient to the anchorites, but it was a very ordinary thing for Martin to vanquish the fury of beasts or the venom of serpents. Or if you quote the case of the man who cured the victims of evil spirits by a word of command or simply through the instrumentality of a shred of his clothing, there are plenty of proofs that

Martin was behind no one in this respect. And even if you fall
back on the man who had his own hair for clothing and was supposed to be visited by angels, Martin conversed with angels every
day.

" As for vanity and boastfulness, he met them with such in-
domitable spirit that no one ever trampled on those vices more
vigorously than he, and yet he was constantly curing at a distance
those possessed by evil spirits and was obeyed not only by counts
and governors but even by emperors. It is true that that is a very
small thing among all his spiritual powers, but you may take it
from me that it was not only actual vanity, but also all possible
causes and occasions of vanity that he fought against more vigorously than anyone else. And I will tell you something very trifling
because it is creditable also to another man, who, holding a very
high position, nevertheless showed such pious eagerness to do
honour to the man of blessings.

" I am thinking of the Prefect Vincentius, a man of very high
rank [1] and as eminent as any man in Gaul for virtues of every
kind. Quite often, when passing through Tours, he used to ask
Martin to let him dine in his monastery and would quote the
example of the blessed Bishop Ambrose[2] who at that time,
according to report, was constantly entertaining consuls and
prefects at his table. But Martin, with deeper understanding,
used to refuse, so as to give no opening for vanity or elation to
creep in.

" So you must admit that Martin had the spiritual powers of
all the people you have told us of, but none of them had Martin's."

XXVI

" But why all this to me? " said Postumianus. "As if I did
not think the same as you, and always have done ! It is true that
so long as I live and think at all I shall speak with admiration of
the monks of Egypt, sing the praises of the anchorites, marvel at
the hermits ; but I shall always put Martin in a class by himself.

---

[1] Latin, " vir egregius ", at one time one of the titles in use for high officials.
[2] St. Ambrose, Bishop of Milan ; see his Life in this volume.

There is no monk I would dare to compare with him, and certainly no bishop! Egypt acknowledges his uniqueness; Syria has discovered it, and the Ethiopian. The Indian has heard of it; the Parthian and the Persian know it. Not even Armenia is ignorant of it; the distant Bosphorus has learnt of it—to say nothing of whoever may dwell in the Island of the Blessed [1] or the ice-bound seas.

"All the more pitiable is this land of ours, which has had so great a man within its borders and has been so unworthy of him that it has not known it. In this accusation I do not include the people; it is only the clergy, only the bishops, who are so ignorant; and they in their envy had good reason to ignore him, for they had only to know of his virtues to discover their own vices. I shudder to repeat what I heard the other day, that some miserable creature (I don't know who) had said that you had told a lot of lies in that book of yours. That is not the language of a man but of a devil, and it is not Martin who is disparaged by that kind of thing; it is the credit of the Gospels that is called in question. For Our Lord Himself declared that mighty works such as Martin accomplished were to be performed by all the faithful, so that if you don't believe that those were Martin's deeds, you don't believe that those were Christ's words.

"But those unhappy men, unworthy men, men half-asleep!—what they cannot do themselves puts them to shame when it is done by Martin, and they prefer denying his spiritual powers to acknowledging their own inertness. But as we are anxious to get on to other things, let us try and forget those people. It is for you now to do what I have been wanting for a long time, and tell us the rest of Martin's mighty works."

"What I think is", said I, "that it is Gallus who should be asked to do that. In the first place, he knows more—a disciple could not fail to know of his master's doings; besides, he owes it both to Martin and to us to take his turn, because I, for my part, have published that book and you, until a moment ago, have been reporting the feats of the Easterners. Let Gallus now unfold the

[1] Latin, " Fortunatae Insulae ", the legendary islands of the Western Ocean, supposed by some to be the Canaries.

tale which is no more than his duty, because, as I said, he owes it to us to take his turn at talking ; and, besides, if I mistake not, to give an account of Martin's doings without complaining is not more than he will do for his hero."

XXVII

" I am really quite unequal to such a task" said Gallus. "At the same time, the examples of obedience which Postumianus has been giving us just now make it impossible for me to refuse the office you lay on me. But when I remember that I am a Gaul and am going to hold forth in front of Aquitanians, I am much afraid that my rather rustic speech may offend your over-civilized ears.[1] However, you will make allowances for me as a simpleton[2] who can't talk in ornamental or dramatic language. After all, you have credited me with being a disciple of Martin, so you must admit that I have the right to follow his example and disdain merely decorative verbal flourishes and figures of speech."

" Speak, if you like in Celtic, or Gallic if you prefer the term," [3] said Postumianus, " so long as you speak about Martin. But, if you ask me, even if you were dumb you would still find words enough to be eloquent about Martin, just as Zachary's tongue was loosened when it came to naming John. But in actual fact you are something of an orator, and you are using an orator's device now, when you plead your lack of skill, because you exude eloquence. But no monk ought to be so crafty or any Gaul so cunning.

" However, you had better be getting on with your story-telling in front of you. We have been spending far too long on

[1] See note I to section I.
[2] Latin, " Gurdonius homo "—" Gurdus ", a Spanish word said to come from the name of a district noted for its boneheads (compare " the wise men of Gotham ").
[3] Latin, " Celtice aut, si mavis, Gallice ". Julius Caesar sometimes used the term *Celticus* to distinguish the inhabitants of central Gaul from the Gauls in general, but the meaning attributed to Sulpicius' phrase in this translation is almost decisively confirmed by the usage of his contemporary, the historian Ammianus Marcellinus, who in his *History* (XV, xi, I) twice in consecutive sentences explicitly equates " Celtae " and " Galli " (" in Celtas eosdemque Gallos ", and " Gallos, qui Celtae sunt ") and explains that their part of the country is separated from the more civilized Aquitaine by the R. Garonne and from the more warlike and independent Belgae by the Marne and the Seine.

other things all this time. The sun is going down and the
shadows are getting longer ; it is a warning that there is not
much of the day left before night is here."

We all fell silent for a little and then Gallus began.

" I think that the first thing for me to beware of ", said he,
" is of repeating what Sulpicius has recorded about Martin's
miracles in his book. So I will leave out what he did in his early
days, when he was in the army, and I won't touch on his doings
as a layman and a monk. Nor will I speak of anything I heard
from other people, but only of what I saw with my own eyes.

(2, I) [1]

" Well then, this happened when I first went to live under the
man of blessings after leaving college. Only a few days after that,
we were accompanying him to the church and a beggar met him,
half-naked, though it was in the winter, and asked to be given
some clothing. The bishop called for his senior deacon[2] and
ordered him to find a garment for the shivering creature without
delay. Then he went into the sacristy and sat there alone, as his
custom was. For even in the church he would secure for himself
this solitude, leaving the clergy complete liberty ; and the priests
used to sit in another sacristy,[3] either spending their leisure in

---

[1] For an explanation of the numbering of this and the remaining sections of
this Dialogue, see the Introductory Note, towards the end.

[2] Latin " archidiaconus ". This was a fourth-century term beginning now
(about A.D. 400) to come into common use. It denoted the chief member of the
body of deacons attached to the bishop. Besides being at the head of the
financial administration of the diocese, the *archidiaconus* stood in a special
relation to the bishop as his deputy in many more strictly ecclesiastical matters
of diocesan administration. Nevertheless, I have not felt justified in using the
obvious transliteration " archdeacon ", because, to English ears, it carries with
it many vivid associations quite alien to the fifth century office, including that
of " priest's orders ".

[3] Large churches at this period commonly had two sacristies, the functions
of which were not always clearly distinguished. The main sacristy, besides
being the place where vestments were kept and the clergy vested, would, in the
case of a cathedral, often be used by the bishop for conferences or his court of
law. The other sacristy was sometimes used for spiritual reading by the clergy
but might also be put to any of the uses of the first sacristy. Moreover, it was
sometimes known by the special name of *salutatorium*, as being the place where
those who took sanctuary were accommodated. The general name for a sacristy
was *secretarium*, which is used for both the sacristies here, and invariably
throughout the Lives in this volume. See the articles under " salutatorium "
and " secretarium " (3) in Ducange, *Glossarium Mediae et Infimae Latinitatis.*

social amenities or occupied with those who came on business, while Martin preserved his solitude unbroken until it was time to celebrate the holy rites in the presence of the congregation.

" And there is a point that I must not forget to mention, that when he sat in the sacristy he never used his chair. And no one ever saw him sit in the church in the way that, not long ago, I was ashamed to see a certain person sitting (as God is my witness) upon a lofty throne raised high upon a kind of royal dais. But Martin would be seen sitting on a rough stool, such as is provided for slaves, which we Gauls call tripets but you learned people, or at least you, Postumianus, who have been in Greece, would call tripods.

" Well, into this retreat of the blessed man there burst the beggar he had picked up on the way. The senior deacon was taking a long time over giving him a tunic and the beggar accused the cleric of tricking him and complained bitterly of the cold. Without a moment's delay the holy man stealthily slipped off his tunic from under his vestment [4] without the beggar seeing, put it on him and told him to be off.

" A little later the senior deacon came in to inform him in the usual way that the congregation was awaiting him in the church and that he ought to be proceeding there to celebrate the holy rites. He replied that the beggar[5] (meaning himself) must first be clothed ; he could not proceed to the church until the beggar had been given a garment. The deacon, not in the least under-

[4] Latin, " amphibalus ", the Gallic equivalent of " casula planeta " (or " paenula ") the name of the garment from which the chasuble was eventually derived. At this period, however, the garment was not distinguished in form from its prototype, the raincoat of the day, although as a rule the priest, on arriving at the church, would change into an *amphibalus* specially kept in the sacristy for liturgical use. The shape of the garment at this period was roughly that of a very small bell tent with the door sewn up and a hole cut at the peak for the head to go through (*casula* actually means " little hut "). It was only later that gaps at the sides, to give more freedom to the arms, were introduced and gradually enlarged, the garment being at the same time shortened until the *casula* became the chasuble of today.

If we bear this in mind, the story told in this section, which would be incredible if St. Martin had been wearing only a modern chasuble over his tunic, becomes perfectly intelligible ; but the rendering of the word *amphibalus* becomes something of a problem. " Chasuble " is obviously impossible on every ground, while " cloak " would be too secular. I have fallen back, therefore, on the vague liturgical term " vestment ".

[5] Latin, " pauper ", as throughout this section ; but " poor man " gives the wrong effect in colloquial English in a context such as this.

standing what he meant, because he could not see that he had
nothing on under the vestment he was wearing, finally pleaded
that the beggar was nowhere to be seen.

" ' Then let the garment which has been found for him be
brought to me,' said Martin. ' There will be a beggar waiting to
wear it.'

" The deacon, by now seething with rage, but finding himself
with no alternative, went and snatched up a bigerrica,[6] short and
shaggy, from the nearest stall (paying five shillings for it) and
angrily laid it out at Martin's feet.

" ' There's your garment,' he said, ' but there's no beggar
here.'

" Quite unmoved, Martin told him to wait outside the door
for a moment, and thus obtained privacy while he stripped and
put on the tunic, making every effort to enable what he had
done to remain a secret. But when have these actions of holy
men ever remained a secret from seekers after truth? Willy nilly,
they all come out.

(2, II)

" Martin, then, proceeded in this garment to the church to
offer sacrifice to God. Now, on that same day (I am coming to
something very wonderful) he had begun to bless the altar in
accordance with the ritual when we saw a ball of fire dart out
from his head, so that, as it rose in the air, the flame drew out
into a hair of enormous length. And although we saw this
happen on a great festival in front of a huge congregation, only
one of the nuns, one of the priests and three monks saw it. Why
the others did not see it, it is not for me to say.

"About that time, my uncle Evanthius, who was a most
Christian man although engaged in worldly business, was taken
seriously ill and before long was in grave danger of death. He
sent for Martin, who hurried there without delay. But while the
man of blessings was still on the road and before he had covered
half the distance, the sick man experienced the effects of his

---

[6] The bigerrica was a rough garment named after the Begerri or Bigerriones,
the inhabitants of a district on the slopes of the Pyrenees, the modern Bigorre,
in which Lourdes is situated.

power. All of a sudden his health returned and he himself came out to meet us as we arrived.

" The next day Martin wished to return but, at my uncle's urgent request, delayed his departure, for in the meantime a snake with a deadly bite had laid low one of the boys of the household. He was almost dead from the effects of the poison when Evanthius himself carried him in on his shoulders and laid him at the feet of the holy man, confident that for him nothing was impossible.

" By now the creeping venom had spread through all his limbs. You could see the skin swollen over all his veins and his vital organs as tight as a drum. Martin put out his hand, felt all the boy's limbs and brought his finger to rest near the tiny wound where the animal had injected the poison. Then—and I am coming to something very wonderful—we saw the poison, drawn from every part of the body, run towards Martin's finger. Then, through that minute aperture in the wound, he pressed out the venom, much as a long thin stream of the abundant milk will flow from the udders of goats or sheep when they are squeezed by the shepherd's hand. The boy rose up sound and well. As for us, we were speechless with wonder at so great a marvel and agreed, as indeed regard for truth required, that there was no one under the sun who could rival Martin.

(2, III)

" We were similarly on the road with him some time after this when he was visiting his parishes and, for some reason I have forgotten, had stopped behind for a short time while he went on ahead. Just then a government coach full of service men came along the highway. But when the mules on Martin's side of the road saw him in his shaggy tunic, with his black cloak swaying, they took fright and swerved a little in the opposite direction. The next moment they had become entangled in the traces and broken the long lines in which the poor beasts were massed together, in the way you have seen often enough.

" They were disentangled with some difficulty, while the impatient travellers were kept waiting. Furious at what they regarded as an injury, the soldiers jumped pell-mell to the ground and proceeded to belabour Martin with whips and sticks. In silence and with incredible patience he submitted to the beating and, at this, the wretches became madder than ever, furious that he should show contempt for them by seeming not to feel their blows.

"And there we caught him up and found him, lying almost lifeless on the ground, all smeared with blood and with wounds all over his body. We at once put him on his donkey and, with maledictions on the place where he had been so brutally assaulted, we hurried away from it with all speed.

"Meanwhile the soldiers, having worked off their anger, had returned to their coach and gave the order for the animals to resume the journey. But they all stood rigid, fixed to the spot like brazen statues. The muleteers shouted at them louder than ever and cracked their whips on either side of them, but they never stirred. Then everybody started beating them and wore out the great Gallic whips in punishing them. The whole wood near by was torn down and the animals were pounded with tree-trunks, but all this savagery achieved nothing whatever. They remained standing like images in precisely the same place.

"The wretched men did not know what to do. They could no longer hide from themselves the fact that, somehow or other, the animals knew in their brute minds that a divine power was forbidding them to move. So at last they paused to reflect and began to speculate as to who it was they had beaten on that same spot a little while before. They made enquiries of some passers-by and learnt that it was Martin they had so cruelly flogged. Then at last the explanation was clear to everybody; they could not blink the fact that it was the injury they had inflicted on that great man that was causing them to be detained.

"All of them, therefore, came after us at a run. Realizing full well what they had done and deserved, overwhelmed with shame, and with tears in their eyes, and their heads and faces stained with the dust with which they had sprinkled themselves, they threw themselves at Martin's knees, begging his pardon and asking to be allowed to go on. They pleaded that they had been sufficiently punished by their own consciences and that they fully realized that the earth might have swallowed them alive on the spot, or, rather, that they ought to have been deprived of their senses and turned as rigid as rocks, in the way they had seen the mules fixed where they stood. They begged and prayed, therefore, that he would grant them pardon for their crime and give them power to go on.

" Even before they had come up with us, the man of blessings had known that they were held fast and had already told us of it. But now he gently forgave them, giving them leave to proceed and restoring to them the use of their mules.

(2, IV)

" I often noticed, Sulpicius, that Martin was in the habit of saying to you that since he had been a bishop he had not possessed the gift of working miracles in anything like the same degree as he could remember possessing it previously. If that is really the case, or rather, since that is really the case, we can imagine what wonders he must have worked as a monk and performed when alone, without witnesses ; we have only to think of what great marvels we saw him perform in front of everybody when he was a bishop.

" It is true that many of those early doings of his could not be hidden and became known to the world ; but there are said to be countless others which, owing to his horror of boasting, never came to light because he never allowed anyone else to hear of them. For having risen above the limits of human nature and being fully conscious of this power of his, he had trodden this world's glory under foot and was perfectly happy with God as an onlooker.

" We can test the truth of this from the things that could not be kept hidden and came to our knowledge. For example, before he became a bishop he restored two dead men to life as your book tells us very fully, but during his episcopate he raised up only one (and this miracle your book rather surprisingly omits). But I was myself a witness of it, and I trust you will accept me as a satisfactory one. At any rate, I will describe the episode to you exactly as it happened.

" For some reason or other we were on the road to Chartres.[1] On the way we passed through a certain country town with a very large population, and a huge crowd came out to meet us. It consisted entirely of pagans, for no one in the district had met a Christian. Nevertheless the report that such a great man was approaching had brought immense numbers streaming from far and wide across the open fields. Martin became aware that there was work to be done, and a deep groan shook him as the Spirit came upon him. Then in inspired utterance he began to preach to the pagans the Word of God, marvelling, with many sighs, that so great a multitude should not know their Lord and Saviour.

" As he preached, with an incredible host standing round us, a woman whose son had died just a little earlier came and presented the lifeless body to the man of blessings with outstretched hands. ' We know that you are a friend of God,' said she ; ' give me back my son, my only son.' All the crowd joined with cries in the mother's supplications and Martin (as he told us afterwards) saw that, to bring salvation to the expectant throng, he would be enabled to perform this act of power.

" He took the body of the dead child into his own hands, then knelt down in the sight of all and, when his prayer was ended, rose and restored a living baby to its mother.

" Then indeed a shout went up to heaven from the whole multitude as they acknowledged Christ to be God. The end of it was that they all came hurrying and crowding around the knees of the man of blessings, asking him in all sincerity to make them Christians. He lost no time in making them all catechumens, in the field, just as they were, by stretching out his hand over all of them together. For, as he said (turning to us), a field where martyrs had often won their crown was no unfitting place for making catechumens."

[1] Latin, " Carnotum (or " Carnutum ") oppidum ". The Latin name for the town was Autricum.

(2, V)

" You win, Gallus, you win ",[1] said Postumianus, " —not a victory over *me*, because I take Martin's part myself and have always known and believed all these things about him, but over all the hermits and anchorites. For none of them had, like this Martin of yours, or rather of ours, command over death. Sulpicius here was quite right to compare him with the Apostles and Prophets, for the power of his faith and the works of power that he accomplished show him to have been like them in everything. But go on, please, although we can hardly hear of anything more magnificent, go on, Gallus, all the same, and let us have what there is still left to tell about Martin. For one has an appetite for even the most trifling and everyday facts about Martin ; for there is no doubt about it, even the least of his doings are greater than the greatest of other people's."

" I will go on," said Gallus, " but what I am coming to now I did not see myself, as it took place before I became his disciple. But it is a celebrated episode which became widely known through reports of reliable brethren who were present.

" It was about the time when he first became Bishop, and the need had arisen for him to visit the Imperial Court. Valentinian the Elder then held the reins of power.[2] When he heard that Martin would be making certain requests that he had no wish to grant, he ordered him to be refused admittance at the palace gates. For his own harsh and arrogant disposition had been reinforced by his Arian wife, who had turned him entirely against

---

[1] Latin, " Vicisti, Galle, vicisti ", a curious echo, just possibly intentional, of the words alleged to have been uttered by Julian the Apostate as death approached (" Vicisti, Galilaee ").

[2] This was Valentinian I, the son of a peasant, Emperor in the West from A.D. 364 to 375, and the father of the Emperor Gratian and (by a second marriage) of Valentinian II (" the Younger "), who appears in the Life of St. Martin (see section XX and the notes there) and frequently in the Life of St. Ambrose in this volume. Valentinian I professed Catholicism but, as Emperor, held himself completely neutral in matters of religion. His northern capital, the scene of the story told in this section, was Trier (Trèves), which was the scene also of the episodes described in section XX of the Life.

the holy man and persuaded him not to treat Martin with proper respect.[3]

" Martin, therefore, after he had more than once attempted to gain access to the haughty prince, resorted to his well-known weapons. He wrapped himself in sackcloth, sprinkled himself with ashes, abstained from food and drink and prayed continuously night and day. On the seventh day an angel appeared to him and ordered him to go confidently to the palace, where the imperial gates, though closed against him, would fly open of their own accord and the proud heart of the Emperor would be softened. Encouraged by such words from an angel visitant, and relying on his help, he made his way to the palace. The gates stood open ; no one challenged him. Eventually he reached the imperial presence without anyone interfering with him.

" When the Emperor from a distance saw him approaching, he ground his teeth as he demanded why he had been admitted ; and he would not for a moment condescend to rise as Martin advanced, until he found that the imperial chair was enveloped in flames and that the fire was attacking that part of his person upon which he sat. Then the proud man was forced off his throne and most unwillingly stood before Martin. And he embraced many times the man he had determined to humiliate and, now that he had learnt his lesson, he admitted that he had been conscious of the presence of divine power.

" Nor did he wait for Martin to proffer his requests before granting everything he asked. He several times invited him to come and talk or to dine with him ; and when eventually Martin was going away he made him many presents. All of these, however, the blessed man refused, ever careful to preserve his poverty.

[3] This was his second wife, Justina, mother of Valentinian the Younger, during whose reign she played a great part, as dowager Empress and a strong partisan of the Arian heresy, in the life of St. Ambrose (see sections XI to XX, *passim*, in the Life of St. Ambrose in this volume, and for Arianism, section VI of the Life of St. Martin, and footnote 2 there).

(2, VI)

" And now that we have made an entry into the palace, perhaps I may put together events from more than one period that took place there. I certainly do not think that I should omit the example of high esteem for Martin set by an Empress holding the true faith. The Emperor Maximus then ruled the state, a man whose whole life would have been praiseworthy if he could have refused the crown illegally thrust upon him by a mutinous army and refrained from waging civil war. But a great Empire cannot be refused without risk or retained without fighting.[1]

" This man often sent for Martin, entertained him in the palace and showed the deepest respect for him. All their talk together was of things present and things to come, of the glory of believers and the immortality of the saints ; and all the time, by day and by night, the Empress hung upon Martin's lips. Indeed, she matched the woman in the Gospels by watering the feet of the holy man with her tears and wiping them with her hair.

" Martin, whom no woman had ever touched, could not escape her constant presence, not to say, her menial service. She took no account of the riches of the realm, the imperial crown and the purple robes. She would seat herself upon the ground, and could not be torn away from Martin's feet. Finally she begged her husband to join with her in compelling Martin to allow her to send all the servants out and wait on him alone at table. Nor could the man of blessings be over-obstinate in his resistance.

" With her own hands the Empress made the modest preparations. It was she who placed Martin's stool and brought his table, poured out the water for his hands and served the meal she had cooked. It was she who, while he ate, stood at a little distance as servants are trained to do, motionless as if rooted to the ground, in everything exhibiting the meekness of a menial, the humble bearing of a maid. When he wished to drink, it was she who

---

[1] For Maximus and his usurpation, see the Life of St. Martin, section XX, and note 1 there. As regards his Empress, there is a story emanating from Welsh sources that, when commanding the army in Britain, he had taken a wife named Helena, the daughter of a wealthy lord of Caernarvon. Gibbon, who quotes the story, is disinclined to believe it, but there really does not seem to be anything intrinsically improbable about it (see *Decline and Fall*, ch. 27).

mixed the cup and she who presented it. When the meal was over, she collected the bread crumbs and the scraps, in her strong faith valuing these leavings above the dainties of the imperial table.

"A truly blessed woman, rightly to be compared for the intensity of her devotion with the one who came from the ends of the earth to visit Solomon[2]—rightly, that is to say, if we consider the outward facts of history. But we ought to compare the two queens in respect of their faith and then, having regard only to the story's deeper and grander meaning, I may be allowed to say that whereas the first queen desired to listen to a wise man, the second was not content merely to listen to the wise man but was privileged to serve him."

(2, VII)

Here Postumianus interposed. "As I have been listening to you, Gallus," said he, " I have been filled with the greatest admiration for the faith of the Empress ; but what becomes of the common belief that no woman ever approached close to Martin ? Here is this Empress not only approaching him but even waiting on him. And I fear that those who take pleasure in female society will be able to some extent to shelter themselves behind this example."

" But why ", replied Gallus, " do you not pay attention to what schoolmasters are always insisting on—the place, the time and the persons ? Picture to yourself Martin trapped in the palace, importuned by the appeals of the Emperor, overborne by the faith of the Empress, compelled by the pressing needs of the moment to obtain, if he could, the release of prisoners, the return of exiles, the restoration of confiscated goods. Do you think that these things should have carried so little weight with the bishop that he should not have modified a little the strictness of his way of life for the sake of them ?

"And if you think that there are some who will make evil use of this example, I can only say that they will be doing very well

[2] See Matt. xii. 42 ; 3 (1) Kings x. 1.

if they do not fall short of the model that that example provides. Let them look at the facts. It happened to Martin only once in a life that went into the sixties.[1] The woman was not an independent widow, nor a wanton girl but was living under her husband's rule, and her husband himself joined in the request. Moreover, she, though an Empress, did not sit down to a banquet with Martin but served and waited on him while he ate, not venturing to share his meal but rendering to him obedience.

" Take that for your model. You may allow a woman, if she is married, to wait on you but not to rule you, to wait on you but not to sit at table with you ; just as Martha waited on Our Lord but was not invited to join in the meal—indeed, the one who chose only to listen was commended more highly than the one who served. But in Martin's case, the Empress played both parts. Like Martha she served and like Mary she listened. So if anyone wants to appeal to this example, let him follow it at every point. There should be the same kind of reason for his action, the same kind of persons taking part, the same kind of service rendered, the same arrangements for the meal, and it should happen once in a whole lifetime."

(2, VIII)

" You have shown most convincingly ", said Postumianus, " that our people here should not press the example beyond the limits observed by Martin, but I can assure you that it will all fall on deaf ears. For, if we were in the habit of following in the footsteps of Martin, we should never have to defend ourselves against charges of kissing and should not have all that scandal talked behind our backs. However, as you say when you are accused of gluttony, we are Gauls ; and so in this matter also we shall never be reformed either by Martin's example or by your disquisitions. But why, Sulpicius, have *you* been so obstinately silent, all the time that we two have been discussing these matters ? "

[1] Latin, " in vita iam septuagenaria " the last word being a conjectural emendation of the " septuagenario " of the MSS.

" Not only am I silent," I replied, " but some time ago I made a resolution to be silent on this subject. For I once rebuked a certain widow—an elegant and expensive little gadabout—for riotous living, and also a girl who was following a young friend of mine about in a rather disgusting way, although I had often heard her rebuking other people for doing the same kind of thing; and by so doing I stirred up such hatred against me amongst all women and all monks that the two armies of them have solemnly declared war on me. So please drop the subject, or even what you two are saying will be put down to my malice. Let us forget them altogether and get back to Martin. Now, Gallus, you've made a start; complete what you've begun."

" I've already told you so much ", he replied, " that you really ought to be satisfied with that. However, I have no choice but to fall in with your wishes, so I will go on talking while the daylight lasts. And, as a matter of fact, that straw I see, which is being got ready for our beds, puts me in mind of a miracle worked in connection with some straw on which Martin had lain.

" This is how it came about. Clion[1] is a small town between Bourges and Tours.[2] The Church there is famous for its holy monks and also for a glorious company of consecrated virgins. Passing through the place on one occasion, Martin lodged in the sacristy of the church. After his departure all the nuns rushed into the sacristy. They kissed every place that the blessed man had sat or stood in, and shared out among themselves the straw on which he had lain. A few days later, one of them took part of the straw that she had collected in order to bring a blessing on herself and put it round the neck of a demoniac tormented by a deceiving spirit. Without a moment's delay, quicker than you could say the words, the demon was expelled and the person was cured.

[1] Latin, " Claudiomagus ".
[2] Latin, " in confinio Biturigum adque Turonum ".

(2, IX)

" About the same period Martin was on his way back from Trier when he encountered a cow which a demon was tormenting. She had left her herd and was attacking human beings and had gored several people dangerously. When she was getting close to us the men who were chasing her began shouting to us to tell us to take care. But when she had come quite near us, her eyes blazing with fury, Martin raised his hand and told the animal to halt. She drew up at his words and then stood motionless. At the same time Martin saw a demon perched on her back and spoke sternly to it.

" ' Get off that animal, you pernicious creature,' said he, ' and stop tormenting an innocent beast.'

" The wicked spirit obeyed and disappeared. The heifer had enough sense to know that she was liberated and, quite quiet now, she lay down at the saint's feet. Then he ordered her to go back to her herd and she rejoined her companions, as placidly as any sheep.

" It was about this time that he found himself with flames all round him but did not feel the fire. But I don't think that I need tell that story because, although Sulpicius left it out of his book, he gave ample details in a letter he afterwards wrote to Eusebius, who was then a priest but is now a bishop.[1] I believe you have read it, Postumianus, or, if you don't know it, you have a copy handy in that chest when you want it. I will confine myself to what he omits altogether.

" Once when Martin was making a round of the parishes we encountered a party of huntsmen. The dogs were chasing a hare and the little thing was by this time exhausted by a long run, and there were open fields on all sides and no escape anywhere. More than once it had been on the point of being caught and it was only by frequent doublings that it was putting off immediate

---

[1] Letter 1 in this volume. Among the many bishops named Eusebius in the Index to Duchesne's *Fastes Episcopaux de l'ancienne Gaule*, only one could by any possibility have been a priest at the time of this Dialogue, namely a bishop of Nantes who was at a Council held at Tours in 461 (II, 361).

death. The man of blessings in his kindliness took compassion on it in its danger and ordered the dogs to leave off following it and let the fugitive get away. They pulled up at once, at the first words of the order. You might have thought them chained or, rather, stuck fast in their own tracks. And so, with its pursuers pinned down, the little hare got safely away.

(2, X)

" It will be well worth while to quote also some of Martin's homely sayings, salty with spiritual wisdom.

" Happening to see a sheep that had just been shorn, he said : ' It has fulfilled the Gospel precept. It had two coats and has given one of them to someone who has none. You ought to do the same.'

"Another time he saw a swineherd shivering with cold and almost naked in his garment of skins. ' Look at Adam ', said he, ' in his garment of skins, thrown out of Paradise and herding swine. But it is for us to strip ourselves of the old Adam that you can still recognize in him, and to put on the new Adam.'

" Oxen had been grazing down part of a certain meadow and another part of it had been rooted up by swine. The rest had not been touched and was rich with verdure and painted with flowers of many colours. ' That part there,' he said, ' where the cattle have been feeding, is a good representation of marriage. It has not altogether lost the beauty of the grass but has not kept any of the glory of the flowers. That part which the pigs—those unclean creatures—have rooted up makes a loathsome picture of fornication. But that part there, which has not been injured at all, shows us the splendour of virginity. It is rich with abundant grass, it will give a luxuriant crop of hay, and it is beautiful beyond comparison, decked out with flowers and shining as if adorned with sparkling gems. A sight most blessed, a sight worthy of God ! For nothing can compare with perfect chastity.

" ' So you see that, on the one hand, those who liken marriage to fornication go terribly wrong and, on the other hand, those who put marriage on the same level as virginity are utterly and miserably foolish. The wise will hold firmly to these distinctions : marriage may be pardoned, virginity looks towards heavenly glory, and fornication is destined to punishment unless it is purged by penance.'

(2, XI)

"A certain soldier had laid aside his sword-belt in the church and entered upon the monastic life. He had built his cell at some distance away in a secluded spot, as if he were going to live the life of a hermit. But the crafty enemy of souls was all the time unsettling his somewhat simple mind with a variety of suggestions to the effect that he should go back on his resolutions and have his wife to live with him (Martin had said that she must be in a convent). So the gallant hermit went to Martin and told him openly what was in his mind.

" Martin, of course, most emphatically refused to let a woman go back in this most irregular fashion to a man who was no longer her husband but a monk. The soldier, however, was insistent and argued that no harm could come of the plan and that all he wanted was the comfort of his wife's company. There was no fear, he said, of their returning to their old life. He was now a soldier of Christ and she also had taken the oath in the same service. Could not the Bishop allow two consecrated persons who, thanks to their faith, had no thought of sex, to serve in Christ's army together ?

" To all this, Martin replied (and I will give you his actual words) : ' Tell me, were you ever on active service and have you ever fought in the front line ? '

" ' I have often fought in the front line,' he replied, ' and I was often on active service.'

" ' Then tell me,' said Martin, ' when weapons were ready and the line was being marshalled for battle, or when contact had been made, swords were drawn and actual fighting was going on with the enemy, did you ever see a woman standing or fighting in the line ? '

" Then the soldier was at last abashed. He blushed, and then thanked Martin for not letting him continue in his mistake and particularly for putting him right by a sound and reasoned analogy instead of by a harsh reproof.

" A number of the brethren had come thronging round and Martin turned to us and said :

" 'A woman should not come near the men's lines. The fighting formations should be kept quite separate and the women should live in their own quarters, far away. It makes an army ridiculous if a troop of women invades the men's battalions. A soldier's place is fighting in the line and on the battle-field ; a woman should keep behind the fortifications. She can win glory too, by living chastely while her husband is away. For her, the first virtue and the crowning victory is that she should not be seen.'

(2, XII)

" I expect, Sulpicius, that you remember (because you were present yourself) the deep feeling with which Martin sang the praises of the consecrated virgin who had withdrawn so completely from the sight of any man whatever that she would not even receive Martin when he wished to pay her the compliment of a visit. He was passing near the little property where she had lived for many years in chaste seclusion and, having heard of her fidelity and her virtues, he turned aside there with the idea that, by this pious act of courtesy performed in his capacity as Bishop, he could do honour to a virgin of such outstanding worth.[1]

" We who were with him had supposed that when a Bishop of such renown modified the strictness of his own rule of life so far as to come and see her, the virgin would be delighted at receiving this recognition of her virtues. But she would not loosen the fetters of her heroic rule even for a sight of Martin. Apologies that were wholly to her credit were sent out to him through

---

[1] It was still common at this period (St. Ambrose's sister provides an example—see his Life, section IV) for consecrated virgins to live in retirement in their own houses instead of as nuns in the still comparatively scarce convents ; and the preceding sections bear witness to the free-and-easy practices to which this practically unsupervised mode of life often led. This must be taken into account before passing judgment on the lengths to which the virgin in this story went in avoiding intercourse with men and dismissing as entirely ridiculous (as the twentieth-century reader will be inclined to do) both the action of the virgin and the author's eulogy of it.

another woman and the man of blessings turned joyfully away from the doors of one who had not allowed him to see or greet her. Glorious virgin! who would not let herself be seen even by Martin. Most blessed Martin! who did not take that repulse as an insult but extolled and exulted in her virtue, delighted that she should have set an example so rare, at least in this part of the world.

" Well, when night came on and we were obliged to stop not far from her little estate she sent a gift to the man of blessings as to a guest. And Martin did a thing he had never done before, for he would accept no parting gift nor any present from anyone. He returned not one of the articles which the revered virgin had sent him. It was certainly not for a bishop, said he, to reject a benefaction from one who should be esteemed above many bishops.

" I trust that all consecrated virgins will take note of that example. If they wish their doors to be closed against evil men, they must shut them even against good men. If blackguards are not to have free access to them, they must not be afraid to shut out even bishops. Let all the world take notice : a virgin would not let herself be seen by Martin !

" It was certainly no common-or-garden bishop that she repelled. The man to whom the virgin would not show herself was one whom it was a saving grace to see. And what bishop besides Martin would not have regarded it as an affront ? Think of the irritation, think of the angry feelings that would have been aroused in his mind against the holy virgin ! He would have pronounced her a heretic and decreed her excommunication. More acceptable to him than that chosen soul would have been those virgins who are always contriving to be where they will meet the bishop and who give expensive banquets at which they even sit with him at table !

" But my tongue is running away with me ! I must put some check on my rather too free speech or I shall be giving offence to certain people. Besides, reproaches will do no good to bad Christians and this example will be enough for good ones.[2] More-

---

[2] Latin, " infidelibus . . . fidelibus ". " Bad Christians . . . good Christians " is a happy rendering from M. C. Watt's translation from the French.

over, when I praise in this way the virtues of this particular virgin, I do not want to be thought to be criticising the many who came long distances to see Martin. For, with the same motives, even angels were constant visitors to the man of blessings.

(2, XIII)

" Now, for what I am going to speak of next, Sulpicius "—and here Gallus looked hard at me—" I have you as witness. One day I and Sulpicius there were keeping watch outside Martin's door. We had already been sitting in silence for several hours, in deep awe and trepidation, as though we had been keeping our allotted watch before an angel's dwelling, though in fact, with the door of his cell closed, he did not know that we were there. We now heard the murmur of conversation and presently there came over us a kind of awe and stupefaction and we could not help being conscious of the presence of the divine.

" About two hours later Martin came out to us and then Sulpicius there, who could always speak to him more easily than anyone else, tried to persuade him to satisfy our pious thirst for knowledge by explaining the meaning of that holy awe which we agreed that we had both felt and telling us who had been in conversation with him in his cell ; for what we had heard outside the door had been a low and practically unintelligible murmur of voices.

" It was a long time before he would tell us, but there was nothing that Sulpicius could not drag out of him, however much against his will. At last he said—and I am going to tell you something scarcely believable, but as Christ is my witness I am not lying and no one would be so blasphemous as to suppose that Martin was lying—he said :

" ' I will tell you, but please tell no one else. Agnes, Thecla and Mary were with me.'

" He proceeded to describe to us the face and general appearance of each of them. He acknowledged also that he had had visits from them, not only that day but frequently. And he had to admit that he had quite often seen the Apostles Peter and

Paul. As for demons, as each one came to him, he would denounce it by its own name. From Mercury he had to endure particular hostility. Jupiter, he used to say, was brutish and obtuse.[1]

" All this used to seem too much to believe, even to many living in Martin's monastery. Still less do I expect that all who hear it by report will believe it. For it was only the superlative excellence of Martin's life and character that persuaded even us to credit him with such glories as these. Nor is it in the least surprising that weak humanity should have its doubts about Martin's mighty works, seeing that in these days we see many not even believing the Gospels.

" But as regards the fact that Martin often saw angels and was on familiar terms with them, we can speak from our own observation and experience. What I am now going to speak of is a very small thing but nevertheless I will speak of it. An episcopal synod was being held at Nîmes[2] to which he had refused to go. He wished, however, to know what took place there. Sulpicius here happened to be travelling with him by boat[3] and Martin, as always, was sitting in a part of the boat well away from everyone else. There an angel brought him news of what had been done at the synod. We made careful enquiries afterwards as to the time the Council had been held, and ascertained definitely that the day of the meeting, and the decrees passed there, corresponded to the day and the details of the angel's announcement to Martin.

[1] It was the common opinion among Christians during the period when paganism was an active force in the Empire, that the gods of the pagans, among which Jupiter and Mercury were prominent, were evil spirits.

[2] Latin, " Nemausus ". This Council was held on October 1st in either 394 or 396. Rauschen in his *Jahrbücher der Christlichen Kirche unter dem Kaiser Theodosius dem Grossen* (p. 421), enters it under the former year, while Duchesne, *Fastes Episcopaux de l'ancienne Gaule* (I, 366) gives a strong reason for favouring 396. J. R. Palanque (in Fliche and Martin, *Histoire de l'Eglise*, III, 469) favours A.D. 396 and affirms that the Council was attended only by bishops of the faction to which Martin was opposed. On the cause of this opposition and Martin's refusal to attend the Council, see the Dialogue *Gallus*, sections XI to XIII.

[3] Presumably on the River Loire, the great highway for much of Martin's visiting and the scene of more than one of Sulpicius' stories.

(2, XIV) [1]

" When we asked Martin about the end of the world, he told us that Nero and Antichrist had first to come. Nero will rule in the West, after subduing ten kings, and will carry persecution to the point of making the worship of the heathen idols compulsory. Antichrist, on the other hand, will first seize supreme power in the East and have his throne and capital at Jerusalem, rebuilding both the city and the temple. He will persecute with the object of compelling men to deny that Christ is God, setting up himself instead as Christ, and will order them all to be circumcised in accordance with the Law of Moses. Nero himself will then be slain by Antichrist and thus the whole world and all the nations will be brought under his rule, until the blasphemer is overthrown by the Second Coming of Christ.

" There was no doubt, he added, that Antichrist was already born, his conception being the work of an evil spirit. He is now a child and will take over supreme power when he comes of age. As it is now more than seven years since we heard Martin say this, you can judge how soon this fearful future may be upon us."

Just when Gallus was in full flood and before he had finished what he had intended to say, a house-boy came in to announce that the priest Refrigerius was at the door. We were in two minds as to whether to go on listening to Gallus or to admit this ever-welcome visitor who was paying us a call. Gallus however settled it.

" Even ", said he, " if the holy priest's arrival had not put an end to our talk, the late hour was quite enough to make us stop at this point. It has been quite impossible to say all there was to say about Martin's spiritual powers, but we have had enough for today. Tomorrow I will tell you the rest."

With that promise from Gallus we all rose from our seats.

[1] The first part of this section was deliberately omitted from many early copies of the Dialogues ; see the Introductory Note.

DIALOGUE 2

GALLUS

I

" It's daylight, Gallus; time to get up! And here comes
Postumianus, as you see; and the priest who missed hearing you
yesterday is waiting for you to keep your promise and give us the
stories about Martin that you put off telling till today. Not that
he is ignorant of any of the things you will be speaking of, but
there is something very pleasant and delightful about being told
such things, even when one is going over old ground, because it
is human nature that one's pleasure in the knowledge of them
should be more unqualified when one can tell from the number
of witnesses that the facts are certain. You see, he was a disciple
of Martin's from his earliest days and knows all about him, but
is always glad to hear it once more. Why, I tell you, Gallus, that
in my own case, though I have heard about Martin's miracles
often enough and have even put a great deal about him into
writing, nevertheless his achievements so amaze me that they are
always new to me, even though I have heard them all before and
they are repeated over and over again.

" Moreover I am all the more glad to have Refrigerius added
to your audience because Postumianus here wants to get back
quickly to the East and is particularly anxious to get the truth
from you with other witnesses present to confirm it."

While I was speaking, Gallus had got ready to begin his story,
when in there burst a large party of monks, the priest Evagrius,
Aper, Sabatius, Agricola and, a little later, the priest Aetherius
accompanied by the deacon Calupio and the sub-deacon Amator;
finally the priest Aurelius, dearest of friends, came hurrying along
very much out of breath, having had a rather long distance to cover.[1]

[1] Aurelius is presumably the recipient of Letter II. None of the other
characters, with the possible exception of Sabatius (see Life of St. Martin,
section XXIII) appears outside this Dialogue.

" Why this sudden and unexpected invasion ", said I, " from so many directions and so early in the morning ? "

" We heard yesterday ", said they, " that Gallus there had been telling stories of Martin's miracles all day long and had put the rest of them off till today because night had overtaken him. That is why we have been hurrying to supply him with a big audience, if he is going to talk on such a grand subject."

While he was speaking, a servant announced that a number of laymen were at the door, and that they would not venture to enter uninvited but begged to be admitted.

" It won't do at all to have them in with us," said Aper, " because they have come to listen out of curiosity more than for the religious interest."

I felt much embarrassed when I thought of those who he considered should not be admitted but at last, with some difficulty, I got everyone to agree to admit one of the Deputy Praetorian Prefects, named Eucherius, and a man of consular rank named Celsus, the rest being sent away.[2] Then we put Gallus in a chair in the centre. For quite a long time the shyness for which he is renowned kept him silent and then at last he began.

II

" You who have come here to listen to me ", he said, " are men of holiness and eloquence but I imagine that you have brought to the listening your piety rather than your learning, expecting to find in me a truthful witness but not a fluent orator. And what I related yesterday, I will not repeat. Those who did not hear it will get it all in writing. Postumianus is waiting for something new, to take an account of it to the East, to make sure that the East does not rank itself above the West when Martin comes into the comparison. And I am inclined to begin with a

[2] The Latin terms are " vicarius " and " consularis ". The former was the title of the governors of the civil " dioceses ", of which there were at this time twelve in the Empire, and the latter denoted the rank of the governors of about a third of the administrative Provinces. However the dialogue form is, as Severus admits, a literary artifice and so, no doubt, is this crowd of magnates on his doorstep at sunrise !

story of which Refrigerius has just whispered a reminder—
something that happened in the city of Chartres.

" There was a father who had a twelve-year-old daughter,
dumb from birth. He brought her to show to Martin, and to ask
that the man of blessings, through his favour with God, would
set her free from her impediment. Two bishops, Valentinus and
Victricius,[1] happened to be on either side of Martin and he tried
to give place to them, declaring that he himself was quite unequal
to so great an undertaking but that to them, with their greater
holiness, nothing was impossible. They, however, added their
own humble requests to the father's entreaties, begging Martin
to satisfy his hopes.

" Then Martin delayed no longer—and he is equally to be
admired for his manifestation of humility and for the promptness
of his kindly action. He ordered all the bystanders to be sent
away and then, with only the bishops and the girl's father present,
he prostrated himself in prayer in his usual way. Next, he
blessed a little oil with the formula used in exorcisms and then
poured the consecrated liquid into the girl's mouth, holding her
tongue with his fingers as he did so.

" Nor did the effects of this act of power disappoint the holy
man. He asked her the name of her father and she replied at
once. Her father cried out with joy mingled with tears as he
clasped Martin's knees, declaring to the astounded onlookers that
that was the first word he had heard his daughter speak. And if
any of you find that too hard to believe, let Evagrius, who is here,
bear witness to its truth, for he was present when the thing took
place.[2]

[1] Probably to be identified respectively with (a) Valentinus, Bishop of
Chartres from at any rate A.D. 344 (Duchesne, op. cit., II, 420,) (b) St. Victricius,
a very eminent Bishop of Rouen, who became Bishop apparently in the decade
before 390 (see Duchesne, op. cit., II, 205), and Butler's *Lives*, under August 7th.
[2] The close parallelism between the circumstances of this miracle and those
of the miracle described in section XVI of the Life led Babut (*Saint Martin de
Tours*, pp. 268, 269) to suggest that the much less circumstantial story in the
Life was a deliberately disguised version of the episode recorded here. Delehaye (loc. cit., p. 40) pointed out the improbability that an " edited " version
should have been inserted in the earlier document and suggested that Sulpicius,
in search of materials for the Dialogues, might easily have come across the
authentic version of the incident, which he had previously known in a form
much distorted after being passed around for several years, and have failed to
recognize it, and therefore included it in this Dialogue as a separate miracle.

III

" What I come to now is a trifling episode that I was recently told about by the priest Arpagius[1] but which I don't think should be omitted. The wife of Count Avitianus[2] had sent Martin some oil such as is required for treating various ailments, for him to bless, as is often done. The glass flask that contained it was round, with a bulge in the middle and an elongated neck, but this projecting neck was not filled with liquid, because it is usual in filling such vessels to leave room at the top of the neck for a stopper. This priest solemnly declared that he saw the oil increase when Martin blessed it, to such an extent that the additional quantity overflowed and ran down from the top of the neck in all directions.

" Moreover, it bubbled up under the same influence when the vessel was being carried back to the mistress of the house. In fact, so much oil overflowed in the hands of the boy who was carrying it that all his clothes were covered with the liquid that escaped. Thus the mistress got the vessel back full to the very brim and to this day (so the priest tells me) there has never been any room in this flask for a stopper, such as is usually used to shut in liquids that have to be preserved.[3]

" That was a wonderful thing, too," went on Gallus, " that I can remember happening to *him* "—and he looked across at me. " He had put down on a rather high window-sill a glass jar containing oil that Martin had blessed. A house-boy, not knowing that the flask was there, unthinkingly pulled away a cloth that had been laid over it and the jar fell on the marble floor. Everyone was terrified to think that God's blessing had been lost, but the flask was found to be uninjured, as if it had fallen on to the softest feathers. And it is to the spiritual power of Martin rather

[1] This is the sole reference to this character.
[2] This may possibly be the same Avitianus that the contemporary historian Ammianus Marcellinus mentions (XXVII. 7. 1) as a former Vicarius (or Deputy Praetorian Prefect) of Africa and whose term of office can be dated by the Theodosian Code (*lex* 15, Juliano IV et Sallustio consulibus) in A.D. 363. He appears again in sections IV and VIII of this Dialogue.
[3] The Latin of most of this paragraph is very confused and one can only try and give the general sense, which is reasonably clear.

than to chance that this must be attributed. His blessing once given could not cease to be.

" There was another thing, too, that was done by someone whose name shall be suppressed because he is here and has forbidden it to be mentioned. Saturninus here was also present on that occasion.[4] A dog was barking at us rather violently and he said to it : ' In the name of Martin I order you to be silent '. And the dog was silent. The barking seemed to stick in its throat ; you might have thought its tongue had been cut off. Yes, indeed ; the fact that Martin himself worked miracles is a small matter ; believe me, many things were done by others using his name.

IV

" You have heard of the barbarous and unspeakably bloody ferocity of the late Count Avitianus. On one occasion he entered Tours in a towering rage, followed by a chain of prisoners looking very dejected.[1] He ordered a number of different tortures to be got ready for their execution and arranged for the dismal proceedings to be carried out before a terrorized city the next day. When this became known to Martin he set out alone a little before midnight for the brute's official residence. But in the dead of night, when all was silent and everybody was asleep, the barred gates denied him entrance and Martin lay down across the blood-stained threshold.

" Avitianus all this time had been sunk in heavy sleep but now he was assailed by an angel who woke him with a blow. ' The servant of God ', said the angel, ' is lying before your threshold— and you are still sleeping ! ' When he heard these words he leapt out of bed in great disturbance of mind. He summoned his slaves and called out to them in panic that Martin was at the gates and that they must go at once and unbar them, or it would be an insult to the servant of God. They, as is the way of all slaves, scarcely went beyond the front door, laughing among themselves at their

---

[4] This character also makes no other appearance.
[1] Avitianus appears to have been employed in crushing the adherents of the Emperor Gratian whom Maximus had overthrown when he usurped power A.D. 383.

master for having been taken in by a dream, and they reported
that there was no one at the outer gates. For they argued from
their own habits that no one could be up so late ; and still less
could they believe that a bishop could be lying across someone
else's threshold during the awful hours of darkness. Nor had
they any difficulty in convincing Avitianus, who went to sleep
again.

"Presently, however, he was struck a still more violent blow and
shouted out that Martin *was* standing at the gates and because of
that he could get no peace for mind or body. And while the slaves
were dawdling he himself went outside the gates. There, as he
had expected, he found Martin. The wretched Avitianus was
appalled at so great a manifestation of spiritual power. 'Why, my
lord, have you done this to me?' he said. 'There is no need for
you to say anything. I know what you want ; I can see what you
have come for. Do go away now at once before the anger of
heaven destroys me for this insult to you. I have already been
punished severely enough. Believe me, it was no light infliction
that brought me out here myself.'

"And after the holy man had gone he summoned his court
officers and ordered them to release all the prisoners, and before
long he was on his way again.

"And so Avitianus was routed and the city rejoiced in its
deliverance.

V

"All this became widely known through Avitianus himself ; and
more recently the priest Refrigerius whom you see in front of you
heard it from one of the tribunes named Dagridius,[1] who is a trustworthy man and who took God's majesty to witness to its truth,
swearing that he had been told it by Avitianus himself.

"But I don't want you to be wondering why I am doing today
what I did not do yesterday, and giving after each miracle, as I
tell it, the names of witnesses, and people who are still alive, to
whom anyone who disbelieves can refer. What has forced me to

[1] For military tribunes see the Life of St. Martin, note 3 to section II ; but
there were also civilian officers bearing that title. Dagridius appears nowhere
else.

do this is the sceptical attitude of a great many people who are said to have doubts about some of the stories told yesterday. So let them appeal to these witnesses, who are still alive and well, and believe them, if they doubt *my* good faith ; although, if they are so unbelieving, I tell you frankly I do not think that they will believe them either.

" But it is amazing to me that anyone with the slightest religious feeling could want to commit such a gross offence as to think that anyone could tell lies about Martin. Anyone who is living a God-fearing life should be exempt from such a suspicion ; for Martin has no need to be bolstered up by lies. But to Thee, O Christ, I pledge my word that in all my story I have told nothing, and will tell nothing, but what I have seen with my own eyes or learnt from sources open to all and very often from Martin himself. It is true that I have adopted the dialogue form to give variety and make it less wearisome for the reader ; but I give the assurance that I attend most religiously to historical truth.

" The scepticism of some people has compelled me, much to my regret, to interpolate this. But to return to our gathering—when I see how eagerly I am listened to, I must admit that Aper acted with sound judgement when he kept away the unbelieving on the principle that only those who believe should be admitted to listen.

VI

" Believe me, it makes me wild and I go all crazy with indignation : there are actually Christians who refuse to believe in the spiritual powers of Martin that were acknowledged even by demons !

" The monastery of the blessed man was two miles distant from the city, but every time he set out to go to the cathedral, no sooner did he put his foot outside his cell door than you could see in all parts of the cathedral demoniacs roaring, and the hosts of the damned trembling as if their judge was coming. In fact, the groans of the demons used to be a warning to the clergy of the arrival of the Bishop, when they did not know that he was coming. I have seen a man, when Martin was approaching, snatched up into the air and hanging with his arms stretched out, quite unable to touch the ground with his feet.

" But if ever Martin undertook the task of exorcising demons, he never touched anyone with his hand or upbraided him, as the clergy so often do, in a whirl of words. He would have the demoniacs brought to him and order everyone else to go out. Then, with the doors barred, he would pray prostrate on the ground in the middle of the church, clothed in sackcloth and sprinkled with ashes.

" Then you would see the various torments inflicted on these unhappy people by the demons as they went out of them. Some would be lifted up by their feet into the air and hang as if from a cloud ; but their clothing would never fall down over their faces, so that there should be no indecency from the uncovering of part of their bodies. In another part of the church you could see the possessed even confessing their crimes without being questioned, and some without questioning would also give their names ; one would declare that he was Jupiter, another Mercury.[1] Finally, you could see that all the servants of the devil shared the tortures inflicted on their master ; and we must admit that those words of Scripture were already fulfilled in Martin : ' For the saints shall judge angels.'[2]

VII

" Every year hail used to do great damage in a certain district near Sens.[1] In their desperate need the population asked for help from Martin. A deputation of men of credit was sent, whose spokesman was an ex-Governor named Auspicius, whose land used to be devasted by the storms with special severity, beyond anyone else's. Martin prayed there and freed the whole district from its harassing scourge so completely that for twenty years, that is to say, while he remained in this world, no one in those parts suffered damage from hailstorms.

---

[1] For the names, see note 1 to section (2, XIII) of Dialogue I. For the way in which the pronouns refer sometimes to the demons, sometimes to their victims, see note 3 to section XVII of the Life of St. Martin.

[2] Not an exact quotation; see 1 Cor. vi. 2, 3.

[1] Latin, " in Senonico ", i.e. in the country of the Senones. Sens itself was Agedincum Senonum. The district was well outside Martin's diocese.

" And, to show that this was not a mere coincidence but the result of Martin's action, in the year he died the bad weather came back and again afflicted the district. Thus even the physical world felt the passing of this man of faith and mourned over his death as it had rightly rejoiced in his life.

" For the rest, if some listener rather weak in faith requires witnesses who can confirm what I have just been saying, I can bring forward, not one man, but many thousands ; in fact, I will call as witnesses, to the miracle that they experienced, the whole district of Sens. But apart from that, you, good priest Refrigerius, will I think remember that not long ago we had a conversation with Romulus, the son of that same Auspicius, a man of high standing and pious as well, about this very matter. He told us the whole story just as if we had never heard it and, when he thought of the danger to future harvests from incessant damage, he was full of regrets (as you saw yourself) that Martin had not been preserved for us until now.

VIII

" But to get back to Avitianus—in every district and every city he stayed in, he left unspeakable evidence of his cruelty ; but at Tours, and Tours alone, he was harmless. Brute beast that he was, who battened on human blood and the deaths of his unhappy victims, he showed himself mild and peaceable where the man of blessings was present.

" I remember one day Martin going to visit him ; and, when he had entered his private office, he saw sitting behind his back a demon of astonishing size. From where he was (I am forced to use a phrase that is hardly Latin[1]) Martin blew at it. Avitianus thought that it was he who was being blown at.

" ' Why, holy man, do you behave to me like this ? ' he asked.

" ' It is not at you,' said Martin, ' but at him, that loathsome creature mounted on your shoulders.'

" The devil capitulated and abandoned his familiar perch ; and it is certainly the case that from that day onwards Avitianus was more gentle, either because he now realized that he had always

---

[1] " exsufflans ", and, in the next line, " exsufflari ".

been the tool of the devil that was riding him, or because the evil spirit, once driven from its seat on him by Martin, was deprived of its power for mischief. For the servant was now ashamed of his master and the master was not goading on its servant.

" In the town of Amboise,[2] that is to say, in the old fortress, now the home of a large community of monks, there used to be (as you will remember) the shrine of an idol. It was a vast and solidly-built edifice—a towering mass of highly polished stones, tapering into a lofty cone ; and the grandeur of the work did much to keep superstition alive in the locality. The man of blessings had frequently given Marcellus, the priest resident in the place, orders for its destruction. Returning there after a considerable interval, he took the priest to task because the idolatrous building was still standing.

" The priest's defence was that the pulling down of such a massive structure would be difficult enough even with the employment of troops or with the aid of a state labour-force ; certainly one could hardly imagine that it could be carried out by some feeble clergy and sickly monks.

" So Martin resorted to his familiar aids and spent all night in prayer. In the morning a storm arose that razed the idol's temple to its foundations. Marcellus can witness to what I have been telling you.

IX

" Now, here is another miracle of much the same character, performed in a similar connection—Refrigerius will be my guarantor. Martin was proposing to throw down an immensely massive column on the top of which an idol stood, but there were no means available for carrying out the plan. Then, in his usual way, he resorted to prayer. It is a certain fact that another column something like the first came hurtling down from heaven and hit the idol and crushed to powder the whole invincible mass. It would seem that it was too small a thing that Martin should employ the powers of heaven invisibly ; the powers themselves had to be seen by human eyes visibly doing Martin's will.

[2] Latin, " vicus Ambatiensis ".

" Refrigerius again will bear me witness that a woman suffering from a haemorrhage, who touched Martin's garment after the example of the woman in the Gospels, was cured on the instant.

" A snake was in the river, cutting through the water and swimming towards the bank where we had settled ourselves. ' In the name of the Lord,' said Martin, ' I order you to go back.' Immediately, at the saint's words, the noxious creature turned round and, as we watched it, swam across to the opposite bank. We could all see that there was something miraculous in this, but Martin sighed deeply. ' Snakes,' he said, ' listen to me, and men refuse to listen.'

X

" During Eastertide Martin generally ate fish and, a little before the time for the meal one day, he asked whether there was a fish ready for it. The deacon Cato, who did the housekeeping for the monastery and was a skilled fisherman, said that he had not had a catch all day and that other fishermen, who fished for the market, had similarly been unable to catch anything.

" ' Go and let down your line,' said Martin, ' and a catch will follow.'

" We lived next to the river, as Sulpicius here has described,[1] and, as we were having holidays for the Feast, we all set off to see the deacon fishing, everybody eagerly hoping that his attempts by Martin's orders to catch a fish for Martin's use would not be in vain. At the first cast he drew out in a very small net an enormous pike and ran joyfully back to the monastery—as some poet has said, I don't know which (being among scholars, I quote a verse scholars will know) :

" To wondering Argos he brought his captive boar.[2]

" Truly this disciple of Christ, in imitating the miracles worked by the Saviour and manifested by Him as an example to His saints, showed Christ at work in himself. For it was Christ who made this saint of His everywhere glorious by bestowing upon one man

---

[1] See the Life of St. Martin, section X.
[2] Statius, *Thebais*, viii, 751. Probably a pun is intended here, for the word for boar (*sus*) also denotes some kind of fish.

so many kinds of gifts. The ex-Governor Arborius[3] declares that
when Martin was offering the holy sacrifice he saw his hand
covered with the most splendid jewels and that when his hand
moved he heard the gems clashing as they struck against one
another.

XI

" I am coming now to an episode which Martin always concealed because it was a disgrace to our times, but from us he could
not keep it secret. There was this much of the miraculous in it,
that an angel spoke to him face to face.

" The Emperor Maximus, in other respects undoubtedly
a good man, was corrupted by listening to the bishops after
the execution of Priscillian.[1] He had used his imperial power
to protect Bishop Ithacius, the chief accuser of Priscillian, and
his colleagues (whom there is no need to name), and to prevent

[3] See the Life of St. Martin, section XIX.
[1] The affair of Priscillian occupies the last 6 sections (46–51) of the *Chronicles*
of Sulpicius Severus, Book II. Priscillian was a Spanish heretic with Gnostic
and Manicheean tendencies (see note 1 to section XXII of the Life of St.
Ambrose and note 9 to section I of the Life of St. Augustine). According to
de Labriolle, it is unlikely that his movement had a definitely dualistic character
from the outset ; he seems to have taught, to begin with, the reality of Christ's
human nature and the responsibility of the human will for sin—two doctrines
entirely contrary to Manicheeism. It was only gradually that his movement
took a form that caused the ecclesiastical authorities to treat it as virtually
identical with Manicheeism and eventually brought it under the criminal law.
He obtained much support in Spain and was elected Bishop of Avila A.D. 380.
But soon after the usurpation of Maximus he was tried at Trier, by an official
appointed by Maximus, on criminal charges of sorcery and obscene teachings
and practices in connection with his religion. In spite of Martin's protests against
a death sentence, and against any trial by a lay court of an issue involving questions of Catholic doctrine, he was sentenced to death and executed (A.D. 385).
Martin, who had left Trier on receiving from Maximus a promise that there
should be no death sentence, now returned to Trier, both to protest against what
had been done and to try and stop the persecution of Priscillianists now beginning (by the Emperor's orders) in Spain. This is the visit to Trier described in
this and the two following sections. It may be added, in further explanation of
the situation, that Ithacus (or Ithacius), the leader of the anti-Priscillianist
bishops in Spain, is described by Sulpicius as a loose-living man whose main
motive was opposition on personal grounds to asceticism in general rather than an
opposition on grounds of Catholic doctrine to the peculiar form of asceticism
taught by Priscillian. St. Martin was naturally (according to Sulpicius) anti-
pathetic to him and he went so far as to allege that Martin's opposition to the
state's action against Priscillian and the Priscillianists was due to the fact that
he had secret Manicheean beliefs himself. It must be remembered, however,
that is only one side of the story and that Ithacius had the support of the Bishop
of Trier, Britonius or Brito, who was subsequently reckoned a saint, see Butler's
Lives (Thurston and Attwater) under May 5th, p. 69.

the charge from being brought against Ithacius that it was through his action that people had been put to death. Meanwhile Martin had been compelled to go to the Court on behalf of many sufferers from grave injustices, and met there the full force of the storm.

" The bishops who had assembled at Trier were still detained there, and they were daily in sacramental communion with Ithacius and made common cause with him. When they were unexpectedly informed that Martin would soon be arriving, their hearts sank and there were many mutterings and quakings. Only the day before, the Emperor had, on their advice, decided to send to Spain tribunes armed with the fullest authority to search out heretics and to put to death those they caught and confiscate their goods. Moreover, it was quite certain that this hurricane would lay low a great many true Christians as well as heretics, without much distinction of persons. For the only test was to be by eye ; and a man was to be judged to be a heretic by the paleness of his face or the peculiarity of his dress rather than by his beliefs.[2]

" The bishops were well aware that all this would be exceedingly displeasing to Martin ; but, to their guilty consciences, their most harassing anxiety was that when he arrived he would refuse to be in communion with them, in which case there would be no lack of persons who, with the authority of so great a man behind them, would imitate his firm stand. They therefore came to an arrangement with the Emperor whereby palace officials[3] should be sent to meet Martin and forbid him to come near the city unless he made a declaration that when he arrived he would be at peace with the bishops who were staying there.

" He dexterously circumvented them by declaring that when he came he would be at peace with Christ. In the end, he entered the city by night and went straight to the cathedral, but simply to pray

[2] As regards the test of paleness, the inner circle of the Manicheeans went in for much fasting and abstained from meat and wine ; and St. Jerome (Ep. xxii, *Ad Eustochium*, section 13), speaks of persons wishing to disparage fasting and abstinence among monks and nuns who, when they see a consecrated virgin looking pale and gloomy, taunt her with being a Manicheean.

[3] Latin, " magistri officiales ". These were minions of the great officer of the Palace known as the *Magister officiorum* (on whom, see note 1 to section XXXVII of the Life of St. Ambrose in this volume). They appear twice in the *Chronicles* of Sulpicius (II, 41 and 49) on errands to bishops.

there. In the morning he made his way to the palace. He had a number of petitions to make, which it would take too long to enumerate ; among the most important were those on behalf of Count Narses and the Governor Leucadius, both of whom had been adherents of Gratian and had incurred the wrath of his conqueror by an unusually obstinate loyalty which this is not the place to enlarge on. But the chief request of all was that tribunes should not be sent into Spain with the power of life and death. For in his kindly anxiety he wished to save, not only Christians, some of whom would be molested if this plan were carried out, but the heretics as well.

" The crafty Emperor, however, kept him waiting both that day and the next, possibly to impress upon him how serious the matter was, possibly because he was too much under the influence of the bishops to relent, or possibly (and this was the reason most people gave at the time) because avarice was the obstacle and he was after the heretics' property. For this man, with all his many good qualities, seems to have given way to avarice all too easily. However, his predecessors at the head of the state had exhausted the Treasury and he himself was living in a state of almost continuous expectation of civil war and preparedness for it, so that in the circumstances he may readily be excused by the state of his Empire for taking any opportunity to accumulate resources for his government.

XII

" Meanwhile the bishops, with whom Martin had refused to join in communion, hurried in great alarm to the Emperor. They complained that if the obstinacy of Theognitus, the only one of their number who had publicly pronounced judgement against them, were reinforced by the authority of Martin, they were as good as condemned already and would all be placed in an impossible position. That man Martin, they said, ought never to have been allowed within the city walls. He was no longer simply a protector of the heretics, but their avenger, and nothing had been gained by the death of Priscillian if Martin were allowed to take revenge for it.

" Finally they threw themselves on the ground and with tears and lamentations begged that Imperial authority should strike with all its force against this one man. Indeed Maximus came very near to being persuaded to condemn Martin to share the fate of the heretics. But although he was altogether too subservient and partial to the bishops, he could not but be aware that Martin, in faith and holiness and spiritual power, surpassed any man alive, and he therefore resorted to another method to overcome the holy man's resistance.

" First he summoned him to a private interview and tried gentle persuasion. The heretics, he said, had been condemned, not by any persecuting bishops, but after a regular trial in the State's court. There was no sufficient reason for holding that communion with Ithacius and the rest of his party should be banned. It was out of hatred rather than for any good reason that Theognitus had separated himself from the rest and in any case he was the only one who had refused communion with them up to now ; none of the others had made any change. Moreover, only a few days ago a synod had been held that had acquitted Ithacius of any blame in the matter.

" All this, however, had little effect on Martin, with the result that the Emperor's anger flared up and he flung out of the room ; and presently executioners were appointed for the men for whom Martin had been interceding.

XIII

" When Martin was told of this, he rushed back to the palace, though by now it was night-time. He promised that if these people were pardoned he would join in communion with the bishops, provided that the tribunes already sent to destroy the Churches in Spain were recalled as well.[1] Maximus granted all his requests without delay. The next day the consecration of Felix as bishop was put through. He was a man of great holiness and, in

---

[1] These bishops had not been excommunicated, so that there was nothing uncanonical in this compromise.

happier times, would have been entirely suited for the episcopate.[2]
On the same day Martin joined the bishops in communion, judging that to make this momentary concession was better than deserting the cause of those whose heads were in jeopardy. But
though the bishops strove with all their might to get him to certify
this communion with his signature, nothing would induce him to
do that.

" The next day he abruptly left the city and began his journey
back, sorrowing and sighing that even for a moment he had taken
part in a guilty communion. When he was not far from a village
named Andethanna, where the woods have recesses pervaded by
utter solitude,[3] he sat down, while his companions went on a little.
There he went over and over in his mind the steps that had led up
to this anguish of mind and the action he had taken, and his
thoughts alternately accused him and defended him. Suddenly an
angel stood before him. ' Martin,' said he, ' you have reason to
feel compunction, but you had no other way out of your predica-
ment. Rebuild your courage, get back your equanimity; or you
will soon be imperilling not only your renown but your salvation.'

" From that time onwards, therefore, he took very good care
not to join in communion again with the party of Ithacius. But
there were times when in curing the demoniacs he took longer than
he used to do, and grace flowed less lavishly, and then he would
confess to us with tears that because of that evil act of participation
he felt a diminution of spiritual power, even though he had taken
part for a mere instant of time, and from necessity and not from
desire. He lived thirteen years after this, without attending a
single synod and keeping away from every gathering of bishops.

[2] This was St. Felix of Trèves (Trier). He was a man of great piety and
generosity to the poor, but was refused recognition by Pope Siricius (384–399)
and St. Ambrose because of his election by the bishops who brought about
Priscillian's execution; and eventually (398) he resigned his see. See Thurston
and Attwater's edition of Butler's *Lives* under March 26.

[3] Halm prints " qua vasta solitudine silvarum secreta patiuntur ", the †
indicating that the text at this point is hopelessly corrupt. But where he con-
jectures " patiuntur ", Babut, on the basis of the MS. in the *Book of Armagh*
(see the Introductory Note), reads " poenetrabantur ", at the same time sub-
stituting " quo " for " qua "; and it is his reconstruction that has been rendered here.

XIV

" Nevertheless it is an undoubted fact, of which I myself had experience, that the grace of God that had been temporarily diminished in him was restored to him with interest. It was after this that I saw a demoniac brought to the back door of the monastery and cured before he touched the threshold. It was only lately that I heard someone testifying how he had been sailing in the Tyrrhenian Sea, heading for Rome, when such a hurricane sprang up that all on board were in the utmost danger of their lives. In the middle of it all a certain Egyptian merchant who was not then a Christian shouted out : ' God of Martin, save us.' At once the storm was stilled, the sea died down and they held on their course in a great calm.

" Lycontius was a believing Christian who had been a deputy Praetorian Prefect.[1] A deadly disease had stricken down his household and all over the house there were people lying sick, portending an unheard-of disaster, and Lycontius wrote to Martin imploring him to help. On this occasion the man of blessings calculated that the boon would be a difficult one to obtain,[2] for he was inwardly conscious that it was by God's particular intention that this house was being scourged. Nevertheless he persevered with prayers and fasts for seven whole days and as many nights, until he obtained what he had been asked to pray for.

" As soon as Lycontius found that God had granted this boon, he travelled at full speed to bring Martin the news and at the same time thank him for ridding the house completely of the danger. He brought also as an offering a hundred pounds' weight of silver. The man of blessings neither refused it nor accepted it, but before the load of silver had reached the threshold of the monastery he had already allocated it for redeeming captives. The brethren suggested to him that some of it should be kept for the expenses

---

[1] See note 2 to section I.
[2] This passage also is marked by Halm with a † as hopelessly corrupt. His conjecture is " rem esse promisit difficilem impetrari ". Babut's reconstruction, based on the *Book of Armagh* (to which Halm had not access), runs " rem mente permensus est difficilem (esse?) impetratu ", and it is this that has been rendered here.

of the monastery, where food was scarce for everybody and many were in need of clothes.

" ' It is for the Church to feed and clothe us ' he said ; ' it is for us to avoid any appearance of seeking anything for our own purposes.'

" At this point some great miracles of his come to my mind which are more easily admitted than described—I am sure you will understand what I refer to : there are many of them which cannot be told in detail. For example, there is this one, which I really do not know how to tell exactly as it happened.

" One of the brethren—you would know the name, but I must not identify him, because we do not want to embarrass the holy man—this brother, then, had found a good supply of coal for his stove and had pulled up his stool and was sitting over the fire with his legs spread out and his person exposed. Martin immediately became aware that the sacred building was being dishonoured and called out loudly : ' Who is defiling our house by exposing himself? ' The brother heard this and his conscience told him that it was he who was being rebuked. He ran to us half fainting and, thanks to this miracle of Martin, confessed his shame.

XV[1]

" Again, one day he had taken his seat on that wooden stool of his, which you all know, in the minute courtyard that surrounded his hut, when he saw two demons sitting on the high rock that overhangs the monastery. They were calling out from there, in eager, gleeful tones, some encouraging phrase like ' Come on, Brictio ; come on, Brictio.'[2] I think they had been watching from a distance the wretched man approaching and were well aware that they had got him worked up to a condition of frenzy.

" Nor, indeed, was there any delay before Brictio burst in raging and, then and there, like a raving lunatic, spat out a thousand

---

[1] This and the next section were omitted from many 5th century manuscripts ; see the Introductory Note to the Dialogues.

[2] Brictio or Bricius had been one of Martin's monks and was now a priest. On Martin's death he succeeded him as Bishop of Tours and was Bishop there at the time Sulpicius wrote these paragraphs. For his later career, see the Introductory Note to the Dialogues.

insults against Martin. For he had been reprimanded by him the day before, for keeping horses and buying slaves, although he had possessed nothing before he was a cleric and had in fact been brought up in the monastery by Martin himself. What is more, it was being freely said of him, at the time we are speaking of, that it was not only boys of barbarian stock that he bought, but also girls with pretty faces.

" Mad with anger, therefore, on this account, and infuriated still further (as I myself believe) by the goading of these demons, this most unhappy man made such an attack upon Martin as scarcely to keep his hands off him, while the holy man, with serene face and unruffled temper, used gentle words to restrain the poor wretch's frenzy. But the wicked spirit had so filled the man to overflowing, that he had no control over his own mind, a shallow one at best.

" With trembling lips and unsteady countenance, and white with fury, he sinned in a whirl of words. He asserted that he was a holier man than Martin. From his earliest years, said he, he had grown up in a monastery, trained by Martin himself in the con-secrated institutions of the Church. Martin, on the other hand, at the beginning of his career had been soiled, as he could not deny, by the life of a soldier ; and now, at the end of it, as the result of baseless superstitions and visions of ridiculous apparitions, had completely sunk into his dotage.

" All this he spat out, and much else besides, even more bitter, which I think it best not to quote. At last, having worked off his rage, he went out with an air of having completely vindicated him-self. He was hurrying back with quick steps in the direction from which he had come when the demons were, as I believe, chased from his heart through Martin's intercession, and he repented of what he had done. Before long he had returned to Martin and was prostrate at his knees. He begged for pardon, he acknow-ledged that he had been wrong and, now that he was at last com-paratively sane, he admitted that a demon had been at work in him.

" There was never any difficulty in getting Martin to forgive those who asked for forgiveness. Then and there, the holy man explained to the penitent, and to all of us, how he had seen him

spurred on by the demons, and that he had not been disturbed by
the insults, which had harmed mainly their author.

" After this episode, although this same Brictio was often
brought before him charged with serious crimes, he could not be
induced to remove him from his priestly office, in case he should
seem to be avenging a personal injury ; and he used often to remark : ' If Christ put up with Judas, why should not I put up with
Brictio ? ' "[3]

XVI

Here Postumianus interposed. " This near neighbour of ours ",
he said, " ought to hear that story. In his wiser moments he takes
no notice of present annoyances and no notice of the future. But
once he has been offended, he loses all control of himself and
raves. He rages against the clergy, makes attacks on the laity, and
stirs up the whole world to avenge him. For three years on end
he has been in this contentious frame of mind and neither the
passage of time, nor argument, allays it.[1] The man's state would
be most painful and pitiable, even if he were not the victim of
other incurable vices. You ought to have been constantly reminding him, Gallus, of these examples of patience and serenity and
then he might learn not to be angry and how to forgive.

" And if he should happen to come to hear of these brief remarks of mine addressed to him and inserted here, I should like
him to know that they are not the words of an enemy but were
spoken with friendly intentions. For I should much prefer, if it
were possible, that people should speak of him as being like
Bishop Martin rather than like the tyrant Phaleris.[2] But let us get
away from a person it is no pleasure to speak of and return, Gallus,
to our Martin."

---

[3] On the attribution of this remark to St. Martin, see the Introductory Note.
[1] It was three years since Sulpicius had published his Life of St. Martin.
[2] A tyrant of Agrigentum in Sicily, proverbial in the ancient world for his
habit of roasting his victims alive in a brazen bull.

XVII

But I had noticed that the sun was already getting low and the evening drawing on. " The day is over, Postumianus " I said ; " we must end our session ; besides, such zealous listeners are owed some supper. As for Martin, it is no use waiting for anyone to be finished who is talking about that man. He spreads into too many things to be disposed of in any conversation.

" Meanwhile, you will be taking what you have been hearing to the East. On your way back there, spread the name and the fame of Martin among the populations of the various coasts and districts and harbours and islands and cities you pass. And, to begin with, remember not to miss out Campania.[1] Even if it takes you a long way out of your way, you must not let any expenditure of time or money that it may involve keep you from visiting a man of such eminence and so universally praised as Paulinus.[2] Please begin by unrolling the scroll containing our talks, both the one we held yesterday and what we have said today. Tell him everything ; read him the whole thing ; and, through him, Rome will get to hear the sacred glories of the holy man, just as he spread that first little book of mine not only through Italy but also through the whole of Illyricum.[3] He is not jealous of Martin's glory and he is a most devout admirer of the sacred miracles that Christ worked through him, so that he will not refuse to set our great patron on the same pedestal as his own Felix.[4]

" If you happen to cross from there to Africa, tell Carthage what you have heard. It is true that she knows of the man already,

---

[1] A coastal region of Italy of which Naples is the centre and in which Nola is situated.

[2] St. Paulinus of Nola ; see the Life of St. Martin, section XXV and note 1 there. See the same note also for the Latin phrase " vir illustris ", here rendered non-technically as " a man of eminence ".

[3] The term Illyricum covered the greater part of what is now Yugoslavia and part of modern Hungary as well.

[4] This Felix is almost certainly not, as Halm's index would suggest, the Felix whose consecration as Bishop of Trier was mentioned in section XIII, but St. Felix of Nola, a remarkable saint of the third century (see Butler's *Lives* under January 14), a devotion to whom played a great part in drawing Paulinus to live at Nola and whose life and miracles he commemorated in a number of verses.

as you told us yourself; all the same, let her this time hear a great deal more about him, so that she learns to admire someone besides her own martyr Cyprian, even though she *is* consecrated by his sacred blood.[5]

" If then you bear a little to your left and enter the Gulf of Achaea, let Corinth know, and Athens too, of one who was as wise as Plato in his Academy and as brave as Socrates in his prison. Happy, indeed, was the lot of Greece, to be thought worthy to hear the Apostle preaching, but let her know that Christ was very far from neglecting Gaul, for He permitted it to have Martin.

" And when you at last reach Egypt, although she can be proud of the numbers and of the miracles of her own saints, she must submit to being told that Europe will not take second place to her, nor to all Asia, for the sufficient reason that she possesses Martin.

XVIII

" Finally, when you set sail from Egypt and make for Jerusalem, my grief sets you a task. Should you ever put ashore at illustrious Ptolemais,[1] make diligent enquiries as to where that Pomponius of mine is buried,[2] and do not disdain to visit those bones laid in a foreign land. And when you find them, shed many heartfelt tears, from *your* heart as well as mine, and, though it be an unprofitable gift, strew the soil there with blood-red flowers and sweetly smelling grasses.

" And as you do so, pardon a man misled and have compassion on a fugitive. Pray that the Lord will be well disposed to him, and for an indulgent judgement on one guilty of such grave offences.[3] Tell him, nevertheless—though not harshly, not bitterly, and in the language of sympathy rather than the rhetoric of rebuke—tell him that if he had only been willing to listen, at one time to you

[5] For the names in this paragraph, see notes 2 and 3 to section III of Dialogue I.

[1] Afterwards Acre or Akka.

[2] See Dialogue I, section XII, and note 1 there.

[3] These two sentences from the MS. in the *Book of Armagh* are conjectured by Babut to belong to the original text (see the Introductory Note to the Dialogue). The Latin of them (somewhat strange at one point) runs as follows : " Simul ignosce decepto, et miserere fugitivo ; placitum illi esse Dominum et indulgens tantis obnoxio erroribus precare iudicium ".

and at any time to me, and had imitated Martin rather than one whom I will not name, he would never have been so cruelly separated from me. He would not now be covered by a heap of alien dust, after meeting death at sea, as might any shipwrecked pirate, and barely securing burial on the very edge of the seashore.

" Let them gaze upon their handiwork—those who took revenge on him in the hope of injuring me. Let them gaze upon their triumph and, sated with their vengeance, let them now forbear to plague me."

All this I sighed out in a voice choked with sobs, and all were moved to tears by my laments. With much marvelling at Martin, but not less moved to sorrow by my weeping, the gathering dispersed.

THE LIFE OF ST. AMBROSE
BY THE DEACON PAULINUS

LITTLE is known for certain about Paulinus. In the view of Dr. F. Homes Dudden, the most authoritative English biographer of St. Ambrose (*The Life and Times of St. Ambrose*, 2 vols., Oxford, 1935), he was probably a native of Florence, who attached himself to Ambrose when the latter visited the city in A.D. 394, and served him as confidential secretary until his death in A.D. 397. At that time he appears to have been a sub-deacon. He was certainly residing at the training-school for clergy attached to the cathedral (see section XLII of the Life). Some years after the death of St. Ambrose, he went to Africa, where he got to know St. Augustine and took part in the anti-Pelagian campaign. At that time he was referred to as Paulinus, deacon of Milan. "At Augustine's suggestion he wrote—almost certainly in A.D. 422—a *Vita Sancti Ambrosii* in imitation of Sulpicius' celebrated work on Martin ", the pattern of which he follows very closely. His only surviving literary composition apart from the Life is a somewhat undistinguished pamphlet written against the Pelagians.

The Life is based on personal acquaintance with St. Ambrose and a careful search for information, which did not extend far, however, into the saint's own correspondence. He shows the disregard for dates usual in biographers of the period. He is not notably credulous and is careful to distinguish between hearsay and first-hand evidence. But, as his editor has said, " we would never gather from the narrative of Paulinus that St. Ambrose was one of the really great figures of his age, one of the last great personalities of the Western Empire." He has no understanding of the saint's political significance, nor do we learn much even of his religious life. Nevertheless the Life is valuable as an honest attempt to tell the truth about St. Ambrose so far as it falls within the writer's mental horizon.

His Latinity is, as we might expect, undistinguished, to use no harsher term ; and its complete lack of style, except perhaps in the closely imitative Preface and at certain moments when he seems to be echoing St. Ambrose's language, makes translation a thankless task.

The present translation is made from the text as revised by Sister M. S. Kaniecka, M.A., of the Felician Sisters, O.S.F., New Jersey, U.S.A., and published as volume 16 of the Catholic University of America Patristic Studies (*Vita Sancti Ambrosii* . . . *a Paulino* . . . *conscripta ;* a Revised Text, and Commentary, with an Introduction and Translation : Washington, 1928). The few occasions on which I have departed from her text are noted where they occur. The editor's pre-occupation with the grammar and syntax of fifth-century Latin makes her commentary less helpful than it might otherwise have been, but she has nevertheless collected much information on other matters besides Latinity, of which I have been glad occasionally to make use. The translation that accompanies the text has nearly always the merit of rendering the grammar correctly. The renderings and paraphrases of the occasional quotations from Paulinus in Dr. Dudden's biography have quite often been helpful and his erudition has been an unfailing stand-by when historical notes have been necessary.

In rendering the Scriptural quotations and allusions I have followed the wording in Paulinus' text, which seldom agrees with the Vulgate, since it follows older versions and often gives the substance rather than the precise language of any version.

The early manuscripts contain no divisions into chapters or sections. After some consideration I have adopted the numbering of sections in the Benedictine text (chiefly for convenience of reference) but not its chapters or chapter headings. I have left some blank spaces at a few points to indicate the divisions into which the text naturally falls in accordance with the hagiographical conventions of the times and the practice of the author's models.

THE LIFE OF ST. AMBROSE, BISHOP OF MILAN
WRITTEN BY HIS AMANUENSIS, PAULINUS
AND DEDICATED TO THE BLESSED AUGUSTINE

PREFACE

I

You tell me, reverend father Augustine,[1] that I should follow the example set by those holy men Bishop Athanasius and Jerome the priest, who penned the Lives of St. Paul and St. Antony,[2] dwellers in the desert, and by Severus, that servant of God, who composed the Life of Martin, the revered Bishop of Tours,[3] and that I should myself pen the life of the blessed Ambrose, Bishop of the Church in Milan. But if you speak of such great men, very bulwarks of the Churches and fountains of eloquence, I know that I can no more match their language than I can their virtues. Nevertheless I think that it would be rather ridiculous of me to refuse to do your bidding. With the help, therefore, of your prayers and of the merits of the great man of whom I write, I shall set down, though it be in unpolished speech, what I learnt from those most reliable men who preceded me in his service and above all from his revered sister Marcellina,[4] and also what I saw for myself when I was in his service, as well as what I heard from those who reported that they had seen him in various Provinces after his death, and what was contained in a letter written to him before it was known that he was dead. And I will be brief and summary, so that even if my style offends the reader, my brevity at least will make him read on.

[1] St. Augustine of Hippo.
[2] St. Athanasius wrote the Life of St. Antony and St. Jerome that of St. Paul, the first hermit, see the Introduction, section III.
[3] In this volume.
[4] See note 2 to section IV.

Nor shall I dress up the truth in ornate language, for while a writer parades his elegant style the reader may be failing to make the acquaintance of very great virtues ; and he would certainly be better occupied in watching virtue in action, and the favours of the Holy Spirit, than a display of words. Besides, we know how travellers are more grateful for a feeble trickle of water when they happen to be thirsty than for a river from a gushing spring whose abundance is not to be found when the thirst is upon them. So too, barley bread is often tasty even to those who regularly belch over the hundred courses of their daily banquet ; and wild flowers often please admirers of the charm of gardens.

II

I therefore beg all of you who handle this book to believe that what I say is true. Let no one suppose that out of affection I have put down anything not wholly trustworthy ; for instead it is better to say nothing at all than to utter anything false, since we know that " we shall have to account for all our words." Nor can I doubt that, though not all the things I tell will be known to everybody, nevertheless some will know of one thing, some another, and there will be some people who know of those things which I myself was not in a position to hear or see. So I shall begin my narrative from the day of his birth, for all to know what favour God showed this man from the cradle.

III

Ambrose, then, was born when his father Ambrose held the office of Prefect of Gaul.[1] When he was a baby, he was sleeping in his cradle with his mouth open, in the courtyard of the governor's palace, when suddenly a swarm of bees came and so covered his face and mouth that they kept on going in and out of

---

[1] He was one of the two Prefects known as Praetorian Prefects who between them exercised, under the Emperor, vice-regal authority over the Western half of the Empire. He ruled almost all the West outside Italy and had his capital at the modern Trèves or Trier. There, in all probability, the younger Ambrose was born. The year of his birth is uncertain. Different interpretations of the evidence give dates ranging from A.D. 333 to 340. Dudden thinks it was A.D. 339.

his mouth in continuous succession. His father was taking a walk near by, with his mother and their daughter, and told the girl who was employed to suckle the babe not to drive the bees away, for he was afraid of their injuring him ; and with a father's solicitude he waited to see how the marvel would end. And presently the bees flew off and soared to such a height in the air that it was impossible for human eyes to see them. It frightened his father. " If that little one lives," he said, " he will be something very big."

For Our Lord, even then when His servant was only an infant, was bringing about the fulfilment of the text : " Words that are good are as honey from a comb." [1] For that swarm of bees was generating for us the honey-combs of his writings, which were to announce to men the gifts of heaven and raise their minds to heaven from earthly things.

IV

Later on, when he was growing up, he lived in Rome with his widowed mother and his sister.[1] The latter had taken the vow of virginity in the company of another girl, whose sister Candida, similarly professed, is now an old woman living in Carthage.[2] He used to see bishops having their hands kissed by members of the family—his sister or mother—and would jokingly put out his hand to this girl and tell her that she ought to do the same to him ; for he used to say that he was going to be a bishop himself. What was speaking through him was the Holy Spirit, who was bringing him up to be a bishop, but the girl used to drive him off, as a boy who was talking nonsense.

[1] Prov. xvi. 24 (pre-Vulgate).
[1] His father had died not later than A.D. 352. His sister, St. Marcellina, was somewhat older than himself and, after the family had moved to Rome after their father's death, she took the vow of virginity, receiving the veil from Pope Liberius at Epiphany A.D. 353. But she remained in the family mansion, living the life of the consecrated virgin at home, as was frequently done at that period, where there was no convent. When her brother became Bishop of Milan, she visited him at his request to help him in fostering the ascetic life in that city, but she continued to reside in Rome. She outlived her brother, dying about the year 398.
[2] Paulinus was writing there, or near by.

V

He received a liberal education and then left Rome to practise as a barrister in the court of the Praetorian Prefect.[1] So magnificently did he plead his cases that he was chosen by his Excellency[2] Probus,[3] then Praetorian Prefect, to be a member of his judicial council. He was next given consular rank as Governor of the Provinces of Liguria and Aemilia and so came to Milan.[4]

VI

During this period [1] Auxentius died; he was a bishop of the Arian sect, who had kept possession of the Church at Milan since Dionysius, Confessor of the faith, of blessed memory, had been sent into exile. [2] Seeing that the people were threatening to riot over the choice of a new bishop, and being responsible for quelling riots, Ambrose proceeded to the cathedral,[3] in case the city populace should be roused to dangerous courses. While he was addressing those assembled there, a child's voice (it is said) suddenly cried out: "Ambrose for Bishop!" Hearing these

---

[1] In this case, the Praetorian Prefect of Italy (see note 1 to section III), whose rule extended N. and N.E. to the Danube and whose capital (where Ambrose practised) was at Sirmium, the modern Mitrovitz, on the R. Save, not far from the modern Belgrade.

[2] Latin, " vir illustris ", a title at this time confined (on the civilian side of the official hierarchy) to the two Praetorian Prefects and six other great officers of the Empire in the West.

[3] Sextus Petronius Probus, a man of enormous wealth, who succeeded to the office of Praetorian Prefect of Italy in A.D. 368, when Ambrose had been at Sirmium perhaps three or four years.

[4] These two Provinces, which were always under one Governor, covered (roughly) all northern Italy north of Tuscany and west of Venetia, and were ruled from Milan. Dudden suggests A.D. 370 as the date of this appointment.

[1] Latin, " per idem tempus ". This phrase, which occurs 13 times in the Life, represents almost its high-water mark of chronological precision. It seems worth while reproducing it by the same formula every time in English for the light its use throws both on the mentality of the writer and on the difficulties of the modern chronologist.

[2] For these persons and events, see notes 3 and 4 to section VI of the Life of St. Martin in this volume. For Arianism, see the Life of St. Martin, section VI and note 2 there.

[3] The chief of the two cathedral churches of Milan, the so-called New Basilica, on the site of the present cathedral. For the rendering of " ecclesia " by " cathedral " here, see note 1 to section XIII below.

words, the whole crowd changed its cry and began clamouring
in unison : "Ambrose for Bishop ! " So it came about that, where
before there had been the most violent dissension, with Arians
and Catholics each wanting the other party to be defeated and a
bishop of their own consecrated, suddenly they agreed on this
man with a miraculous and incredible unanimity.

VII

Realizing this, Ambrose left the church and had his dais[1] got
ready for him (being about to become a bishop he naturally
mounted to a higher place). Then, contrary to his usual practice,
he ordered some people to be put to the torture.[2] But even while
he was doing this, the crowd kept clamouring for him and saying :
" Your sin be upon *us*." But the cry of this crowd was not like
that of the Jewish crowd, who by their words shed Our Lord's
blood, when they said : " His blood be upon us." These people,
knowing him to be only a catechumen, were assuring him, with
the voice of faith, of the forgiveness of all his sins by the grace
of baptism.[3]

Really disturbed by now, and back at home, he proposed to
dedicate himself to philosophical meditation. But he was to
become a true philosopher, in the school of Christ, for he was
going to spurn the pomps of this world and follow in the
footsteps of the fishermen, who gathered in the peoples for
Christ, not by ornate language, but by unsophisticated speech
and the reasonableness of the true faith. Sent without wallet
and without staff, they converted even the philosophers themselves.

Failing to obtain leave to do this, he had some of the common
women of the town brought openly into his house, for the sole

[1] Such as judges used : Latin, " tribunal ". It might be erected anywhere.
The comment of Paulinus shows that the word must here be taken literally.
[2] The use of torture to exact confessions was a recognized part of judicial
procedure in grave cases.
[3] Ambrose, though a good-living Catholic, had, like many others in a like
position at that period, put off baptism, in accordance with the popular but
theologically erroneous opinions of the day, for which see note 8 to section II
of the Life of St. Martin.

purpose of inducing the people to change their minds at the sight of them. But they only shouted more insistently than ever : " Your sin be upon *us*."

VIII

When he saw that nothing brought him nearer his purpose, he took to flight, leaving the city in the middle of the night. But when he thought he was heading for Pavia,[1] he found himself in the morning at what is known as the Roman gate of Milan. For God prevented his flight, for He was providing for His Catholic Church a wall against His enemies and erecting " a tower of David " to face " towards Damascus ", that is to say, towards the unbelief of the heretics. And when the people found Ambrose they kept him under guard, while a message was sent to the most gracious Emperor, at that time Valentinian.[2] The latter was highly gratified to learn that the judges he had himself appointed were in demand as bishops. The Prefect Probus was also delighted that his words about Ambrose were coming true ; for when Ambrose had been setting off and he had been giving him his instructions in the usual way, he had used the words : " Go and act as a bishop, not as a judge."

IX

While the outcome of the message was being awaited, Ambrose again resorted to flight and stayed secretly for a time on the estate of a certain gentleman of rank[1] named Leontius. But when the answer to the message came, Leontius handed him over to the authorities. For the Vicarius[2] had been ordered to press on with the completion of the business and, as he wished to carry

---

[1] Latin, " Ticinum ". The name was changed to Papia (whence Pavia) by Charlemagne.

[2] Valentinian I, the son of a peasant, who was proclaimed Emperor A.D. 364 and died A.D. 375. He professed Catholicism. His ratification of an election to the episcopate was not ordinarily required, but Ambrose was a high official in the Imperial service and, moreover, Milan was the capital of Italy.

[1] Latin, " vir clarissimus ", the third rank in the official hierarchy.

[2] The official who governed the civil " Diocese ", or group of Provinces, as the deputy of the Praetorian Prefect.

out these instructions, he had issued a proclamation warning everybody that if they had any regard for themselves or their possessions they had better hand the man over.

So he was handed over and brought back to Milan and then he recognized that it was God's will for him and that he could not continue to resist. He insisted, however, that he must be baptized by a Catholic bishop, for he was most carefully on his guard against the Arian heresy. After his baptism he passed through (it is said) all the grades of the Church's ministry[3] and was consecrated bishop on the eighth day amid universal goodwill and rejoicing.[4]

Now, some years after his consecration he made a journey to Rome (to his own estate, that is to say) and found there that holy maiden I spoke of above, to whom he used to offer his hand. She was in the house with his sister, just as he had left her (his mother was now dead), and when she kissed his hand he said to her with a smile: " There now, I told you, you are kissing the hand of a bishop ! "

X

During this period [1] he was invited to the home of a lady of rank across the Tiber, to offer the holy sacrifice in her house. A manageress at the baths, who had become paralysed and bed-ridden, heard that a priest [2] of the Lord was in the neighbourhood and had herself carried in a litter to the house to which he had been invited. During his prayer and imposition of hands she touched his clothes. Then she began kissing them and at once she recovered her health and began to walk. Thus was fulfilled Our Lord's words to the Apostles : " You who put faith in My name will do even greater things than these." [3] It was a

---

[3] Latin, " omnis ecclesiastica officia ", meaning here, almost certainly, the minor and the major orders.

[4] The traditional date is 7.12.374 but Dudden (op. cit., pp. 68, 69), following J. R. Palanque, argues for 1.12.373.

[1] See note 1 to section VI.

[2] Latin, " sacerdos ", here used in the sense of one possessing the fulness of the priesthood, i.e. a bishop ; see the Introduction, section I.

[3] Based on John xiv. 12.

marvellous manifestation of healing and it was not kept secret. I myself learnt of it from the account of holy men in the same district when stopping in the City very many years later.

XI

On one occasion he had gone to Sirmium to consecrate Anemius as bishop and there was a plan, authorized by Justina, at that time Empress, to have him driven from the cathedral by a crowd collected for the purpose, so that, instead of his consecrating, the heretics should consecrate an Arian bishop in the cathedral itself.[1] He had taken his seat on the dais,[2] disregarding the woman's[3] attempt to stir up trouble, when one of the consecrated virgins of the Arian party, more shameless than the rest, mounted the dais and took hold of the bishop's robe, meaning to drag him to the women's part of the church, for them to beat

---

[1] The Bishop of Milan had the status of an Archbishop and one of his duties was to consecrate bishops within his Province. For Sirmium, see note 1 to section V. Justina was the second wife, and now the widow, of the Emperor Valentinian I (see note 2 to section VIII). She had one son, also called Valentinian. When Valentinian I died in A.D. 375, the Empire was divided between his brother Valens, who took the East, his son by his first marriage, Gratian, who took (roughly) the territories ruled by the Praetorian Prefect of the Gauls (see note 1 to section III), and Valentinian II to whom were allotted (roughly) the territories ruled by the Praetorian Prefect of Italy (see note 1 to section V). But as Valentinian was at this time only 4 or 5 years old, his share was administered from Trier by Gratian, acting as regent. Justina, however, wielded considerable power within her little son's share of the Empire and particularly at Sirmium, where she resided at his court, and she used it to further the cause of Arianism, which appealed to her as " a manageable and accommodating form of state religion " (Dudden, I, p. 188). Gratian, on the other hand, had been brought up a Catholic by his father and under the influence of St. Ambrose became an increasingly convinced and fervent one as he grew to full manhood (he was only sixteen when his father died). In this way, Sirmium acquired great importance as a last rallying-point for Arianism, now rapidly losing ground elsewhere in the Western part of the Empire ; and when its Arian bishop Germinius died, probably in A.D. 380, Justina, with strong support from the women of the city, was determined to secure an Arian successor, while the Catholic party in the city put up Anemius as their candidate. " Ambrose realized that the fate of orthodoxy in the whole region of the Danube Provinces was at stake, and, in great anxiety, went himself to Sirmium to superintend the election and consecration " (Dudden, p. 196). This resulted in the first of a series of clashes between Ambrose and Justina, who did not forgive him for his victory on this occasion, as will be seen.

[2] Latin, " tribunal ", meaning here probably the dais on which the episcopal chair (" cathedra ") was set in the apse at the end of the cathedral beyond the high altar ; it has the same meaning in section XLVIII.

[3] Justina's, as again in section XIII.

him and put him out. But, as he used to relate, she was met by
the warning words :[4]

" Even if I am unworthy of the great office of bishop, it ill
becomes you or your religious profession to lay hands upon a
bishop, whoever he may be. You ought to be afraid of what
may come upon you by the judgement of God."

The outcome justified his words, for the next day she was
dead ; and he repaid insult by kindness by conducting her to the
grave. This event struck no little terror into the hearts of his
opponents and enabled the Catholics to proceed with the consecration of a bishop in complete peace.

XII

With a Catholic bishop duly consecrated, Ambrose returned
to Milan and there had to withstand innumerable stratagems on
the part of the woman Justina we have been speaking of.[1] She
tried to rouse the people against the holy man by distributing
offices and honours. Those of weak character were, indeed,
deceived by these promises, which included tribuneships and
various other dignities for those who would kidnap him from the
cathedral and carry him off into exile.

Many attempted this but, with God protecting him, could not
achieve it. One man named Euthymius, even more luckless than
the rest, was worked up to such a frenzy that he acquired a house
next to the cathedral and installed a light cart there, with the
object of seizing him and putting him on the chaise and taking
him into exile more easily. But " his wickedness descended on

[4] Latin, simply " audivit ", a curious locution which occurs four times in this
Life. There seems to be no natural English equivalent for it, but in each case
Paulinus seems to be using it to call attention to some particularly remarkable
or oracular pronouncement or admonition, and it has been paraphrased accordingly.

[1] Not long after the episode recorded in the last section, Gratian moved his
court from Trier to Milan, largely to be near Ambrose. But in August 383 he
was murdered by a supporter of the usurper Maximus, who made Trier his
headquarters. (On Maximus, see the Life of St. Martin in this volume, section
XX, and the footnotes there, and also section XIX below, with note 2.) Justina
and Valentinian II then moved their court from Sirmium to Milan. The disorders
over the basilicas mentioned in the next section arose out of their attempt to
obtain one of the churches of Milan for Arian worship.

his own head ",[2] for a year later, on the anniversary of the day
on which he had planned to kidnap him, he was put into the
same chaise and taken off into exile from that very house. He
reflected then on the justice of God's judgements that so turned
the tables on him that he was sent off into exile in the same
chaise as he had got ready for the Bishop, who, however, did
much to alleviate his sufferings by providing the expenses and
other necessaries.

XIII

But the man's acknowledgement of his guilt did nothing to
abate the woman's frenzy nor the folly of the half-crazed Arians.
Indeed, they got worked up to still greater folly when they tried
to break into the Portian Basilica.[1] Soldiers were even sent to
guard the doors of the cathedral church, so that no one should
dare to enter the Catholic cathedral. But Our Lord has a way
of enabling His Church to triumph over its enemies and He so
moved the hearts of the soldiers that they became a support for
His Church and, in guarding the cathedral doors, turned their
shields so as to prevent anyone going out but did nothing to stop
the Catholic congregation going into the cathedral. But even
this was not enough for the soldiers detailed for this duty ; they
also joined with the congregation in lifting up their voices on
behalf of the Catholic faith.

It was on this occasion that the antiphonal chanting of the
psalms, the singing of hymns and the chanting of the night

[2] Ps. vii. 17.
[1] This basilica was outside the walls. Dudden places this episode in Lent,
385, and distinguishes it from the siege described in the following sentences,
which he places a year later and interprets as an attempt to seize the cathedral
church, the New Basilica (see note 3 to section VI). The Latin is ambiguous,
and many biographers, including (oddly enough) Dudden himself (p. 271, note
1) suppose Paulinus to be describing only one episode, either (as Dudden thinks)
because he has confused two separate episodes or because there was in reality
only one. But the rendering I have adopted, which makes Paulinus distinguish
between the two episodes, seems to be fully consistent with the Latin as well
as with the evidence from other sources. It turns on rendering " ecclesia "
here by " cathedral " in contradistinction to the basilica just mentioned and
this is not only consistent with Paulinus' usual use of the term but (it seems to
me) almost required by it. Towards the end of the fifth century, St. Gregory
of Tours was regularly using the term " ecclesia " for the cathedral church, to
distinguish it from the ordinary church, which he calls " basilica ", e.g. *History
of the Franks*, II, 38 ; III, 10 ; V, 4, 11.

office were first introduced into the cathedral church of Milan.[2] These liturgical devotions are still practised, not only in that cathedral, but in almost all the Provinces of the West.

XIV

During this period [1] the holy martyrs Protasius and Gervasius revealed themselves to the Bishop. They were lying in the basilica in which the bodies of the martyrs Nabor and Felix are today ; but, whereas the holy martyrs Nabor and Felix were constantly visited, neither the names nor the graves of the martyrs Protasius and Gervasius were known—so much so that their graves were walked over by everybody who wanted to get to the gratings that protected the graves of the holy martyrs Nabor and Felix. But when the bodies of these holy martyrs were taken up and placed upon biers, many sick persons are credibly reported to have been cured.

One case was that of a blind man named Severus, who to this day serves devoutly in that same basilica (known as the Ambrosian) into which the bodies of the martyrs were moved. When he touched their clothing, immediately he got back his sight.[2] Similarly, those whose bodies were possessed were cured and returned home full of gratitude. And through the benefits

[2] By Ambrose himself, who was shut up in the cathedral with the congregation and took this course to alleviate for them the tedium of the siege. St. Augustine, not yet a Christian, was also there, with his mother, and describes the scene and the singing in his *Confessions* (IX, vii). The antiphonal (i.e. alternate) chanting of the psalms by the two halves of the choir was borrowed from the practice of the Eastern Churches, as was the singing (as part of the liturgy) of metrical hymns, of which St. Ambrose was one of the earliest as well as one of the best composers in Latin.

[1] See note 1 to section VI. The occasion of this episode was the completion and dedication of a new basilica St. Ambrose had been building, known afterwards as the Ambrosian Basilica. The date was June, 386. The martyrs whose relics were discovered were brothers who suffered martyrdom in Milan in the first century but had in the course of time been forgotten. The church of SS. Felix and Nabor where the relics were found was known originally as the Basilica Philippi and stood on the site of an ancient Christian cemetery. The bodies of SS. Felix and Nabor had been enshrined there by St. Ambrose himself. On the cultus of the relics of the martyrs, see the Introduction, section III.

[2] St. Augustine, who was in Milan at the time, makes several references to this cure in his writings, especially in the *Confessions*, IX. 7, and *De Civitate Dei*, XXII. 8.

obtained through these martyrs the faith of the Catholic Church continued to spread, and the Arian sect correspondingly dwindled.

XV

Indeed, from this time onwards, the persecution which Justina in her frenzy had stirred up to drive the Bishop from his cathedral began to subside. Nevertheless there were a number of Arians in Justina's court who scoffed at the great grace that the Lord Jesus had vouchsafed to His Catholic Church through the merits of His martyrs and put about a story that Ambrose, that revered man, had bribed people to pretend that they were troubled by evil spirits and to say that both the Bishop and the martyrs were tormenting them.[1]

But in saying this the Arians were using the language of the Jews, being indeed very much like them. For the Jews used to say of Our Lord that He drove out demons in union with Beelzebub, the chief of the demons, and the Arians said of the martyrs and of the priest of the Lord that the evil spirits were not driven out by the grace of God working through them but that people took bribes to pretend that they were being tormented. For the demons kept calling out : " We know you, you martyrs ", and the Arians kept saying : " We do *not* know they are martyrs." So also we read in the Gospel that the demons said to Our Lord : " We know you to be the Son of God ", while the Jews said : " Where this man comes from we do not know." [2] Not that one takes the words of demons as evidence ; nevertheless, they are an admission. All the more shame to the Arians and the Jews that they should deny what demons admit.

---

[1] Here and throughout this Life it is taken for granted that for the demoniacs to cry out in torment is commonly a sign of the presence of great sanctity and often the prelude to a cure. Compare the cry of the demoniacs to Our Lord : " Have you come to torment us before our time ? " (Matt. viii. 29).

[2] Mark i. 24 ; John ix. 29.

XVI

However, God, who is continually enlarging His favours to His Church, did not long allow His saints to be insulted by heretics. So it came about that one of their number was suddenly seized upon by an evil spirit and began to cry out that those who denied the martyrs, or did not believe in the unity of the Trinity as Ambrose taught it, were in the same torments as he himself was. The Arians found these cries embarrassing and, though they ought to have been converted and done penance to match such a striking admission, they pushed the man into a pond and killed him, adding murder to heresy. " For the logic of events had deservedly brought them to this." [1] But the holy Ambrose had increased in humility as bishop, so that he lost nothing of the graces that Our Lord gave him and grew daily in faith and love in the eyes of God and men.

XVII

During this period there was a member of the Arian sect who was a very keen controversialist and too hardened to be converted to the Catholic faith. Being in the cathedral when the Bishop was preaching, he saw, as he used afterwards to tell, an angel speaking into the Bishop's ear as he preached, so that the Bishop seemed to be repeating the angel's words to the congregation. By this vision he was converted to the faith he had been attacking and became one of its defenders.

XVIII

There were also two chamberlains of Gratian when he was Emperor,[1] who belonged to the Arian sect. They had submitted to the Bishop a question for him to deal with and had promised

---

[1] Wisd. xix. 4.
[1] We have gone back several years, for this episode must belong to the period (from Easter 381 to autumn 383) when Gratian's court was at Milan. Paulinus is, as often, grouping his episodes partly by topics.

to be present in the Portian Basilica the next day to hear him on it ; it was a question about the Incarnation of Our Lord. But the next day the wretched men, swollen with pride and heedless of their promise, got into a carriage and left the city for a drive, slighting God in the person of His priest and disregarding the injustice to the waiting congregation, and forgetting, too, Our Lord's words : " Whoever is an occasion of sin to one of these little ones ought to have a millstone of the largest size fastened to his neck and be sunk in the depths of the sea." [2] Meanwhile the Bishop waited for them with the congregation in the church.

But I shudder to relate the end of this defiance, for suddenly they were thrown out of the carriage and lost their lives, and their bodies were taken for burial. But the holy Ambrose, knowing nothing of what had happened and unable to keep the congregation waiting any longer, came to the front of the dais and began a sermon on the question that had been put to him. " Brethren," he began, " I wish to pay my debt, but I do not find here my creditors of yesterday," with the rest, as it is written in the book entitled *On the Incarnation of Our Lord.* [3]

XIX

After the murder of the Emperor Gratian, Ambrose undertook a second embassy to Maximus for the purpose of recovering his body.[1] Anyone who would like to see how firmly he acted

[2] Based on Matt. xviii. 6.

[3] The full title is *De Incarnationis Dominicae Sacramento.*

[1] See note 1 to section XII. Maximus was a Spaniard and a Catholic, who in A.D. 383 revolted but at the head of the army in Britain, crossed the Channel and overthrew Gratian. His next step was to try to get Valentinian II, now about twelve years old and the sole legitimate Emperor in the West, to come to him at Trier and live there as his ward and puppet. Justina, by now established at Milan, so far suppressed her hatred of Ambrose as to make the request (then unprecedented in the case of a Christian bishop) that he should go as an ambassador to Maximus to negotiate peace. Ambrose undertook the mission and before the end of 383 succeeded in negotiating peace without committing Valentinian to going to Trier but at the price of recognizing Maximus as legitimate Emperor ruling west of Italy and the Alps—a recognition in which Theodosius, now Emperor in the East, reluctantly joined in the following year. (On Theodosius, see note 1, section XXII below.)

In A.D. 386, to which Paulinus' narrative has returned, Maximus was again threatening to invade Italy, partly on the ground that Valentinian had never towards him will get proof if he reads the letter reporting the mission, which was sent to Valentinian the Younger. (It seemed to me that to insert it would be inconsistent with my promise, as the length of the letter, if it were added here, would weary the reader.) He actually excluded Maximus from communion, warning him that if he wished to stand well with God he must do penance for shedding the blood of one who was his master and (what was still more serious) an innocent man.[2] But he in his pride refused to do penance and forfeited his salvation in this world as well as in the next ; and he laid down in fear, like a woman, the realm that he had wickedly usurped, thereby acknowledging that he had been merely the administrator, not the sovereign, of the state.[3]

XX

After the death of Justina,[1] a certain fortune-teller, Innocent by name but not in reality, was being put to the torture by a judge in connection with his witchcraft and began to confess to something quite different from what he was being questioned about. He kept screaming that he was suffering even worse torments from the angel who guarded Ambrose ; because in

come to Trier, partly on the ground that the court at Milan was persecuting the Catholics. Once more (following Dudden's reconstruction, p. 345 sqq.) Ambrose was asked by Justina to go as ambassador to negotiate peace and also to recover the remains of Gratian, which had been kept in Gaul, one of her motives being that if he failed, he could be charged with collusion with Maximus, the enemy of his country, and thus be discredited with the Catholics. But Ambrose, conscious of this motive, conducted his mission in such a way as to avoid all grounds for such a charge.

The letter referred to by Paulinus in the next sentence was written by Ambrose on his journey back (Ep. XXIV).

[2] The actual ground of the excommunication seems to have been, not the murder of Gratian, which Maximus had never been proved to have instigated, but his joint responsibility with some bishops of Gaul for the execution of certain Priscillianist heretics, see sections XI to XIII of the Dialogue *Gallus* (on St. Martin) in this volume, and the notes there.

[3] Maximus, in the year following Ambrose's second embassy, had carried out his threatened invasion and made himself master of Italy, Justina and the young Valentinian taking refuge with Theodosius in the East. There Valentinian (but not Justina) was reconciled to the Church. Then, in A.D. 388, Theodosius invaded Italy and overthrew Maximus, who was taken captive and executed by the soldiers. For Theodosius, see note 1, section XXII below.

[1] Apparently A.D. 388, about the time of her son's restoration to his throne in the West.

Justina's time he had climbed to the top of the roof of the cathedral and offered sacrifices in the middle of the night to stir up people's hatred against the Bishop. But the more assiduously and zealously he had persevered in these malicious practices, the stronger had grown the love of the people for the Catholic faith and for the priest of the Lord.

He confessed also that he had sent demons to kill him but that the demons had reported that they were quite unable to get close to him or even to the doors of the Bishop's residence, because an impassable fire protected the whole building, so that they were burnt even while they were a long way off. For that reason he had given up those magic arts with which he had once thought he could do something against a priest of the Lord.

Another man went carrying a sword to the Bishop's bedroom to kill him but when he had raised his hand he stayed with his right arm stiffened, with the drawn sword in it. He then confessed that he had been sent by Justina ; and the arm that had stiffened when it was stretched out to do an evil deed was healed by his confession.

XXI

During this period his Excellency Probus[1] sent to the Bishop a young member of his secretariat who was seriously troubled by an evil spirit. But when he had left Rome the demon went out of him, dreading an encounter with the holy man. Consequently, while the youth was at Milan with the Bishop he showed no signs of being under diabolical influence. But when he had left Milan and was drawing near Rome, the same spirit that had possessed him before began to trouble him again. When the demon was asked by the exorcists[2] why it had not shown itself while he was in Milan, it admitted that it dreaded Ambrose, and so had withdrawn for a time. But it had waited in the place

[1] See note 3, section V. Probus, after filling many high offices, was now living in magnificent retirement in Rome ; see section XXV, below.
[2] The minor order known as exorcists actually exercised at that time the function of exorcism, which is still in use in the Church but now reserved to priests.

where it had withdrawn from the youth, until he returned, and on his return had resumed possession of the utensil it had abandoned.

XXII

It was after Maximus had been put to death, when the Emperor Theodosius was at Milan and Bishop Ambrose at Aquileia, that the Christians in a certain military stronghold in the East burnt down the Jewish synagogue and the sacred grove of the Valentinians, because the Jews and the Valentinians had insulted some Christian monks (for the Valentinian sect worships thirty gods).[1] The Count of the East [2] sent a report of this to

[1] Theodosius I was one of the great personalities of his time and his relations with Ambrose were of crucial importance in the lives of both and also for the future relations of Church and Empire (see the Introduction, section I). He was a Spaniard, born about A.D. 345, and a Catholic, though not baptized till A.D. 380 (see note 3 to section VII). His father had been one of the generals of Valentinian I. After the death, in 378, of Valens, the uncle of Gratian and his colleague in the East, Theodosius had been invited by Gratian to take Valens' place. He was proclaimed Emperor in January, 379, and made Thessalonica (now Salonika) his headquarters. His first great political achievement was a settlement with the Goths, who had settled within the Empire south of the Danube, become restive, and gained an overwhelming victory over Valens at Adrianople in August, 378. His first great acts in the ecclesiastical sphere were (a) the severance by edict of the long association of the Empire in the East with Arianism, the Nicene creed being taken as the test of orthodoxy; (b) the summoning of the first General Council of Constantinople (381).

He first came into close contact with Ambrose after his victory over Maximus in July, 388 (see note 3, section XIX). He had then added the dominions usurped by Maximus to those ruled by Valentinian II, who had thereupon gone off to Trier. Theodosius himself remained in Italy for three years, mainly at Milan. It was during this period that the two clashes with St. Ambrose here took place, the first of them in December, 388. When the episode opens, Ambrose is apparently presiding over the election of a new bishop at Aquileia (at the head of the Adriatic Sea, the parent town of Venice). The " stronghold " mentioned is Callinicum (now Av-Rakka) on the Upper Euphrates. The Valentinians were the followers of a Christian Gnostic named Valentine, powerful at Rome c. 140. Gnosticism in general was a movement whose representatives claimed to possess, or have the means of acquiring, an esoteric or inner knowledge of religious truth hidden from the ordinary man, the word " Gnostic " itself being the Greek for " knowledgeable " or " enlightened ". The knowledge was supposed to be obtained, partly through a secret chain of initiates going back to a divine revelation, and partly in ecstasy, by devotees in the highest grades. What was made known to the ordinary disciple was cast in a philosophical framework partly derived from Neo-Platonism and partly from oriental magic and asceticism and Greek and Egyptian mystery cults, embellished to a fantastic degree of elaboration, particularly with the genealogies of the intermediate beings, usually called aeons, supposed to be generated as a pre-

[2] In the case of the civil Diocese known as " Oriens ", the title " Comes " (" Count ") was used as the equivalent of " Vicarius " (Deputy Praetorian Prefect) used elsewhere.

the Emperor, who on receipt of it ordered the synagogue to be rebuilt by the bishop of the place and the monks to be punished. But when the purport of this order had come to the ears of that revered man, Bishop Ambrose, as he could not hurry off himself at the moment, he sent the Emperor a letter in which he represented to him that his decree should be withdrawn and that he himself should be granted an audience. He added that, if he were not a fit person to receive a hearing from the Emperor, he would not be a fit person to receive a hearing from the Lord on his behalf or to have prayers and petitions entrusted to him by the Emperor. He was even ready to face death over this issue rather than disguise his thoughts, if that was going to make an apostate of the Emperor, who had issued an order so unjust to the Church.

XXIII

Then, after his return to Milan, he dealt with the same question before the congregation, with the Emperor present in the cathedral. In this discourse he represented Our Lord Himself as speaking to the Emperor and saying : " I myself raised you from the place of the youngest to be Emperor ; I delivered the army of your enemy into your hands ; I gave you the troops he had collected for his own army against you ; I put your enemy himself into your power ; I established one of your offspring upon the throne ; I enabled you to enjoy the triumph without the toil. And are you allowing My enemies to enjoy a triumph over Me ? " [1]

As the Bishop came down from his throne, the Emperor said to him : " Your sermon was against me today." He replied that he had not spoken against him, but for his good.

---

liminary to the creation of the world. Christian Gnosticism was thus a sort of Modernism which attempted to defend Catholicism by refining its dogmas into " higher truths " and reducing to allegories such concrete historical facts as seemed to be stumbling-blocks. The Valentinians were a leading group among the Christian Gnostics, and believed in a series of fifteen pairs of semi-divine aeons (which had added a sixteenth pair to themselves) standing between God the Father and the man Jesus, the Saviour.

[1] Paulinus seems to be following the phrasing of the letter (Ep. XL) rather than the sermon. The son referred to was Arcadius, who had been given the rank of Augustus (Emperor) in A.D. 383, though only a little boy at the time.

" It is true ", said the Emperor, " that my order to the bishop about rebuilding the synagogue was too harsh, but the monks really must be punished."

The courtiers who were in attendance expressed their agreement but the Bishop retorted : " I am now conferring with the Emperor. With you I shall have to deal very differently."

And he continued to hold his ground and would not approach the altar until the Emperor had given a pledge that would make it right for him to celebrate. " Then I celebrate in reliance on your word ? " said the Bishop. " You may celebrate in reliance on my word," replied the Emperor. And when this promise had been repeated, the Bishop celebrated the sacred mysteries with his mind set at rest.

All this is to be found in a letter[2] which he wrote to his sister, in which he enclosed a discourse he delivered the same day on the nut stick which is described as having been seen by the prophet Jeremias.[3]

XXIV

During this period [1] the Bishop suffered great distress on account of the city of Thessalonica, when he heard that it had been almost wiped out. For the Emperor had promised him that he would pardon the citizens of the city in question, but the courtiers had worked on the Emperor secretly, behind the Bishop's back, and for three hours the city had been given over to the sword and many innocent people had been butchered.

When the Bishop learnt what had happened, he refused the Emperor admission to the cathedral, nor would he pronounce him fit to sit in the congregation or to receive the Sacraments until he had done public penance. When the Emperor remonstrated that David had committed adultery and murder, both together, his immediate reply was : "As you imitated him in his

[2] Ep. XLI.
[3] Jer. i. 11, Septuagint ; the Vulgate has a different rendering.
[1] See note 1, section VI. This episode was in the late summer of 390. The inhabitants of Thessalonica had broken out into murderous rioting against Theodosius' commandant.

transgressions, imitate him in his amendment." The Emperor
took these words so much to heart that he did not shrink even
from public penance ; and the effect of his making amends was
to give the Bishop a second victory.[2]

XXV

During this period [1] two Persians, eminent for their rank and
learning, came to Milan, drawn by the fame of its Bishop. They
brought with them many questions to test his wisdom. From
six in the morning till nine at night they discussed these with
him through an interpreter and went away marvelling. And to
prove that they had come for no other reason than to get to know
at first hand the man they had known of by report, they took
their leave of the Emperor the next day and set off for Rome.
They wished to see there the magnificence of his Excellency
Probus,[2] and when they had done so they went back to their own
country.

XXVI

When Theodosius had left Italy and taken up his residence in
Constantinople, Symmachus, then Prefect of the city of Rome
and acting in the name of the Senate, sent an embassy to the
Emperor Valentinian in Gaul regarding the restoration of the
Altar of Victory and the subsidies for its ceremonial.[1] When the

----

[2] The Latin is obscure ; this seems on the whole the most probable interpretation.
[1] This was apparently in A.D. 391, which could still be within the " period "
of Theodosius' stay in Italy (see note 1, section XXII).
[2] See note 3 to section V, and note 1 to section XXI.
[1] Towards the end of A.D. 382 the young Gratian, the first Emperor to refuse
the pagan title of Pontifex Maximus (" High Priest "), had abolished the state
subsidies to the pagan shrines and rites still maintained in Rome and ordered
the removal of the ancient Altar of Victory from the Senate House. Quintus
Aurelius Symmachus, a relative of Ambrose but leader of the conservative and
pagan section of the Roman aristocracy, had arranged with his friends to replace
the subsidies by private subscription but failed to get the Altar put back. The
next year Gratian was murdered and the year following (A.D. 384) Symmachus
was made Prefect of Rome and on behalf of the Senate drew up a magnificently
worded petition which was sent to the boy Emperor Valentinian II, then resident
in Milan. In it he once more pleaded for the restoration of the Altar. This
petition made such a strong impression on the court that only the hasty and
forceful intervention of Ambrose, who threatened Valentinian with exclusion

questing that a copy of the petition should be sent to him, to which he would reply from his point of view. On receiving it he composed such a splendid memorial that Symmachus, man of eloquence though he was, dared not make any kind of reply to it.

But after Valentinian of sacred memory had ended his life at Vienne, which is a city in Gaul, Eugenius became Emperor.[2] It was not long after he had begun to reign that he was petitioned by Flavian, then Prefect,[3] and Count Arbogast, to restore the Altar of Victory and the subsidies for its ceremonial ; and what Valentinian of sacred memory, in spite of his youth, had refused to the petitioners, he so far forgot his faith as to concede.

XXVII

When the Bishop heard this, he left Milan, towards which Eugenius was hastening, and retired to Bologna and from there moved on to Faenza. After spending a few days there, he received an invitation from the Florentines and so came down to Tuscany. It was not that he feared injury from the Emperor but that he

---

from the cathedral, secured its rejection. (It was in this year, incidentally, that Symmachus obtained for Augustine the professorship that brought him to Milan.)

In the winter of 389–390 Symmachus made a third attempt, this time going in person to Milan, where Theodosius was then reigning, but was again unsuccessful. Moreover, in February, 391, Theodosius sent from Milan to the then Prefect of Rome a law forbidding all the external observances of paganism. But after the return of Theodosius to the East, in July 391, and before the end of that year, Symmachus and his friends in the Senate made a fourth attempt, sending a deputation to Valentinian, now in Gaul and without Ambrose to advise or support him. But this time Valentinian, now about twenty years old and a Catholic (though not baptized), though his whole court was against him, stubbornly refused to undo his half-brother Gratian's work.

Paulinus in this section confuses the two embassies to Valentinian, of A.D. 384 and A.D 391.

[2] Valentinian died a violent death in May, 392. It is uncertain whether he was murdered or was driven to suicide by Count Arbogast, the pagan barbarian who commanded his army in Gaul, and dominated his court. In any case Arbogast, three months later, had his own nominee, Eugenius, crowned Emperor in Valentinian's place. Then early in 393, Eugenius, finding that Theodosius refused to recognize him, made the bid for the support of the pagan party which Paulinus records and then marched into Italy with Arbogast, as implied in the next section.

[3] i.e. of Rome.

refused to meet so sacrilegious a man. For he sent him a letter in which he appealed to his conscience, and I think that a few of its many points should be quoted here :

" The imperial power may be great, but consider, Emperor, how great is God. He sees into the hearts of men, He examines their innermost consciences, He knows everything before it happens ; He knows the secrets locked in your breast. You do not allow *yourself* to be deceived, and do you expect to hide things from God? Has no such thought occurred to you? And, granted that they were very persistent, was it not for you, Emperor, to be still more persistent, in resisting and refusing what plainly violated His holy Law? " And again : " Since, then, my words are binding on me in the sight of both God and man, I concluded that, as I could do nothing for *your* welfare, the only course open to me or required of me was to see to my own ! "

XXVIII

While he was in the above-mentioned city of Florence[1] he stayed with the late Decens, a gentleman of rank and, what is more, a Christian. This man's son, Pansophius by name, then quite a little thing, was troubled by an evil spirit but was cured by the Bishop's repeated prayers and his laying on of hands. But some days later this baby was seized with a sudden illness and passed away. His mother was a most pious woman, full of faith and the fear of God, and she brought him downstairs from the top of the house and laid him on the Bishop's bed in his absence.

When the Bishop returned—he had been out of the house at the time—he found him on his bed and, out of pity for the mother and having in mind her faith, he laid himself like Eliseus over the baby's body and prayed, and was privileged to restore to the mother, alive, one he had found dead. He also wrote a little book for the child, so that he might learn through reading what he could not take in as an infant. But he made no mention of this

---

[1] March to July, 394. So Dudden, who thinks that it was on this occasion that the author first met Ambrose and entered his service.

event in his writings, though from what motive he refrained it is not for me to judge.

XXIX

In this same city he dedicated a basilica in which he deposited the relics of the martyrs Vitalis and Agricola, whose bodies he had exhumed in Bologna.[1] For these martyrs' bodies had been laid among the bodies of the Jews, and this would never have been known to the Christians if the holy martyrs had not revealed themselves to the Bishop himself[2]. When the relics were placed under the altar which stands in this basilica, there was great delight and rejoicing on the part of all the faithful and, for the demons, the pain of having to acknowledge the merits of the martyrs.

XXX

During this period[1] Count Arbogast made war on his own people, namely the Franks. In this fighting he routed a great host in a pitched battle and concluded peace with the rest. At a subsequent banquet he was asked by the chieftains of his people whether he knew Ambrose. He answered that he knew the man and was a friend of his and had very often dined with him, and received the remarkable reply :[2]

" No wonder you win battles, Count, if you are a friend

---

[1] These martyrs were a slave and his master who suffered under Diocletian, about A.D. 304. The Church in Florence where their remains were deposited came to be known (like the one that St. Ambrose built and dedicated in Milan) as the Ambrosian Basilica (see section L), but is now San Lorenzo. On the cultus of the relics of the martyrs, see the Introduction, section III.

[2] Kaniecka reads " sacerdoti ipsius ecclesiae ", meaning " to the bishop of that Church." The alternative reading " sacerdoti ipsi ", rendered here, is supported, not only by the general probabilities of the case (the Bishop of Bologna is not likely to have agreed to the removal to Florence of relics revealed to himself), but by a definite statement that Ambrose was the discoverer, made in an account of the affair purporting to be written by Ambrose and certainly very early. And St. Ambrose had recently passed through Bologna (section XXVII).

[1] See note 1 to section VI. Paulinus' " period " seems this time to cover the whole period of Eugenius' usurpation, for we now return to the winter of 392-3, after his usurpation but when the question of his recognition by Theodosius was still in suspense and before the breach with Ambrose had taken place over the restoration of pagan worship (see note 1 to section XXVI). The narrative returns to St. Ambrose's Italian journey in the next section.

[2] See note 4 to section XI.

of that man, who says to the sun ' Stand still,' and it stands still ! "

I set this down so that the reader may see what fame the holy man had, even among the barbarian nations. My own knowledge of this episode comes from what I was told by a young man in Count Arbogast's service, a most pious youth, who was present, because at the time when the conversation took place he was cup-bearer.

XXXI

Eventually the Bishop left Tuscany and returned to Milan, from which Eugenius had by this time set out to do battle with Theodosius.[1] There he awaited the arrival of the Christian Emperor, confident that God, in His might, would not deliver a believer into the hands of wicked men, " nor allow the rod of the sinner to be the portion of the just, or the just might set their own hands to wicked deeds."[2] For the late Count Arbogast and the Prefect Flavian had threatened, as they were leaving Milan, that when they returned victorious they would stable their horses in the basilica of the Church in Milan and would enlist the clergy in the army.

But when wretched men wickedly put their trust in demons and " open their mouths to blaspheme against God ",[3] they destroy their hope of victory. What had so infuriated them had been the fact that the Church had rejected the offerings made by the Emperor and refused him the privilege of praying with the Church. But Our Lord, whose way it is to protect His Church, " hurled down His judgement from heaven " and gave the completest of victories to the pious Emperor Theodosius.[4]

After Eugenius and his satellites had thus been disposed of, the Bishop received a letter from the Emperor ; and his chief concern

---

[1] Theodosius was at last marching on Italy to depose Eugenius. St. Ambrose arrived in Milan 1.8.394.

[2] Ps. cxxiv. (cxxv.) 3.

[3] Apoc. xiii. 6.

[4] The quotation is (substantially) from Ps. lxxv. 9 (lxxvi. 8) (pre-Vulgate), and would seem to be an allusion to the blinding hurricane which blew in the faces of Eugenius' troops and materially assisted Theodosius to annihilate his army on the second day of a two-day battle (5th and 6th September, 394) not far east of the R. Isonzo, the Italian line of defence, 1915-1917.

after that was to intercede for those whom he had found to be liable to punishment.[5] He first made his request by letter, which he sent to the Emperor by a deacon ; then he sent John, at that time one of the secretaries to the Privy Council[6] but now a Prefect, to secure the safety of those who had taken refuge in the cathedral. Finally he went himself to Aquileia to plead for them. And he easily obtained pardon for them, for the Christian Emperor prostrated himself at the Bishop's feet and declared that he had been preserved by his merits and his prayers.

XXXII

He then returned from Aquileia and arrived in Milan a day before the Emperor. But the Emperor Theodosius of most gracious memory, was not much longer in this world. He left his sons in the fold of the Church and under the care of the Bishop, who survived him less than three years.[1] It was during this period that the Bishop exhumed the body of the holy martyr Nazarius, which had been buried in a garden outside the city, and had it moved to the Basilica of the Apostles, by the Roman Gate.[2] In the grave in which the martyr's body was lying we saw the martyr's blood as fresh as if it had been shed that day (and when he actually suffered we have not even yet been able to learn). His head, moreover, which had been cut off by the impious men, was so complete and uncorrupted, with its hair and beard, that it had the appearance of having been washed and laid in the grave at the very hour it was taken out. And why wonder, seeing that Our Lord promised in the Gospel that " not a hair of their heads shall

[5] i.e. for complicity in the usurpation of Eugenius.
[6] Latin, " tribunus et notarius ", a phrase having at this period a technical meaning, roughly indicated by this rendering.
[1] Theodosius died 17.1.395, leaving his sons Arcadius, aged 18, and Honorius, aged 11, as Emperors in East and West respectively, with Stilicho (see note 2, section XXXIV) as the actual ruler in the West. St. Ambrose died two years and two and a half months later.
[2] This was in A.D. 395. Near the body of Nazarius was found the body of his fellow-martyr Celsus (see next section). Little is known of them for certain ; as the next sentence shows, the story of their martyrdom under Nero was unknown to Paulinus.

perish " ? [3] We were surrounded also by a strong scent that surpassed all perfumes in sweetness.

XXXIII

When this martyr's body had been exhumed and placed on a bier, we at once went with the holy Bishop to the holy martyr Celsus, who was buried in the same garden, to pray there. I have since found, however, that he had never been to pray at that spot before. It was, in fact, a sign that a martyr would be discovered if the holy Bishop went to pray at a spot he had never been to before. I was told, moreover, by the people who looked after the place, that it was a family tradition with them that they should stay on the place so long as the family lasted, because great treasures were deposited there. And indeed there were great treasures there, of the kind that " neither rust nor moth destroys nor thieves break in and steal," for Christ is their guardian and the halls of heaven their store-room, and, for them, " to live is Christ, to die is gain ".[1]

So then, the body of the martyr was moved to the Basilica of the Apostles, where the relics of the holy Apostles had recently been deposited with great and universal devotion. While the Bishop was preaching, one of the congregation, filled with an evil spirit, began to shout that he was being tormented by Ambrose. The latter turned to him and said :

" Silence, demon. It is not Ambrose tormenting you but the faith of the saints and your own envy, because you see men ascending to those heights from which you were hurled down." (For Ambrose did not know how to be puffed up).[2]

At these words the man who had been shouting became silent and prostrated himself on the ground and uttered no more sounds that could cause a disturbance.

[3] Luke xxi. 18.
[1] Matt. vi. 20 ; Phil. i. 21
[2] Taking " nescit inflari " to be a slip for " nesciit inflari ", the present tense (" nescit ") makes the sentence part of the speech (where, indeed, Kaniecka prints it) but it seems impossible there.

XXXIV

During this period the Emperor Honorius gave a show of wild beasts from Libya in Milan, on the occasion of his consulship.[1] As the people were assembling for it, soldiers were sent by Count Stilicho at the request of the Prefect Eusebius, and authorised to carry off a man named Cresconius from the cathedral.[2] Since he had taken refuge at the altar of the Lord, the holy Bishop with such clergy as were there at the time surrounded him to protect him. But the soldiers, who were commanded by officers of the Arian sect, were too many for a mere handful of men. They carried off Cresconius and returned to the amphitheatre with great rejoicings, leaving the cathedral plunged in gloom ; and the Bishop long lay prostrate before the altar of the Lord, shedding tears over the deed.

But when the soldiers had returned and reported to those who had sent them, some leopards that had been let loose made a swift leap, right up to the very place where the triumphant victors over the Church had taken their seats, and left them severely mauled. Stilicho saw this, and it brought him to repentance, so much so that, for a long time afterwards, he did his best to make amends to the Bishop. As for the man who had been carried off, he let him go unscathed, although, as he was guilty of the gravest crimes and there was no other way of punishing him, he sent him into exile, a pardon following not long after.

[1] The ancient Roman office of consul was now merely honorary and was the gift of the Emperor, but its bestowal was regarded as a very great honour. In some years an Emperor would hold one of the two consulships himself. Honorius was consul three times during St. Ambrose's lifetime, twice as a child before his accession and for a third time in A.D. 396, and it is clearly this third consulship that is in question here.

[2] Stilicho was a Vandal by race who had risen in the Imperial service to be Commander-in-Chief of the forces in the West and had been nominated by the dying Theodosius as guardian of his two sons, particularly of the boy Emperor Honorius. Eusebius was the Praetorian Prefect of Italy that year (see note 1 to section V). Cresconius was one of the criminals who had been sentenced to be devoured by the wild beasts at the show. He had escaped from the amphitheatre before the show began.

XXXV

During this period, the Bishop was going to the palace and I was following him in my official capacity, when someone accidentally slipped and fell at full length on the ground. Theodulus, then one of his secretaries, who afterwards won great esteem in the government of the Church at Modena, burst out laughing. The Bishop turned round and said to him: "Take care, or you who stand will fall." Even as he spoke, the one who had laughed at another's fall had to bewail his own.

XXXVI

During this period, again, Frigitil, Queen of the Marcomanni, heard of his reputation from a Christian who happened to have come to her from Italy.[1] Being given to understand that he was a servant of Christ, she herself became a believer in Christ and sent emissaries with gifts for the Church and a request that he would write something to instruct her in the faith. He wrote her a remarkable letter in the form of a catechism[2] and in the same letter urged her to persuade her husband to remain at peace with the Romans.

On receiving this letter, the woman succeeded in persuading her husband to put himself and his people under the protection of the Romans, and she also came to Milan. But to her deep grief she failed, for all her haste, to find the holy Bishop, for he had departed this life.

XXXVII

Finally, in Gratian's time (if I may retrace my steps), he once went to the official residence of Macedonius, then Master of the Offices,[1] to intercede for someone, but found the doors closed by

---

[1] The Marcomanni were a Teutonic people who occupied most of what is now Czechoslovakia. The year was A.D. 396.

[2] It has not survived.

[1] This official was practically the head of the Imperial civil service, and one of the eight civilian *Illustres* in the West (see note 2 to section V).

Macedonius' orders, and failed to obtain admittance. " One day you will come to the cathedral," he said, " and though the doors will not be closed you will not find entry."[2] And this came true at the death of Gratian, when Macedonius fled for safety to the cathedral and, though the doors were open, could not gain an entrance.[3]

XXXVIII

This revered Bishop was a man of much fasting, and many vigils and labours. He wore out his body by fasting daily, never taking breakfast except on Saturdays and Sundays and on the festivals of the principal martyrs.[1] He was most constant in prayer by day and by night. He did not shirk the labour of writing his books out with his own hand, unless he was physically incapacitated. His, also, was " the anxious care for all the Churches "[2] and an unwearying zeal and perseverance when his intervention was required. In fulfilling his priestly duties he was a tower of strength, so much so, that he used to get through by himself, in connection with those who were to be baptized, an amount of work that five bishops could hardly get through after his death.

He had constant thought also for the poor and for captives, and on the occasion of his consecration as Bishop he gave away to the Church or to the poor all the gold and silver that was at his disposal. He also presented his estates to the Church, after arranging for his sister to retain the use of them. He left nothing for himself he could call his own here below, for it was as a soldier stripped and unhampered that he wished to follow Christ Our Lord, " Who, although He was rich, became for our sakes poor, that we through His destitution might be enriched."[3]

---

[2] Following an alternative reading which inserts a second negative.
[3] He was cut down outside.
[1] The Church at Milan followed the Eastern usage in keeping Saturday as a feast day, instead of as a fast day as was the custom at Rome and in the West generally.
[2] 2 Cor. xi. 28.
[3] 2 Cor. viii. 9.

XXXIX

He was one of those, too, who " rejoice with the joyful and weep with the weeping."[1] Thus, whenever anyone confessed his transgressions to him to receive a penance, his own weeping compelled the other to weep ; for it was as if he lay prostrate with the prostrate sinner. But of the nature of the crimes that were confessed to him he said nothing to anyone except to God, when he interceded with Him, leaving a good example to future bishops of acting as intercessors before God rather than as accusers before men.[2]

For, as the Apostle says again, our charity should be intensified towards a man in that position,[3] because he has been his own accuser, speaking first instead of waiting to be accused, so as to mitigate his offence by confession and have nothing with which the adversary can charge him. And so Scripture says : " The just man speaks first and accuses himself."[4] For he takes the words out of the adversary's mouth and, by confessing his sins, breaks (as it were) the teeth that are ready to prey by malicious accusations.[5] Moreover, he gives God His due, " to whom all things are naked ",[6] and who wishes the sinner to live rather than to die.[7] For confession of itself is not enough for the penitent, who must also amend his ways and not, upon repenting, commit what needs repentance, but humble himself as did holy David after he heard the prophet say " Your sin has been forgiven." For he became still more humble in making amends for his sin, " eating ashes like bread and mingling tears with his drink."[8]

[1] Rom. xii. 15.
[2] In the fourth century the practice of public confession was giving way to private confession, and this brought into prominence the need for the seal of the confessional, but it was not until A.D. 459 that St. Leo I issued the first Papal pronouncement enjoining private confession, and silence on the part of the priest (Denzinger, 145).
[3] See 2 Cor. ii. 8.
[4] Prov. xviii. 17.
[5] These phrases seem to be a reminiscence of Ps. iii. 8.
[6] Heb. iv. 13.
[7] See, e.g., Ezech. xxxiii. 11.
[8] Ps. ci. (cii). 10.

XL

He used also to weep most bitterly whenever he was told of the death of any of the holy bishops, so much so, that we would try and console him. But we did not realize the piety of his nature or understand the real reason why he wept so, and he would explain to us that he was not weeping because the man reported dead had passed away but because he had passed away before him, and also because it was difficult to find a man fit for the fulness of the priesthood. As regards his own death, he foretold that he would be with us till Easter, and he did indeed obtain by his prayers to Our Lord the privilege of being more speedily released from this life.

XLI

For it was the greatest grief to him to see how avarice flourished, " a root of all evils "[1] which neither plenty nor poverty can diminish, and how it went on increasing everywhere and particularly among those in positions of authority, so that any business with them caused him endless trouble, because everything was retailed at a price.

First, the vice brought " every evil " to Italy and, from that beginning, everything has changed for the worse. And how can I say anything about the mania it rouses in people who can put forward the needs of their children or relatives " as excuses to excuse their sins ",[2] when it has seized also upon numbers of celibates—" priests and Levites " " who have God for their portion,"[3] so that they too get the craving? And alas! for us wretched creatures in whom even the thought of the end of the world does not stir a desire to shake off such a heavy yoke of servitude, which submerges us in the depths of hell, nor move us to " use illgotten wealth to make friends for ourselves who will give us a welcome in eternal homes."[4] Happy indeed is he who is converted and breaks the chains and throws off the yoke of this tyranny, and

---

[1] I Tim. vi. 10.
[2] Ps. cxl (cxli). 4.
[3] See Deut. xviii. 1, 2.
[4] Based on Luke xvi. 9.

" will take and dash his little ones against the rock,"[5] that is to say, will dash all his cravings against Christ, who, according to the Apostle,[6] is the rock, which destroys all who are dashed against it, remaining itself imperishable. And he who dashes against it the ignobler offspring of his evil womb is not rendered guilty thereby, but blameless, and can say with confidence : " The Lord is my portion." For those who have nothing in this world truly have Christ for their portion and those who disdain the unimportant things will receive many things " and have life in eternity as well."[7]

XLII

A few days before he was confined to his bed,[1] he was dictating the 43rd Psalm and I was taking it down and watching him, when suddenly a flame, shaped like a short shield, spread over his head and little by little entered in through his mouth, like someone going into his own house. His face then became as white as snow, but afterwards his features resumed their normal appearance.

While this was going on I was petrified with amazement and unable to write down what was being dictated, though I did so after the vision had passed. For at the time in question he was quoting the testimony of holy Scripture, which I retained in my mind particularly well because that was his last day of writing or dictating ; indeed, he could not even finish that Psalm. As for myself, I immediately related what I had seen to that most estimable man, the deacon Castus, under whom I was living at the time.[2] Full of the grace of God, he showed me, by reading from the Acts of the Apostles, that I had seen the coming of the Holy Spirit upon the Bishop.

---

[5] Compare Ps. cxxxvi (cxxxvii). 9.
[6] 1 Cor. x. 4 may be meant, but there is no reference to the psalm there.
[7] Compare Matt. xix. 29.
[1] February, 397.
[2] In a training school which St. Ambrose had established in Milan for his clergy, in which Castus seems to have held some kind of office.

XLIII

Some time before this, a slave of the late Count Stilicho, who had been plagued by a demon and had been cured, was living at the Ambrosian Basilica, where he had been placed under supervision by his master. It was reported of him, and readily believed by his master, that he was forging army commissions, and men were even being arrested who were proceeding to take up their duties. But, when Count Stilicho came to the case of his slave, he would not punish him himself. At the Bishop's intercession he discharged the men who had been acting under a misapprehension, but as regards the slave, he made a complaint to the Bishop.

The holy man sent after the slave as he was getting away from the Ambrosian Basilica and had him brought to him. After examining him and finding that he had in fact committed this very grave crime, he said : " He must be given over to Satan for the destruction of his body as a deterrent against the committing of such crimes in the future." At that very moment, before the words had left the Bishop's mouth, the evil spirit seized him and began to tear him ; and we were filled with wonder and with no little fear at the sight. We saw also at that time many purged from evil spirits at his command and at the laying on of his hands.

XLIV

During this period a former secretary to the Privy Council named Nicentius, who was so crippled with pain in the feet that he seldom appeared in public, approached the altar to receive the Sacrament and was accidentally trodden on by the Bishop. He yelled, and received the remarkable assurance :[1]

" Go back, and you will be all right for the future."

And he used to bear witness with tears, after the holy Bishop had departed this life, that he had had no more pain in his feet.

[1] See note 4, section XI.

XLV

But the time came when, after consecrating a bishop for the Church at Pavia, he fell ill. When after many days he was still confined to his bed, Count Stilicho (it is said) declared that the passing of so great a man would be the ruin of Italy. So he sent for some of the nobles of the city whom he knew to be friends of the holy Bishop and persuaded them, partly by threats and partly by soft words, to go to the Bishop and urge him to ask God for his life to be prolonged. He heard them out and replied :

" I have not lived among you in such a way that I am ashamed to be living ; at the same time, I am not afraid to die, for we have a very good Master."[1]

XLVI

During this period Castus, Polemius, Venerius and Felix, then all deacons, were talking together at the far end of the veranda on which he was lying. They were discussing, in voices so low that they could hardly hear one another, who would be consecrated bishop after his death. When they came to the name of the holy Simplician,[1] the Bishop, as if he were taking part in the discussion, although he was lying a long way off, ejaculated approvingly three times : " Old, but good." For Simplician was of a ripe age.

Hearing his voice, they fled in terror. But, when he was dead, it was none other than the one he had three times designated as a good old man who succeeded him in the episcopate. And Simplician was succeeded by Venerius whom we have just mentioned, and Felix now governs the Church at Bologna. As for Castus and Polemius, nurslings of Ambrose and the good fruit of

---

[1] For St. Augustine's comments on these words, see section XXVII of the Life of him in this volume.

[1] One of the spiritual fathers of St. Ambrose and also of St. Augustine, whose conversion he helped to bring about.

a good tree, they are performing the duties of the diaconate in the Church at Milan.[2]

XLVII

We learnt, moreover, from the holy Bishop Bassian of Lodi,[1] who had it from our bishop, that, in that same place where he was lying, when he was praying with Bishop Bassian, he had seen the Lord Jesus approach him and smile on him. And it was not many days after that, that he was taken from us.[2] As he was passing from us to Our Lord, from about five in the afternoon until the hour he expired, he prayed with his arms stretched out in the form of a cross. We could see his lips moving but heard no sound.

Then Honoratus, Bishop of the Church at Vercelli,[3] who had retired to the top of the house to get some rest, heard three times a voice calling him and saying : " Make haste and get up ; he is at the point of death." He came down and administered the Lord's Body to the holy man, who took it and swallowed it and breathed his last. Thus he took with him a good viaticum and, all the more vigorous for this food, his soul now enjoys the company of the angels, whose life he had lived on earth, and the fellowship also of Elias ; for Elias, fearing God, was never afraid to speak to kings or any potentates, and neither was he.

XLVIII

From there his body was carried before dawn on the day of his death to the principal cathedral ;[1] and it was there during the night when we celebrated the vigil of Easter. Many neophytes saw him as they came back from the font after baptism, some

[2] It was still a common thing in the Church at this period for deacons to remain all their lives in that office, to which important administrative duties were attached ; see the Introduction, section I.

[1] Now patron saint of Lodi, where he was Bishop from 377 to 412. His Feast Day is on January 19th. (Pétin, *Dictionnaire Hagiographique*.)

[2] He died in the early hours of Holy Saturday, A.D. 397.

[3] St. Honoratus, whose feast is on 29th October.

[1] See note 3 to section VI.

saying they saw him sitting on his throne on the dais[2] and others pointing him out to their sponsors as he walked about ; but the latter looked and could see nothing because they had not had their eyes purified. Many, however, reported seeing a star over his body.

But at dawn on Sunday, after the celebration of the holy mysteries, his body was taken out of the cathedral to be carried to the Ambrosian Basilica, where it was deposited, amid such a clamour from a host of demons crying out that they were being tormented by him that their shrieks could hardly be borne. And, to this day, grace works thus through the Bishop, not only there, but also in a great many Provinces. Moreover, crowds of men and women kept throwing their handkerchiefs and aprons at the body of the saint in the hope that they would touch it. The crowd at the funeral was, indeed, countless, comprising every rank and sex and almost every age, and not only Christians but even Jews and pagans, though the ranks of the baptized, in their higher state of grace, led the way.

XLIX

Moreover, on the very day he died, he appeared to some holy men and prayed with them and laid his hands on them. This is stated in a letter, still preserved in the monastery at Milan, which was received by his successor, the revered Simplician, but had been addressed to him from the East as if he were still living amongst us. The letter thus sent gives the day and, when I read it, I found it to be the day of his death.

L

Again, in Tuscany, in the city of Florence, where that holy man Zenobius is now Bishop,[1] I learnt from the holy Bishop himself, that in fulfilment of a promise made, in response to requests, that he would often visit them, he has frequently been seen praying at the altar in the Ambrosian Basilica there, which he

[2] See note 2 to section XI.
[1] St. Zenobius, whose feast is on 25th May.

dedicated.[2] In the house, too, where he stayed when he was avoiding Eugenius,[3] he appeared to someone in a vision, at the time when Radagasius was besieging the city we are speaking of[4] and the citizens were reduced to complete despair, and he promised that deliverance would come to them the next day. When the man reported this, the citizens took heart ; and the next day the late Count Stilicho arrived with an army, and the enemy were defeated. I know this through that very pious woman Pansophia, the mother of the boy Pansophius.[5]

LI

He appeared also, holding a staff in his hand, in a vision at night to Mascezel when he was despairing of the safety of himself and the army he was leading against Gildo.[1] When Mascezel threw himself at the feet of the saint, the latter, who had appeared to him in the form of an old man, struck three times on the ground with the staff with which his steps were guided, saying : " Here, here, here ", and marking a place. At the same time he enabled the man whom he had deemed worthy of this visit to understand from this that he would win a victory in three days' time on the very spot where he had seen the holy priest of the Lord. With his mind thus set at rest, Mascezel entered upon the campaign and brought it to a successful conclusion. I myself was in Milan at the time, but I know of this from Mascezel's own account of it. For in this very Province where I am now writing[2] he told the story to a number of bishops ; and having them also as witnesses, I think I can all the more safely add to this book what I know about the matter.

[2] See section XXIX, and note 1 there.
[3] See sections XXVII and XXVIII.
[4] Radagasius was a barbarian leader who besieged Florence A.D. 406.
[5] See section XXVIII.
[1] Mascezel was a Moorish chieftain who in A.D. 398 was in command of the Imperial forces operating against his brother Gildo, who was in revolt.
[2] i.e. the administrative Province known as Africa, corresponding roughly to the modern Tunisia.

LII

Again, we were one day welcoming at Milan with the deepest devotion the relics of the martyrs Sisinius and Alexander, who in our own time, that is to say, after the death of the holy Ambrose, had won the crown of martyrdom at the hands of pagans in the district of Anaunia.[1] A blind man had received sight that day by touching the chest in which the relics of the saints were being carried and he came and told us that this was because he had seen a vision in the night of a ship approaching the shore with a number of white-clad men on board. As they were disembarking, someone in the crowd had asked to know who they were, and he heard that they were Ambrose and his companions. On hearing this name, he begged that he might get his sight and received the remarkable reply:[2] " Make a journey to Milan and meet my brethren who will be going there " (and he named the day), " and you will receive your sight." The man, as he told us himself, came from the coast of Dalmatia and had never previously been to the city of Milan before he met the relics of the saints on the highway. He was then still unable to see, and began to see after touching the chest.

LIII

I am at the end of my story, but I do not think that it will be regarded as a grave offence if I overstep a little the limits I promised to observe to show how the word of the Lord has been fulfilled which He spoke through the mouth of His holy prophets : " On those who sat in judgement on their brethren, or disparaged them in private, my hand was heavy " ;[1] and in another place : " Seek not delight in disparaging others or you may be uprooted."[2] For those who may be the victims of this habit, if they read how judgement overtook those who dared to disparage

---

[1] The Val di Non (Nonsberg), near Trent, in the Southern Tyrol. The date was May, 397, on the occasion of a festival of the pagan rustics.
[2] See note 4 to section XI.
[1] Ps. c (ci). 5.
[2] Prov. xx. 13 (after the Septuagint).

this holy man, may be brought with the others to amend their ways.

LIV

A certain Donatus, then, an African by birth but a priest of the Church at Milan, was at a banquet where there were some very pious army men and began disparaging the Bishop's reputation. The others would have nothing to do with it, and broke off the malicious conversation, and he was suddenly prostrated by a deadly stroke. He was taken up by the hands of strangers from the place where he lay and laid upon a couch and from there was taken to his grave. Again, in the city of Carthage, I had gone to dine with the deacon Fortunatus, brother of the revered bishop Aurelius,[1] together with Vincentius, Bishop of Culustinum, and Muranus, Bishop of Bolita,[2] as well as other bishops and deacons. Bishop Muranus began disparaging the holy man and I told him the story of the end of the priest I have been speaking of ; and he, by his own speedy death, demonstrated that the words spoken about another were God's warning to himself. For he, too, was suddenly prostrated by a very severe stroke and was carried to a bed by the hands of strangers from the place where he was lying. From there he was taken to the house where he was staying and that day was his last. Such has been the end of men who disparage the holy Bishop ; and those who were present and saw it could not but marvel at it.

LV

So I urge and beseech every reader of this book, if he would rather be in the company of Ambrose at the resurrection than undergo in the company of disparagers a punishment that every wise man will avoid, to imitate his life and praise the grace of God in him, and keep clear of disparaging tongues.

---

[1] St. Aurelius, Archbishop of Carthage from 388 to 423 ; a friend and collaborator of St. Augustine.
[2] Other sees in North Africa, where Paulinus was then living.

LVI

Finally, my father Augustine, I beseech your Beatitude, together with all those holy men who in your company call upon the name of Our Lord Jesus Christ in sincerity, to condescend to pray for me Paulinus, the lowliest of sinners, that since it is not for me to emulate so great a man in winning God's favours, I may, after winning forgiveness for my sins, be rewarded by not being punished.

THE LIFE OF ST. AUGUSTINE OF HIPPO
BY ST. POSSIDIUS, BISHOP OF CALAMA

Possidius was born in North Africa, then one of the most flourishing territories of the Catholic Church (and, for that matter, of the Roman Empire). The year is uncertain but must have been between A.D. 360 and 370. (These figures and most of the particulars that follow are taken from pages 11-23 of the Introduction to H. T. Weiskotten's edition of the Life—see the end of this note). He entered St. Augustine's community at Hippo immediately, or very soon, after the latter's ordination as priest in A.D. 391. He remained in it till, on St. Augustine's recommendation, he was made Bishop of Calama (a town about 40 miles S.W. of Hippo). This was in A.D. 397. He remained in close touch with Augustine and was a constant collaborator with him as a fellow-bishop, especially against the Donatists. In 428, when the Vandals invaded Africa and captured Calama, he took refuge in Hippo and once more resided with St. Augustine, witnessing his death in A.D. 430. When, in the following year, the Vandals abandoned the siege of Hippo, he returned to his see but in 437 was driven out again by the Vandal ruler, who was trying to enforce Arianism. This is the last that is certainly known of him, though it is probable that he died in Italy. His feast-day is on May 17th.

He wrote his Life of St. Augustine, with a bibliography attached, probably within two or three years of Augustine's death. He was qualified for the task by an intimate and unbroken friendship of nearly forty years (seven or eight of which were spent under the same roof) and complete fidelity to the facts. According to his editor, who is not a Catholic, " wherever Possidius' statements can be checked by the writings of St. Augustine or the Acts of Councils, they are always fully corroborated " (Weiskotten, p. 19). He does not attempt to deal with Augustine's life before his conversion or with his interior development, taking it for granted that his readers will have read Augustine's own account of these things in the *Confessions*. Nor were his education and culture sufficient to enable him to give any real picture of Augustine's intellectual stature and achievements or to visualize the nature of his future influence. For example, he makes no reference to *The City of God*, Augustine's greatest work, the writing of which was one of his principal activities, on and off, for thirteen years. Nor, in his narrative and style, does he often rise above the prosaic and his Latin is frequently awkward and faulty. (The contrast between his style and Latinity and that of St. Augustine as exhibited in the letter incorporated in Chapter XXX of the Life presents no small problem to the translator). But his work must always have the fascination attaching to an intimate and truthful account of a very great man.

The present translation is made from the text as reconstructed by Herbert T. Weiskotten of Princeton (*Sancti Augustini Vita Scripta a Possidio Episcopo*, edited with a revised text, introduction, notes and an English version by Herbert T. Weiskotten, Princeton University Press, 1919). He describes it as " a text written in a manner somewhat more uncouth, abrupt and awkward than is found in the editions where the text abounds in smooth corrections of editors " but " nevertheless evidently the truer text." The translation that accompanies it has not infrequently been of service to the present translator in elucidating the author's obscurities (though it is not always possible to agree with its interpretations) and occasionally in suggesting a happy turn of phrase. And there are, of course, a certain number of the inevitable but accidental coincidences between the two versions. But the approach to the problems of translation has been so different in the two cases that close verbal resemblances are few and direct dependence of the later version on the earlier very rare indeed.

Another English version of the Life is in existence, by the Very Reverend E. A. Foran, O.S.A., prefixed to his history of his Order, entitled *The Augustinians from St. Augustine to the Union, 1256*, Burns, Oates and Washbourne Ltd., 1938. It has been used occasionally in checking the ecclesiastical terminology.

THE LIFE OF SAINT AUGUSTINE WRITTEN BY BISHOP POSSIDIUS

PREFACE

I WRITE at the prompting of God, the Maker and Ruler of all things, and in accordance with my resolution, first as a layman and now as a bishop, to serve in the faith, by the grace of the Saviour, the omnipotent and divine Trinity, desiring to use such talents and literary gifts as I possess to promote the welfare of the true and holy Catholic Church of Christ Our Lord. My subject is the life and character of that best of bishops, Augustine, a man predestined from eternity to be given to us when his time came, and I must keep back nothing of what I saw in him and heard from him.

And indeed we may learn from our reading that the same kind of thing was repeatedly done in times past by the most devout sons of our Holy Mother, the Catholic Church. Inspired by the Holy Spirit, but in their own language and style, by speech or by pen they addressed similar narratives to the ears or the eyes of those who wished to be informed, and thus enabled the student to learn of the great and remarkable men who were privileged to share in the grace of the Lord while living amidst the affairs of men, and to persevere in it to the end of their days.

I, too, therefore, though the least of God's stewards, but in that unfeigned good faith with which the Lord of Lords wishes all good Christians to serve and please Him, have undertaken to trace, so far as He allows me, the beginnings, the career and the fitting end of this venerable man, as I have learnt them from him or observed them for myself through many years of close friendship. And I beseech the infinite Majesty that in the execution and completion of the task I have begun I may neither sin against the truth as it is known to " the Father of all enlightenment " [1] nor appear at any point to depart from charity towards good sons of the Church.

I have no intention of entering into all those things that the most blessed Augustine recorded of himself in his *Confessions*, concerning the kind of man he was before he received grace and the kind of life he lived afterwards. He wrote as he did in order that (as the Apostle says[2]) no man should believe or imagine anything better of him than he knew for himself or had heard about him. So, with his customary holy humility, he would deceive in nothing. It was not his own glory but his Lord's that he sought in respect of the benefits he had already received—his own deliverance and vocation ; and, for what he hoped to receive further, he looked to the prayers of his brethren. For we have it on the authority of the angel : " It is good to keep a king's secret but honourable to reveal and acknowledge the works of the Lord." [3]

I [1]

He was born, then, in the city of Tagaste in the Province of Africa.[2] His parents were of good standing, and of senatorial rank,[3] and Christians.[4] They carefully attended to his upbringing themselves and he was educated at their expense, chiefly in secular literature ; in other words, he took all the subjects that are included in what we call a liberal education. Thus equipped, he first of all taught literature[5] in his own town and then oratory at

[1] Jas.i. 17.
[2] 2 Cor. xii. 6, paraphrased.
[3] Tobias xii. 7.
[1] The text in the MSS. is continuous. The division into sections followed here was made in the first separate printed edition, that of Salinas, 1713.
[2] The date was 13th November, 354. Tagaste, now Suk Arras, was about 150 miles S.W. of Carthage, or of the modern Tunis. The administrative Province known as Africa comprised roughly the modern Tunisia and a small portion of eastern Algeria, in which Suk Arras is situated.
[3] Latin, " curiales ", a term which in the Provinces denoted landowners entitled by a property qualification to sit on the local Senates, though a *curialis* might at this period be, in actual fact, far from well off, as was, indeed, the case with Augustine's father, who had the utmost difficulty in paying for his education.
[4] His father only became a Christian when Augustine was at college.
[5] Latin, " grammatica ", but " grammar " would be a more misleading term than " literature " because it did not include the elements but consisted chiefly of the study of the masterpieces of Latin and Greek literature much as they used to be studied in English public schools.

Carthage, the capital of the Province,[6] and, later still, overseas, in Rome and at Milan, where at that time the Emperor, Valentinian the Younger,[7] had established his court.

In this city the office of bishop was then held by Ambrose, a priest most dear to God and outstanding even among men of the first quality.[8] From time to time Augustine, standing in the congregation, used to listen with fixed attention to the discourses frequently delivered in the church by this preacher of God's word. Now, at one time, when only a youth at Carthage, he had been attracted by the Manicheean heresy.[9] For that reason he was, more than most people, on the look-out for anything said either for or against it ; and the day came when God so worked upon the heart of His priest that certain problems of the divine law were solved that bore upon those errors.

Thanks to this instruction, the heresy was slowly and step by step driven out from Augustine's soul. Then, as soon as he was convinced of the truth of the Catholic faith, there was born in him a burning desire to go forward in it, and with the coming of the

[6] Near the site of the modern Tunis. It had been rebuilt after its destruction by the Romans at the end of the Punic wars.

[7] Valentinian II. He had been nominally one of the Emperors since about the age of four. On his half-brother Gratian's death in August 383 he became, at about the age of twelve, sole Emperor in the West and was brought by his mother to Milan. See the Life of St. Ambrose in this volume. The date of Augustine's arrival in Milan was probably the autumn of 384 (see note 1 to section XXVI of the Life of St. Ambrose).

[8] Ambrose, saint and Doctor of the Church, was Bishop of Milan from 373 or 374 to 397. See his Life in this volume.

[9] So called after its founder, a Persian named Mani or Manichee, who was teaching (at Ctesiphon in Mesopotamia, where he was born, and in exile) from A.D. 242 to 275. It was the product of a self-conscious and deliberate attempt to create a religion which should include the truths of all previous religions, Christianity among them. Its starting point was, however, characteristically Persian, namely the root idea of the old religion of Zoroaster, that there are two gods, one good and one evil, ruling two co-eternal kingdoms of light and darkness, with man, in whose composition good and evil are mixed, as a kind of perpetual battle-ground between them. Angels and demons fight on either side : Noah, Abraham, Zoroaster, Buddha, Jesus and Mani (himself the Paraclete promised by Jesus) come to aid man in the struggle. The inner circle of the Manicheea is set for themselves, and outwardly practised, a standard of asceticism which was extremely high ; but the Manicheean distinction between spirit and matter (which taught that spirit was wholly good and matter—hence the body and its sexuality—was intrinsically evil) also taught by implication that evil, deriving from matter, could not affect the spirit of the Elect, and thus licensed for them the worst sins of the flesh. As a result Manicheeism was proscribed as a public danger in almost every country that it entered, and it of course provided a special danger to the ascetic movement within the Church.

holy season of Easter he received the saving waters of baptism.[10] In this way it came about, through God's ordering, that he received both the saving truths of the Catholic Church and the divinely instituted sacraments through that great and remarkable prelate Ambrose.

II

Soon after this, with every fibre of his being he renounced all his ambitions for this world. He no longer thought of wife or children or wealth or worldly honours but resolved to serve God amongst God's people, desiring to be one of that " little flock " whom the Lord was addressing when He said : " Fear not, little flock, for it is the Father's pleasure to give you the Kingdom. Sell your possessions and give alms, making purses for yourselves that do not grow old and a treasure in heaven that never fails," [1] and so on. And what Our Lord said on another occasion, this holy man conceived the desire to act on : " If you wish for perfection, sell all that you have and give it to the poor, and you will have treasure in heaven. Come now, follow in my steps." [2] It was on the foundation of faith that he wished to build ; not on wood or hay or straw, but on gold and silver and precious stones.[3]

He was then over thirty years old.[4] Only his mother was surviving and still close to him (for his father had died some time before this[5]) and *she* had more joy in his resolution to give himself to the service of God than in the thought of grandchildren. And he duly gave notice to his pupils in oratory that, as he himself had decided to enter God's service, they must find another teacher.

III

His next step after being admitted to the sacrament, was to return to Africa and his own house and estate, in the company of some fellow-countrymen and friends of his who were joining

[10] In the year 387.
[1] Luke xii. 32-3.
[2] Matt. xix. 21.
[3] Compare I Cor. iii. 1-13.
[4] He was thirty-two.
[5] In A.D. 371, St. Augustine's mother, St. Monica, died a few months after his baptism.

him in God's service. On arriving there, he settled down there for about three years, selling his property and, with his companions, giving himself to God in a life of fasting, prayer and good works, and " meditating on God's Law day and night." [6] And what God revealed to his understanding as he reflected and prayed, he taught by sermons to those who were with him and by books to those who were not.

Now, it so happened that during this period his good name and his teaching came to the knowledge of one of those people known as " public executive officers," [7] appointed to Hippo-Regius,[8] a man living as a good Christian in the fear of God. He conceived a strong desire to see Augustine and asserted that he could defy all the lusts and allurements of this world if only he might, some time or other, have the privilege of hearing the Word of God from his lips.

A report of this came to Augustine from a reliable source and he longed for this soul to be rescued from the dangers of this life and from eternal death. So without being asked he went at once to the city now so famous, and saw the man. He had several talks with him and urged him, with all the force God gave him, to see that his promises to God were kept. The man kept promising from day to day to do this but never carried it out during this visit of Augustine. But we may be certain that there was some benefit and profit derived from the action of divine Providence, which was now operating everywhere through this " instrument cleansed for honourable use, serviceable to the Lord and ready for any good work." [9]

IV

At this time the office of bishop in the Catholic Church at Hippo was held by that holy man Valerius. He was now

---

[6] Ps. i. 2.

[7] Latin, " agentes in rebus ", of whom Weiskotten says : " These officers had various duties, principally as messengers, tax-collectors and police-agents." But their real work was to constitute an Imperial secret service.

[8] The full name of the city of Hippo of which Augustine was soon to become Bishop. It was about fifty miles north-west of Tagaste, on the coast, near the site of the modern Bone or Bona.

[9] 2 Tim. ii. 21.

impelled by the pressing needs of the Church to address his
flock and impress upon them the necessity of finding and
ordaining a priest for the city. The Catholics were by now
aware of the holy Augustine's teaching and way of life and they
seized hold of him—he was standing in the congregation quite
unconcerned and with no idea of what was going to happen to
him. (While a layman, as he used to tell us, he used to keep
away from churches where the bishopric was vacant but only
from these[1]). Holding him fast they brought him, as their custom
was, to the Bishop for ordination, for they were unanimous in asking for this to be done then and there. And while they were
demanding this with eager shouts, he was weeping copiously.

At the time, indeed, some of them, as he told us himself,
attributed his tears to wounded pride and, by way of consoling
him, told him that the priesthood, though he was certainly
worthy of something better, was not much below the episcopate.
But the man of God, as he told us, was viewing the situation with
more understanding and was bemoaning the many great dangers
to his way of life that he anticipated would come crowding on
him if he had to govern and direct the Church, and that was why
he was weeping. But they had their way.[2]

V

Once a priest, it was not long before he established a
monastery within the precincts of the church[1] and entered upon
a life with the servants of God in accordance with the method
and rule established under the holy Apostles. Above all, no one
in that community might have anything of his own but they
were to "hold everything in common" and it was to be
"distributed to each one as he had need of it." [2] He himself

[1] With the case of St. Ambrose in mind (see sections VI to IX of his Life.
Compare also the commandeering of St. Germanus to be bishop (see section II
of his Life in this volume). See the Introduction, section I.

[2] This was in 391.

[1] In a garden given for the purpose by the Bishop. Its first members were
probably the brethren from Tagaste.

[2] Acts ii. 44–5 ; iv. 35. It appears that Augustine's priestly duties prevented
him from taking any great share in the daily life of the community in the garden
and that Possidius acted for him as Superior. See Foran, *The Augustinians*,
pp. 55, 84.

had done this before, when he returned from across the sea to his own home.

The holy Valerius, who had ordained him and was a devout man living in the fear of God, was filled with joy and gave God thanks. He used to tell people how the Lord had heard the prayers he had so often sent up to Him that heaven would send him just such a man as this, who would help to build up the Lord's Church by his invigorating teaching of the Word of God. For this was a work for which he knew himself to be less fitted, being a Greek by birth and less versed in the Latin language and literature.

He even gave his priest permission to preach the Gospel in his presence in the church and very frequently to hold public discussions also, contrary to the custom and practice of the Churches of Africa.[3] Some bishops found fault with him for this. But this venerable and far-seeing man, who knew for certain that this was the practice in the Eastern Churches and thought only of the good of the Church, cared nothing for nagging tongues so long as the priest was getting done what the Bishop could see could never be done by himself.

Thus, lit and burning and "raised upon a candlestick" Augustine continued to "give light to all who were in the house ".[4] Presently the news of it got about everywhere and, such was the force of good example, other priests were given permission by their bishops and began to hold forth to the people in their bishop's presence.

VI

Now, at the time we are speaking of, in this city of Hippo the plague of Manicheeism had infected and taken hold of both

[3] The term " Africa " in this context would cover almost the whole of Roman Africa, that is to say the coastal regions of N. Africa west of the modern district of Benghazi. Within this area, nearly coterminous with the civil " Diocese of Africa " (see note 1 to section XX), the Churches formed a well-organised and semi-autonomous group under the primacy of the Bishop of Carthage. (The Churches east of Benghazi fell within the Patriarchate of Alexandria and within a different civil Diocese also, and the term " Africa " is never used in this Life so as to include them.)

[4] Matt. v. 15.

citizens and visitors in great numbers. They had been attracted to it and ensnared by a certain priest of that heresy named Fortunatus, who had settled there. In due course the Christian citizens and visitors to Hippo, Catholics and even Donatists,[1] came to our priest and demanded that he should meet this Manicheean priest, whom they regarded as a learned man, and hold a discussion with him about the Law of God. He made no objection to this, being, in the words of Scripture,[2] " ready to give an answer to anyone asking him to account for the faith and hope he had " in God, and " well able to inspire with sound doctrine and refute objectors ". But he enquired whether Fortunatus would agree to this.

They at once reported the position to Fortunatus, asking, pressing and indeed demanding that he should on no account refuse. But this Fortunatus had known the holy Augustine before this, at Carthage, when he had been involved with him in the same errors, and dreaded an encounter with him. However, hard-pressed and embarrassed by this insistence, particularly from his own people, he promised to meet him face to face and oppose him in debate.

So a day and place were fixed [3] and they met in the presence

[1] The Donatist schism arose out of the great persecution by Diocletian, which in Africa had lasted from 303 to 305 and in which the demand had been made for the surrender of the sacred books and vessels. There had been many who had surrendered them—the so-called *traditores*—and among those accused or suspected of this was the Primate of Africa, the Bishop of Carthage ; and some of those who had suffered imprisonment for the faith took upon themselves to excommunicate him. When he died in A.D. 312, they did the same with his successor, whose consecrator had been among the suspects. Moreover, these self-appointed excommunicators made the breach worse by taking the view, particularly congenial to African Christianity though not confined to it, that the loss of grace incurred by apostasy involved the loss of validity in all the sacraments administered by the former apostate, even baptism. In this way they made null and void all the sacraments, from the priest's orders to the layman's Communion, of as much of the Church in Africa as derived its orders from the Catholic Primate or from any suspected apostates among his colleagues. To fill the supposed gap, a complete opposition Church was created by a great organizer and propagandist, Bishop Donatus from Numidia. A hundred years of almost incredibly violent and bitter controversy followed, in which the Donatists rose to be the most powerful force in North Africa, alternately persecuting the Catholics and being rounded up practically as bandits by the civil power. When St. Augustine was ordained priest at Hippo the Donatists had an opposition bishop in almost all of the three hundred sees of the civil Diocese.

[2] I Pet. iii. 15 ; Titus i. 9.

[3] 28th August, 392.

of a large and interested audience and a crowd drawn by curiosity. The shorthand reporters opened their notebooks and the debate was opened on one day and concluded on the next. In the course of it, as the record of the proceedings shows,[4] the exponent of Manicheeism could neither refute the Catholic case nor succeed in proving that the sect of the Manichees was founded upon truth. When he broke down in his final reply, he undertook to consult his superiors about the arguments he had been unable to answer and, if by any chance they failed to satisfy him, well, he would look to his own soul.

The result was that this man, whom everybody had thought so great and learned, was considered to have entirely failed in the defence of his sect. His embarrassment was such that, when soon afterwards he left Hippo, he left it never to return. Thus, through this remarkable man of God, these errors were uprooted from the minds of all, whether they had been present at the debate, or had not been present but had heard about the proceedings ; and the Catholic religion was admitted to be manifestly the genuine one.

VII

Augustine continued to teach and preach the message of salvation both privately and publicly, in his home and in the church. He opposed with the fullest confidence the African heresies and especially the Donatists, the Manicheeans and the pagans, in carefully finished books and in extempore sermons. The Christians admired him beyond words and were full of his praises. They could not keep silent about it but made it known wherever they could. In fact, by God's good gift, the Catholic Church in Africa began to lift its head again after a long period during which it had lain prostrate—led astray, overpowered and oppressed, while the heretics grew strong, especially the rebaptizing Donatist party, which comprised the majority of Africans.[1]

As for these books and pamphlets of his, which by the marvellous grace of God issued from his pen in a constant flow, they

[4] *Acta contra Fortunatum* (Migne, P. L., vol. 42, 111).
[1] The Donatist re-baptized because they denied the validity of the sacraments of the Catholics ; see note 1 to the previous section.

were founded upon an abundance of reasoned argument and the
authority of Holy Scripture, and the heretics themselves used to
come hurrying with the Catholics with intense eagerness to hear
them read aloud. Those who wished to have what they heard
taken down, and could afford to do so, brought shorthand writers
with them. Thus the splendid teaching and " the sweet odour of
Christ " was spread abroad and made known through the length
and breadth of Africa ;[2] and the Church of God across the seas
rejoiced also when they heard of it. For " just as, when one limb
suffers, all the limbs suffer, so, when one limb is held in honour,
all the limbs rejoice with it." [3]

VIII

That man of blessings, the aged Valerius, rejoiced over all this
even more than the rest and thanked God for the special favour
conferred upon him. But he began to be afraid, such is human
nature, that Augustine might be wanted as bishop by some other
Church, which had lost its own, and thus taken away from him.
Indeed, this would actually have happened if our Bishop had not
got to know of it and succeeded in hiding him, so that he was not
found by the searchers. After this, the venerable old man grew
still more nervous and, realizing how very infirm he had become
through old age, he approached the Archbishop-Primate of
Carthage[1] by a private letter in which he pleaded his bodily
weakness and the weight of his years and asked that Augustine
might be consecrated as a bishop of the Church at Hippo, not so
much to succeed him in the see as to serve with him as Coadjutor.
And what he hoped for, and had taken such trouble to get, was
formally granted.

Accordingly when, after this, Megalius, Bishop of Calama, the

[2] See note 3 to section V.
[3] I Cor. xii. 26.
[1] This was St. Aurelius, Archbishop of Carthage from 388 to 423. For his
life, his dealings with the Donatists and the Pelagians and his friendship with
St. Augustine, see Butler's *Lives of the Saints* (Thurston and Attwater) under
July 20th. The confirmation of the Primate was needed for the election of a
bishop in any city of Roman Africa (see note 3 to section V).

then Primate of Numidia,[2] came by invitation to visit the Church of Hippo, Bishop Valerius surprised the bishops who happened to be present, as well as all the clergy of Hippo and his whole flock, by intimating to them his intention. His audience was delighted and clamoured eagerly for the business to be put through then and there. But our priest refused to receive the episcopate contrary to the practice of the Church, while his bishop was still living.

All set to work to persuade him that the thing was constantly done and appealed to examples from Churches across the sea and in Africa, which he had not known about. Under this pressure and constraint he gave in and received consecration to the higher office. In later years he said, and wrote, that they ought not to have done this to him, namely consecrate him while his bishop was living, since it had been prohibited by a General Council, as he had discovered after his consecration.[3] As he did not want others to have done to them what he had been sorry to have done to himself, he made efforts to have it decreed by an episcopal synod that the Canons relating to priests should be brought to the knowledge of ordinands and already ordained priests by the ordaining bishops, and this was done.[4]

IX

As Bishop he preached the message of eternal salvation more insistently and fervently than ever and with greater authority, and no longer in one district only but in others where he went by invitation ; and the Church of the Lord blossomed and expanded, briskly and busily.

---

[2] The office of primate in the various Provinces of the African Church was not attached to any particular see but went by seniority. Thus Possidius, the author of this Life, soon after this succeeded Megalius in the see of Calama, but without the primacy.

[3] St. Augustine seems to have been mistaken in this. The Canon of the Council of Nicaea to which he was referring provided against two bishops occupying one see but did not forbid a bishop to obtain a coadjutor. There was nothing unlawful, therefore, in the consecration of St. Augustine (see Weiskotten *in loco*.). This was in A.D. 395. In 396 Valerius died and Augustine succeeded him as Bishop of Hippo.

[4] By the Third Council of Carthage, A.D. 397.

He was always " ready to give an account, to anyone who asked, of the faith and hope he had " in God ;[1] and Donatists in particular, if they lived in Hippo or one of the neighbouring towns, used to bring along to their bishops things they had heard him say. When the bishops had heard these, and perhaps made some sort of reply, either they were answered by their own followers or their replies were brought to the holy Augustine. He used to examine them patiently and gently (as Scripture says : " in fear and trembling " he " worked for men's salvation ") and showed how these bishops were neither willing nor able to attempt a proper refutation and how true and clear are the things we hold and learn in the faith of the Church of God.

He laboured at this task day and night continually. He even wrote personal letters to some of the bishops of that heresy—the more prominent, that is to say—and to laymen, trying to persuade them by reasoned argument that they ought either to alter their perverse opinions or else meet him in debate. But they had too little confidence in their own case even to answer his letters, but merely raged against him in their anger, denouncing him in private and in public as a seducer and deceiver of souls. They used to say, and argue at length, that he was a wolf to be killed in defence of their flock and that there could be no doubt whatever that God would forgive all the sins of those who could achieve this feat ; for they felt neither fear of God nor shame before men. Augustine for his part took pains that everyone should know of their lack of confidence in their own cause and they, when they met him on public bodies, dared not enter into a discussion with him.

X

These same Donatists had in almost all their congregations men of an unheard-of kind, perverted and violent, who made a profession of celibacy and were called Circumcellions.[1] They were

---

[1] I Pet. iii. 15.

[1] St. Augustine (*Contra Gaudentium* I, xxviii, end) derives this name from *circum*, "around", and *cella*, a " cell " or " hut ", because they went round the huts of the country-folk to get food. Their own name for themselves was *Milites Christi Agonistici*.

very numerous, and there were organized bands of them all over Africa. Evil teachers had inspired them with an insolent audacity and a reckless lawlessness. They spared neither their own people nor strangers and interfered with justice in defiance of all law and right. If they were not obeyed, they inflicted fearful loss and injuries, for, armed with various weapons, they ran raving over the farm-lands and estates, restrained by no fears from going as far as bloodshed. And though the Word of God was unremittingly preached and " with those who hated peace, peacemaking was attempted, against him who spoke of it they made war without a reason."[2]

Nevertheless, when the truth began to make headway against their teaching, there were some who were glad to break away from them as opportunity arose, either openly or by stealth, and to enter the peace and unity of the Church with as many as they could bring with them. Seeing their heretical congregations growing smaller as a result, and envious of the growth of the Church, they became more angry and inflamed than ever and banded themselves together in an intolerable persecution of the undivided Church. They made daily and nightly attacks even upon Catholic priests and clerics, plundering them of all their goods. Many servants of God they beat till they crippled them. They even threw lime mixed with vinegar into people's eyes, and others they killed outright. In the end, these re-baptizers came to be hated even by their fellow Donatists.

XI

As divine truth made headway, those who had been serving God in the monastery with the holy Augustine, and under his rule, began to be ordained as clergy for the Church at Hippo.[1] The result was to make better known and more evident every day the truths preached by the Catholic Church, the way of life of the

---

[2] Ps. cxix. 7 (cxx. 6, 7).

[1] Augustine, after his consecration as Bishop, had had to leave " the monastery in the garden " and take up his residence with the cathedral clergy, but had continued to keep in close touch with it. According to Foran (p. 56), it was from this drawing of priests from the monastery that the introduction of a religious rule of life into the cathedral clergy-house began.

holy servants of God, their chastity and their utter poverty. Then, in the Church of peace and unity, there grew up a strong desire for bishops and clergy from the monastery founded by, and flourishing under, this remarkable man. They began to be asked for, and presently what was asked was obtained.

For no less than ten men,[2] known to us as holy and venerable, chaste and learned, were supplied by the most blessed Augustine to various Churches, including some of the most important, in response to requests. These in their turn, having come from the religious life, founded fresh monasteries as the Churches of the Lord multiplied ; and then, as zeal for the spread of God's Word went on growing, they supplied brethren to yet other Churches for promotion to the priesthood.

Thus through many agents and to many hearers, the saving faith, hope and charity taught by the Church became known, not only through every part of Africa, but also across the seas, especially through his books that were published and translated into Greek ; and it was from this one man, and to the many through him, that all this knowledge flowed. And, as Scripture says : " The sinner saw it and was furious ; he gnashed his teeth and pined away."[3] But, as it says again, Thy servants " with those who hated peace played the peacemaker ; and against them, when they spoke of it, they made war without a reason."[4]

XII

Now, the Circumcellions we have been speaking of lay in wait by the road with weapons several times for God's servant Augustine, when he happened to have been asked to go and pay a visit, or to instruct or preach to Catholic congregations, as he very often was. On one occasion they failed to capture him although they had come out in full force ; for, as it turned out, by the Providence of God acting through a mistake of the guide, the Bishop and his companions reached their destination by the wrong road and, as he learnt afterwards, by this mistake had just

---

[2] Including Possidius himself.
[3] Ps. cxi (cxii). 10.
[4] Ps. cxix. 7 (cxx. 6, 7).

missed falling into the hands of the wicked, for which they all gave thanks to the God who delivers us. For it was certainly not the way of the Circumcellions to spare either laity or clergy, as the public records bear witness.

In this connection it is impossible to pass over in silence certain measures taken and carried through, to the glory of God, against these re-baptizing Donatists through the energy of this outstanding churchman and his " zeal for the House of God ".

On this occasion one of the bishops he had provided for the Church from the clergy of his monastery[5] was making a round of the diocese of Calama, of which he had charge, and for the peace of the Church was preaching against this heresy what he had learnt from Augustine. In the course of his journey he fell into one of their ambushes. He and all his companions got away but their beasts and their baggage were taken and he himself was most seriously injured.

This time, to remove a real hindrance to the Church's peace and progress, the Church's representative[6] appealed to the law ; and Crispinus, who was Bishop of the Donatists in the city and district of Calama and for a long time had a reputation for learning, was pronounced liable to a fine of gold under the state's laws against heretics.[7] He appealed against this and, when he appeared before the proconsul, denied that he was a heretic.

The Church's representative[8] had by this time withdrawn from the case but this plea made it absolutely necessary for Crispinus to be opposed by the Catholic bishop and convicted of being what he denied he was. For if his pretence had been allowed to stand, the Catholic bishop might have been taken by the simple to be a heretic, since the heretic denied that he was one, so that letting the case go by default would have created a hindrance to the faith of the weak.

[5] The author himself. The year was 403. The subsequent conviction of Crispinus as a heretic took place in 404.
[6] Latin, " Defensor Ecclesiae ", a phrase repeated a few lines further on. The sequel seems to show that St. Possidius is still speaking of himself, but the passage is full of obscurities.
[7] Those of Theodosius I, Emperor in the East from 379 ; sole Emperor 387–395. See the Introduction, section I.
[8] See note 2 above.

Indeed, that unforgettable prelate Augustine firmly insisted on this course, so both Bishops of Calama came into the case—the third clash that had occurred between them in connection with their religious differences.[9] Vast numbers of Christians, not only in Carthage[10] but all over Africa, awaited the result of the trial, which was that Crispinus was pronounced a heretic by a written judgement of the proconsul.

The Catholic bishop, however, interceded on his behalf with the judge, to remit the fine of gold ; and this favour was granted. But the ungrateful man appealed to the most gracious sovereign[11] and his statement of his case duly brought from the Emperor a general ruling, in conformity with which an injunction was issued to the effect that the Donatist heretics were not to be tolerated in any place and that all the laws passed against heretics were to be enforced against them everywhere. It also ordered the judges and officers of the court and Crispinus himself, since he had not been fined before, to pay ten pounds weight of gold apiece to the credit of the imperial treasury.

However, speedy steps were taken by the Catholic bishops, and particularly by Augustine of holy memory, to get this sentence on all of them remitted by a pardon from the sovereign and this, by the Lord's help, was achieved. And all this vigilance and holy zeal contributed greatly to the growth of the Church.

XIII

For all this work in the cause of peace in the Church, Our Lord rewarded Augustine with triumphs here on earth and kept a crown for his well-doing in readiness for him in heaven. More and more every day, unity in peace—the true brotherhood of the

---

[9] Weiskotten suggests that " the first is apparently the assault of the followers of Crispinus on Possidius, the second the public notice to Crispinus that he was subject to the fine imposed upon heretics and the third the debate [sic] here mentioned." But this is not altogether satisfactory and there may well have been earlier clashes more naturally described by Possidius' words. For example, Weiskotten himself records in his Introduction (pp. 12, 13) that Possidius had just made two abortive attempts to bring Crispinus to a public debate.

[10] The capital, where the Court of Appeal would sit.

[11] The Emperor Honorius, who reigned in the West from 395 to 423. The edict here recorded was issued in February, 405.

Church of God—"grew and spread widely".[1] This was particularly the case after the Conference which was held at Carthage some time later between all the Catholic bishops and the bishops of the Donatists by the orders of the most glorious and gracious Emperor Honorius, who had sent Marcellinus, one of the secretaries to the Privy Council, to Africa as his personal representative to act as judge and see the thing through.[2]

In the debates on this occasion the Donatists were completely out-argued.[3] They were convicted of heresy by the Catholics and formally censured by the arbitrator. They appealed against this, and these evil men were then condemned as heretics by the decision of the most gracious sovereign himself. The effect of this was to make it a more common event than before for their bishops, as well as their clergy and laity, to enter the Catholic communion; and these men, being now at peace with the Church, endured much persecution from the Donatists, even to the loss of life and limb. And all this good work was, as I said, begun and carried through by this holy man, with our fellow-bishops glad to play their part.

XIV

However, after this Conference with the Donatists there were some to be found who said that their bishops had not been allowed to put their case fully before the magistrate who presided, since the arbitrator belonged to the Catholic communion and favoured his Church. As a matter of fact they only put forward this excuse after they had failed and been defeated, for these heretics had known before the discussions began that he belonged to the Catholic communion, yet, when they had been summoned by him to the public proceedings for the trial of strength, they

[1] Acts xii. 24.

[2] A.D. 411. The edict of 405 had not been consistently applied, the sect of the Donatists had survived and in 410 an edict of toleration had been published; see Hughes, *A History of the Church*, vol. II, p. 13.

[3] Almost entirely by Augustine, though seven bishops, of whom Possidius was one, were chosen to carry on the discussion on the Catholic side. In all there were 286 Catholic bishops present. The Donatist bishops numbered 279, so that there were "two bishops for almost every see in the country" (Hughes).

had agreed to it. After all, if they had mistrusted him, they could have declined the encounter.

However, the providence of Almighty God brought it about that some time afterwards[1] Augustine of revered memory was staying in the city of Caesarea in Mauretania.[2] A letter from the Apostolic See had obliged him and some of his fellow-bishops [3] to go there to settle some other difficulties of the Church. In this way he met Emeritus, the Donatist bishop of the place, who was looked on as having been the chief defender of their sect at the Conference. He reasoned with him publicly in the church on this very point with people of both communions present, and challenged him to a trial of the issues, to be conducted in the church, so that, if (as they said) there was something that Emeritus could have put forward at the Conference but had not been allowed to, he need have no anxiety about saying it there and then, with no magistrate present to prohibit or obstruct, and he should not refuse to defend his own communion boldly in his own city with all his fellow-citizens present.

In spite of this appeal and the pressing requests of his relations and townsfolk, he was unwilling to do this, though they promised him that they would return to his communion, even at the risk of losing their property and their temporal prosperity, if he refuted the Catholic arguments. He was neither willing nor able to add anything to the former proceedings except to say : " The records of the Episcopal Conference at Carthage are enough to show whether we won or lost." And when from another direction came a warning from a reporter that he had better make some reply, he said " Do what you like ! " [4] His

---

[1] A.D. 418. The scene described here took place on 20th September, as the shorthand report notes.

[2] Mauretania—Morocco, but the Province of which Julia Caesarea was the capital corresponded roughly to the modern Spanish Zone and part of Algeria.

[3] Including the author.

[4] This rendering is based on a conjectural emendation of the Latin text, in which there is almost certainly an original copyist's error here, for " ait " (" said ") with nothing following is impossible. Weiskotten is doubtless right in rejecting such editorial smoothings as the insertion of " nihil " (" nothing ") or the conversion of " ait " into " tacuit " (" was silent ") ; but the shorthand report of the dialogue, which Possidius evidently had in front of him when he wrote and to which he refers a few lines further on, seems a safe source from which to supply the missing word, namely " Fac " (" do it "). By combining the two accounts we then get a vivid picture of Emeritus sitting sullenly silent

subsequent silence and the publicity given to his doings through his lack of confidence in his own position caused the growth of the Church, and the strength of its case, to stand out plainly.

But anyone who would like to know more of the care and industry that Augustine of blessed memory devoted to upholding the dignity of the Church of God should read those proceedings.[5] He will discover there the nature of the arguments he brought forward in challenging and appealing to that learned, eloquent and illustrious man to say whatever he wished in defence of his faction and he will see Emeritus vanquished.

XV

Here is an incident, known not only to me personally but also to other brethren and fellow-servants of God who at that time were living with us in the Church at Hippo with this holy man. He said to us as we were seated at table :

" Did you notice in my sermon in church today that the beginning and ending went differently to my usual method? Because I did not continue my explanation of the subject to the end, but left it in the air."

" Yes," we replied, " we know, and we remember that we wondered at it at the time."

" I should not be surprised ", he said, " if the Lord was wanting some wanderer from the flock to be taught and cured through my own forgetfulness and wandering. We are all in His hands, and our sermons too. It was when I was dealing with something on the border-line of my subject that I went off from my sermon to something else. That is why I never brought my

under Augustine's exhortations and pleadings from the pulpit and making only the shortest and most evasive replies, and then hearing a reporter near him threaten him with the power of publicity and angrily snapping out a mono-syllabic defiance—in effect : " All right, publish." The words that follow, with their strange Latinity (but the text is, again, almost certainly corrupt), can then be interpreted so as to fall into place.

The report in question is entitled *De Gestis cum Emerito* and is printed among St. Augustine's works in Migne, P. L., vol. 43, columns 698–706. It may be added that in two or three other cases in this passage where Possidius' language is ambiguous, I have allowed the choice of renderings to be settled by this report.

[5] i.e. in the *De Gestis cum Emerito* referred to in the preceding footnote.

explanation of the question to a proper conclusion but ended
with an argument against the errors of the Manicheeans, which
I had had no intention of discussing, instead of with what I had
planned to say."

It was after this and, if I am not mistaken, within the next
day or two, that there came, if you please, a certain business man
named Firmus. The holy Augustine was in the monastery,
sitting with us round him, and the man flung himself down on
his knees at his feet and, with tears falling, asked the Bishop to
intercede, together with the saints, with the Lord for his sins.
He confessed that he had been a follower of the Manicheean
sect and had lived in it for many years, which meant that he had
spent a great deal of money on the Manicheeans and their so-
called " Elect " [1] which was all wasted. He had just lately, by
the mercy of God, been shown his errors by Augustine's
arguments in church and been made a Catholic.

Our revered Augustine and those of us who were present carefully enquired of him what exactly in the sermon had especially
satisfied his mind. He told us, and it brought back to all of us
the whole course of the sermon. We contemplated with wonder
and stupefaction the depth of God's plans for the salvation of
souls ; and we glorified and blessed the holy Name of Him who
brings about the salvation of souls just at the time He wishes, just
from the direction He wishes, and just by the method He wishes,
through those who know what they are doing and through those
who know it not. [2]

From that day the man followed the way of life of the servants
of God. He gave up his business and made such progress as a
member of the Church that, in another land, by the will of God
he was summoned and even constrained to enter the priesthood.
He continued faithfully in the religious life and, for all I know, is
still alive and active among men across the seas.

[1] See note 9 to section I of the Life of St. Augustine.
[2] The Latin reads like an echo of Augustine's own words.

XVI

To go back to Carthage, a certain Controller of the Imperial Household named Ursus, a Catholic by faith, had a visit of inspection paid to a gathering of Manicheeans of the kind they call the Elect, both men and women. They were removed by him to the church, where they were examined by the bishops, a record being taken of the proceedings. Among the bishops was Augustine of holy memory, who knew the abominable sect better than the rest and could produce their damnable blasphemies from passages in books which they acknowledge. By this means he brought them to confess these blasphemies; and the shameful and foul rites which they practise to their utter undoing were brought to light in the ecclesiastical proceedings through the disclosures of these women—Elect forsooth!

Thus, through the vigilance of its shepherds, the Lord's flock grew in numbers and an adequate defence was maintained against the " thieves and robbers ".

Augustine held a public debate also with a man named Felix, another of those the Manicheeans call the Elect. This was in the church at Hippo, with the people present and reporters taking it down.[1] After the second or third session, when the unrealities and fallacies of the sect had been laid bare, the Manicheean was converted to the faith of our Church, as the records in question will show if consulted.[2]

XVII

There was also an officer of the Imperial Household named Pascentius, who was an Arian.[1] He was a ruthless collector of the imperial taxes and used his position to wage cruel and continuous war upon the Catholic faith. Both by his sarcasms and his official powers, he used to harass and distress great numbers of God's priests who were living lives of faith in all simplicity. Through

---

[1] 7th and 12th December, 404. Here, as frequently, there is little attempt to preserve the order of time.

[2] *De Actis cum Felice Manichaeo* (Migne, P. L., xlii, 519).

[1] See the Life of St. Martin, section VI, and footnote 2 there.

certain men of noble rank who acted as intermediaries, Augustine had been challenged by him, and met him publicly at Carthage.

But this heretic absolutely refused to have notebook or pen in the place, though our master expressed the strongest desire for it both before and at the encounter. And he persisted in his refusal, on the ground that he did not want to run the risk of written records for fear of the state's laws, and appealed to the intermediaries. Eventually Bishop Augustine agreed to hold the discussion, as his colleagues who were present thought that there had better be a private debate without reporters. But he prophesied what did afterwards come about, that, once the conference had dispersed, anyone would be free to say, in the absence of written proof, that he had said what perhaps he did not say, or had not said what he did say.

He then plunged into the argument. He stated his own beliefs, heard from his opponent what *he* held, and then brought forward solid arguments and the authority of Scripture to teach and demonstrate the foundations of our faith. He also explained how the assertions of his opponent were unsupported either by the truth of reason or by the authority of Holy Scripture and thereby showed their worthlessness. Then, when the two parties had gone their separate ways, the Arian's anger worked itself up into a frenzy and he began hurling about numbers of lies in support of his false faith and proclaimed that Augustine, the much-praised Augustine, had really been vanquished by him.

All this was bound to become public and Augustine was compelled to write to Pascentius himself. In deference to the latter's fears he omitted the names of those present at the conference but in this letter he set out faithfully all that had passed between the two parties. If his assertions were denied he had, in readiness to prove them, plenty of witnesses, namely the illustrious men of rank who had been present. But Pascentius, in reply to the two letters addressed to him, wrote one, and what was hardly a reply at all. In it he contrived to offer insults rather than to present the case for his sect, as anyone can verify who is willing and able to read it.[2]

[2] The correspondence, consisting of four letters (Augustine wrote a third letter, a reply to the letter of Pascentius) comprises those numbered 238 to 241 in the *Epistolae*.

Augustine also held a debate with a bishop of these same
Arians. This was Maximin, who had come to Africa with the
Goths.[3] It was held at Hippo, at the wish and request, and
through the mediation, of a number of distinguished men ; and
what was said on either side was taken down.[4] Anyone who is
sufficiently interested to read the report carefully will undoubtedly
get a good idea of what this plausible but illogical heresy puts
forward to ensnare and deceive, and also of what the Catholic
Church holds and teaches about the divine Trinity.

But when this heretic got back to Carthage from Hippo he
boasted that, thanks to his interminable flow of speech in the
debate, he had come away from it victorious. He was lying but,
of course, he could not easily be cross-examined and exposed by
people ignorant of theology. Our revered Augustine, therefore,
subsequently put into writing a summary of all the points made
and answers given in the course of the debate. Moreover, how
completely unable Maximin had been to answer objections was
shown in a supplementary section containing matter that it had
been impossible to introduce and have taken down in the short
time available at the conference. For the malice of the man had
contrived that all that remained of the day had been taken up with
his last and by far his longest speech.

XVIII

The most recent heresy of our times is that of the Pelagians,[1]
plausible debaters, still more subtle and pernicious writers, and

[3] Maximin had become the Arian Bishop of Hippo and the debate was held
in 427 or 428.

[4] In the *Collatio cum Maximino* (Migne, P. L., xiii, 709–742).

[1] So named after the originator of the heresy, Pelagius, of whom little is
known for certain save that he came to Rome from Britain around the year 380.
Its essence lay in an unbounded confidence in the capacity of human nature,
unaided by supernatural grace, to live virtuously and attain perfection. Man's
loss of supernatural grace through the Fall and his rebirth to the supernatural
life in baptism were alike denied ; and Christ's life, death and present glory
were held to be no more than an example to us. Human free-will was made
all-sufficient ; and humility ceased to have a place in the spiritual life. Pelagianism, like Arianism, proved itself fertile in subtle compromises and ambiguities, which made the refutation, and even the detection, of its errors at times
exceedingly difficult. Definite condemnation of Pelagianism both by the Pope
of the day and by a Council at Antioch came in 418.

untiring talkers in public and in the homes of the people. Against these, Augustine laboured for nearly ten years,[2] writing and publishing many books and frequently holding debates in the church with people holding those errors. When these perverted minds tried by flattery to force their false faith upon the Apostolic See, the most urgent measures were taken by Councils of the holy bishops of Africa, to impress upon the holy Pope of Rome, first on the Venerable Innocent,[3] then on his successor, the holy Zosimus,[4] how strongly this sect should be reprobated and condemned by the Catholic faith. And the bishops of that great See did, at various times, censure them and cut them off from the body of the Church and sent letters to the African Churches of the West and to the Churches of the East decreeing that they should be anathematized, and shunned by all Catholics.

Moreover, the most gracious Emperor Honorius, when he heard of this judgement passed on them by the Catholic Church of God, followed its lead. He condemned them by his own laws and decreed that they should be treated as heretics. As a result, some of them returned to the bosom of Holy Mother Church, out of which they had flung themselves ; and others are still returning, as the truth of the orthodox faith stands out ever more clearly and victoriously against their abominable errors.[5]

But indeed, this unforgettable man, this outstanding member of the Lord's Body, was unceasingly solicitous and vigilant in all that concerned the welfare of the Church universal. And God granted him the joy of seeing even in this life the fruit of his labours, first in the establishment of unity and peace in the diocese of Hippo, his own particular charge, then in other parts of Africa. There he could see the Church of the Lord budding and extending, either through his own action or through that of others (including priests he had himself provided), and rejoice over Manicheeans, Donatists, Pelagians and pagans losing much of their strength as numbers of them returned to the Church of God.

[2] The years 412–421. Four other anti-Pelagian treatises appeared from 426–429.
[3] St. Innocent I, Pope from 402–407.
[4] Pope from March 417 to December 418.
[5] The final condemnation of Pelagianism by the General Council of Ephesus took place in A.D. 431, when St. Possidius was probably setting to work on the composition of this biography.

He loved to see enterprise and zeal, and delighted in all that was good. He had a kind and holy patience with the irregularities of the brethren and sighed over the wickedness of evil men, both those within the Church and those outside it, for, as I said, the Lord's gains always brought him joy and His losses grief.

As for all that he dictated and published, and all the debates in the cathedral that were taken down and revised, some were against heretics of various kinds, others were expositions of the canonical books for the instruction of holy sons of the Church, but there are so many that there is hardly a student who has been able to read and get acquainted with them all. However, not to be thought in any way to fail those who are particularly eager for the words of truth, I have decided, if God furthers it, to append to this little work of mine a catalogue of these books, pamphlets and letters. Anyone who reads it, and who cares more for God's truth than for earthly riches, will be able to pick out for himself the book he wants to read. If he wants to make himself a copy of it, he should apply to the Church at Hippo, where the best texts can generally be found. Or he may make enquiries anywhere else he can and should make a copy of what he finds and preserve it and not grudge lending it in his turn to someone else asking to copy it.

XIX

In another matter also he followed the teaching of the Apostle :[1] " Do any of you dare, when you have a quarrel with another of you, to go to law in a court of the unregenerate instead of bringing it before consecrated men ? Or do you not know that it is for the consecrated to sit in judgment on the world ? And if you are to be judges of the world, are you unfit to judge in trifles ? Do you not know that we shall judge angels ? How much more, then, in everyday matters ! If it is an everyday matter that has come up for arbitration among you, take the most insignificant people in the Church and set *them* to preside. I am saying this to make you ashamed of yourselves. Is there really no one among you wise enough to settle the case of one of

[1] I Cor. vi, 1–6.

his own brethren? Must one brother go to law with another, and do so before a court of unbelievers? "

When, therefore, he was appealed to by Christians or men of any sect,[2] he used to listen carefully and conscientiously, keeping in mind the maxim of someone who said that he would rather hear cases between strangers than between friends, because he could gain one of the strangers as a friend when he gave a just decision in his favour but would lose one of his friends when the judgement had gone against him.

And he would always go into these cases until he had settled them, even though it meant fasting till dinner-time or sometimes all day long. He studied in them the movements of Christian souls, and how one would be advancing in faith and morals and another falling back. When the business in hand provided an opportunity, he would teach the parties to the actions truths about the Law of God and impress these upon them, and remind them how to obtain eternal life. The only payment he asked of them for giving up his time to them was the Christian obedience and devotion they owed to God and men. Sinners he would " rebuke in public, for the others to learn to fear." [3]

He did all this as one appointed by the Lord as " a watchman for the house of Israel." [4] He " preached the message, insistent in season and out of season, convincing, exhorting, rebuking, always patiently teaching." [5] He took special pains to train those " who might be suitable for teaching others." [6] He used also, in response to requests, to write letters to various people about their temporal affairs. But this he regarded as forced labour that took him away from better things. What he really enjoyed was addressing or conversing with the brethren about the things of God in the intimacy of the home circle.

[2] During the lifetime of St. Augustine, the Christian bishops in a constantly increasing degree exercised judicial functions over their flock (and often outside it) in both civil and criminal cases ; see the Introduction, section I.

[3] I Timothy, v. 20.

[4] Ezech. iii. 17.

[5] 2 Timothy, iv. 2.

[6] 2 Timothy, ii. 2.

XX

We know, also, how he refused requests to write letters petitioning the civil authorities even on behalf of his dearest friends. He used to say that one should go by the wisdom of a certain sage of whom it is recorded that he had too much regard for his own reputation to vouch for his friends. But he used to add a reason of his own, which was that an official of whom you ask favours generally becomes overbearing.

Nevertheless, when he saw that the intervention for which he was asked was really required, he conducted it with such dignity and reasonableness that, so far from being regarded as giving trouble or annoyance, he actually aroused admiration. Thus, he interceded once in his usual way in a case of necessity, on behalf of a petitioner, in a letter to a Deputy Praetorian Prefect of Africa [1] named Macedonius. The latter, in acceding to the request, wrote in this strain :

" I am amazingly impressed by the wisdom I find, first in the books you have published, and now in this letter you have not thought it too much trouble to send me, interceding for people in trouble. The books show a penetration, a learning and a piety to which nothing can be added ; and the letter is written with such delicate restraint that, if I did not do what you tell me, I should have to put the blame on myself and not on the case. For you, my lord—' venerable ' indeed—and most esteemed father in God, do not, like most men in your position, insist on extracting everything the petitioner wants, but confine yourself to what you think can rightly be asked of a judge with so many responsibilities, and recommend it with that accommodating tact that is the best way of settling difficulties amongst men of good will. For this reason I have given immediate effect to your recommendations, as, indeed, I had given you reason to expect."

[1] Latin, " Africae Vicarius ", *Africa* being here the civil Diocese and *Vicarius* (or " Deputy ") the title of its governor. See note 3 to section V.

XXI

Whenever he could, he attended the Councils of the holy bishops held in the various Provinces, not " seeking his own interests " but " those of Jesus Christ," [1] as, for example, in preserving inviolate the faith of the holy Catholic Church, or in absolving or casting out priests and clerics rightly or wrongly excommunicated. When it came to ordaining priests and clerics, he thought it best to follow the common opinion of our Christian ancestors and the custom of the Church.

XXII

His clothes and food, and bedclothes also, were simple and adequate, neither ostentatious nor particularly poor. For it is in these matters, more than in most, that men are apt either to show off or to demean themselves, in either case " seeking their own interests, not Jesus Christ's." So he, as I said, held a middle course, " turning aside neither to the right hand nor to the left." [1] His diet was frugal and economical. With the herbs and pulse he sometimes had meat for the sake of his guests or the delicate brethren, and always wine, for he recognized and taught that, as the Apostle says, " everything created by God is good and nothing need be rejected that can be taken with thanksgiving, for it is hallowed when we ask for God's blessing." [2] As Augustine himself put it in his *Confessions* : [3] " It is defilement from greed, not defilement from food, that I fear. I know that Noe had permission to eat any kind of flesh fit for food, that Elias was refreshed by flesh-food, and that John, who was capable of marvellous austerity, was not defiled by the animals (the locusts, that is) which fell to his lot for food. I know that Esau, on the other hand, *was* ensnared by a craving for lentils, that David found fault with himself for wanting water, and that, when our King was tested, it was not with meat but with bread. Similarly, when the people earned a rebuke in the wilderness, it

[1] Phil. ii. 21.   [1] Prov. iv. 27.   [2] I Tim. iv. 4, 5.   [3] xxxi. 46.

was not because they desired meat but because, in their desire for meat, they muttered against God."

As regards taking wine, there is the dictum of the Apostle writing to Timothy, and saying : " Do not go on drinking water but take a little wine for your stomach's sake, and your constant ill-health." [4]

Only his spoons were of silver ; the dishes in which the food was served were either earthenware or wood or marble, not under the compulsion of poverty, but from choice. And he was always hospitable. Moreover, what he loved at table was not feasting and drinking but reading and discussion ; as a preventative against a common pest of human intercourse he had these words inscribed on it :

Let him who takes pleasure in mauling the lives of the absent
Know his own is not such as to fit him to sit at this table.

By this he warned all the company to refrain from wanton and damaging anecdotes. And once, when some most intimate friends among his fellow-bishops forgot the inscription and broke the rule, he was so upset that he rebuked them really sharply, saying that either those lines must be erased from the table or he would get up from the middle of the meal and go to his own room. I myself and others who were with him at table were witnesses of this.

XXIII

He never forgot his companions in poverty ; and what he spent on them came from the same fund as supported him and those who lived with him,[1] namely the income from the Church's property and the offerings of the faithful. When, as often happened, this property roused the envy of the clergy, he would address his flock and tell them that he would rather live on the contributions of the people of God than be burdened with the care and administration of this property and that he was quite

[4] I Tim. v. 23.
[1] At this time, the parochial clergy ; see note I to Chapter XI.

ready to hand it over to them and let all God's servants and
ministers live in the way we read of in the Old Testament,[2] that
those who serve the altar share in its offerings. But the laity
were never willing to undertake it.

XXIV

He used to delegate the care of the Church house and all the
property to the more capable clergy, entrusting it to them in
turn. He never kept the keys or wore the signet-ring, and all the
accounts were kept by these household stewards. At the end of
the year they were read to him so that he could know the amount
received and spent and the balance in hand. Many documents
he took on trust from the steward instead of checking and
inspecting them for himself.

He was never willing to buy a house or land or an estate. If,
however, anything of that sort happened to be given to the
Church by someone of his own accord, or came as a legacy, he
would not refuse it and gave orders for it to be accepted. But I
have known him refuse to be the heir to inheritances, not because
they could not be used for the poor, but because it seemed only
right and fair that they should go to the children or relatives or
connections of the deceased, even though the latter had not
wanted to leave them to them.[1]

Once one of the leading citizens of Hippo, who was living at
Carthage, wished to present his estate to the Church at Hippo.
Retaining the income from it for himself, he sent, quite
spontaneously, the title-deeds duly executed to this same
Augustine of holy memory. The latter gladly accepted his
offering and congratulated him on thinking of his eternal
salvation. But some years later, when I happened to be staying
with him, what should the donor do but send his son with a

[2] Deut. xviii. 1 sqq.; cf. 1 Cor. ix. 13.
[1] Two Latin legal terms, " legatum " (legacy) and " hereditas " (inheritance),
are involved in this passage. St. Augustine did not mind receiving, as legatee,
money or properties separated from an inheritance by specific bequest but he
was careful about succeeding to an inheritance as the result of being designated
as heir, perhaps in place of the natural heirs. The same distinction is involved
three paragraphs further on.

letter requesting that the title-deeds should be handed over to the son and giving directions for distributing one hundred gold pieces to the poor.

When the holy man was told of this he was deeply grieved, for either the original donation had been a sham or the man had regretted his good deed. In his distress of mind at this perversity, he gave utterance as far as he could to what God put into his heart to say, by way of censuring and reproving him. Moreover, he immediately returned the deeds (which the man had sent of his own accord, unasked and under no necessity) and at the same time refused to touch the money. He wrote a letter, too, in which he reprimanded and reproached him, as was only right. He warned him that he had better atone to God by doing humble penance for what was either double-dealing or a wanton injury, so as not to depart from this life with so heavy a burden of sin.

He used also quite often to say that the Church could accept legacies much more confidently and safely than she could succeed to inheritances,[2] that might bring anxiety and loss. Furthermore, the legacies themselves should be offered, not extracted. Nor would he himself accept property to be held in trust, though he would not stop his clergy doing so if they wished.

But in none of these holdings or possessions of the Church did he allow his affections to become fixed or entangled ; all that happened was that, with the whole bent of his mind upon higher and spiritual things, he did occasionally relax from the contemplation of things eternal to turn to these temporal affairs ; then, once they had been settled and put in order, his mind drew back from them as if from a sting or an irritant and reverted to interior and higher thoughts, either to discover new truths of theology or to dictate what he had discovered or perhaps to revise what had previously been dictated and transcribed.

He got through it all by living laborious days and working far into the night. He was a type of the Church in heaven, like that ever glorious Mary of whom it is written that she sat at the feet of the Lord listening intently to His words ; and, when her sister complained of her that she got no help from her when she was

---

[2] See preceding footnote.

overwhelmed by all the household work, she heard Him say : "Martha! Martha! Mary has chosen the better part and it shall not be taken away from her." [3]

He never had the passion for erecting new buildings, not wishing to have his mind taken up with them. He liked to have it always free from all mundane anxieties. Nevertheless he did not stop those who wished to build from doing so, unless they did it to excess.

Occasionally, when the funds of the Church gave out, he would announce this to his flock, telling them he had nothing to bestow upon the needy. He would even order some of the sacred vessels to be broken up and melted down, for the benefit of captives and of as many of the poor as possible, and to be distributed to them. I would not have mentioned this if I had not seen that it was done against the all too human judgement of some. I may add that Ambrose of revered memory said and wrote that it was unquestionably a thing that ought to be done in such extremities. So, too, if the faithful had been neglecting the collections for the sacristy (for supplying the needs of the altar), he would sometimes speak warningly in church about it, and he once told us how he had been present in the church when the most blessed Ambrose had dealt with the same subject.

XXV

The clergy and he were all fed and clothed in the same house, at the same table and from a common purse.

In view of the danger of slipping from thoughtless swearing into perjury, he used to tell the people in his sermons in church, and made it a rule for his own household, that no one should swear, and certainly not at table. If anyone offended against this, he lost one drink from his allowance (for there was a fixed number of cups allowed to each person living and dining with him). So, too, with irregularities among his household and offences against rules or good manners, whether he rebuked them or overlooked them, it was to the extent that was fitting and right. He was

[3] Luke x. 41–2.

particularly insistent, in such matters, that no one should " lower himself to petty lies in making excuses for his sins."[1]

Again, if anyone was " making his offering at the altar and there remembered that his brother had ground of complaint against him, the offering was to be left at the altar and he was to go and be reconciled to his brother and then come and make the offering at the altar."[2] But if he had ground of complaint against his brother, he ought to " take him to task in private and, if he listens to him, he has won his brother. But, if he does not, he should take with him one or two others. If he disregards them also, the Church should be told ; and if he will not obey the Church he should be regarded as a heathen or an outcast."[3]

He used to add that a brother who sins and asks forgiveness for his offence should be pardoned " not seven times but seventy times seven,"[4] just as each of us asks the Lord for pardon for himself every day.

XXVI

No woman ever lived in his house, or stayed there, not even his own sister, who as a widow in the service of God lived for many years, to the very day of her death, as prioress of God's hand-maidens. It was the same with his brother's daughters, who were also enrolled in God's service, although the Councils of the holy bishops had allowed an exception to be made of them. He used to say that even though no suspicion of evil could arise from his sister or his nieces stopping with him, *they* would have to have other women attending on them and staying with them, and other women again would be coming to see them from outside, and all this might give scandal or prove a temptation to the weak. Thus, the men who happened to be staying with the Bishop or with one of the clergy, when all these women were stopping there together or coming and going, might fall victims to the common tempta-tions of mankind and would certainly suffer the grossest defama-tion by suspicious people.

For these reasons he used to say that the servants of God, how-ever chaste they might be, ought never to have women staying in

[1] Ps. cxl. (cxli). 4.   [2] Matt. v. 23, 24.   [3] Matt. xviii. 15–17.   [4] Matt. xviii. 22.

the same house with them, for fear (as I have said) of setting an example that might give scandal or prove a temptation to the weak. Even when women asked to interview him, or just to pay their respects, they might never come into his room unless there were clergy there as witnesses. He would never talk to them alone even if the matter were strictly private.

XXVII

In the matter of visiting, he held to the rule laid down by the Apostle, to visit only " widows and orphans in their affliction."[1] If he were specially asked by people who were ill to pray to the Lord for them in their presence and lay his hands on them, he would go at once. He would only visit convents of nuns if there were urgent need.

He used also to quote, as a rule to be observed in the life and conduct of every man of God, what he had learnt from the practice of Ambrose of holy memory : never ask a woman's hand for another man ; never give a recommendation to a man who wants to join the army or advise him to accept an invitation to a banquet in his home town. And he would give his reasons in each case. Thus, when a married couple quarrel, they are likely to curse the man who brought them together. (But of course, if the two parties have already agreed to marry and have asked the priest, he ought to be there, so that their compact and consent may be ratified and blessed.) As to military service, the man who has been recommended and then misconducted himself is likely to say that it is the fault of the man who recommended him. Finally, by constant attendance at banquets with fellow citizens, the habit of temperance is easily lost.

He once told us how he had heard of the very wise and very pious reply which the above-mentioned man of blessed memory made in the last moments of his life ; and he used often to praise and commend it. When that venerable man was on his death-bed, the leading members of the Church were standing round his bed. Seeing that he was on the point of passing from this world to

---

[1] Jas. i. 27, but there is no " only " there.

God, they were full of grief that the Church was being deprived of the teaching and the administration of the sacraments by so great and remarkable a prelate, and they tearfully asked him to petition God for an extension of his life.

" I have not lived in such a way," he said, " that I am ashamed to be living among you ; at the same time, I am not afraid to die, for we have a very good God."[2]

Our Augustine, when he was an old man himself, used to marvel at, and praise, the lapidary and balanced phrases of this reply. Ambrose (he said) must be understood to have added the words " I am not afraid to die, because we have a very good God" so that it should not be thought that it was from overconfidence in the immaculateness of his own character that he had said first " I have not lived in such a way that I am ashamed to be living among you." When he said that, he had been referring to what men could know of a fellow-man, but when it came to the scrutiny of Divine Justice, for any goodness he preferred to trust to God, to whom, indeed, he said in his daily prayer " Forgive us our sins ".

In the same connection he was constantly repeating towards the end of his life the words of a certain fellow-bishop and most intimate friend. He had been going frequently to visit him as his death drew near, and his friend by a gesture of the hand had indicated that he was on the point of leaving the world. Augustine had replied that his life was perhaps still necessary to the Church ; but he answered, so as not to be thought to be clinging to this life, " Yes, if I need never die ; but, if some day, why not now ? "

Augustine marvelled at the saying and used to praise the man who uttered it—a God-fearing man, certainly, but brought up on a country estate and without much education or reading. Contrast the attitude of another sick bishop, of whom the holy martyr Cyprian told this story in the letter he wrote on Mortality :[3]

" One of our colleagues in the episcopate, worn out by illness and disturbed by the approach of death, was praying for an extension of his life. As he prayed, and was almost on the point of death, there stood before him a youth of such awe-inspiring

[2] See the Life of St. Ambrose, section XLV.
[3] St. Cyprian of Carthage, who lived from about 210 to 258 and was martyred at Carthage. The story here quoted is from his *De Mortalitate*, ch. xix.

dignity and majesty, and so tall and radiant, that human vision and
mortal eyes could hardly have looked upon him as he stood there if
the one who looked had not been about to leave this world. With
a certain disgust in his expression and voice the youth sighed and
said : ' You are afraid to suffer ; you are unwilling to die. What
am I to do with you ? ' "

XXVIII

Shortly before his death he made a survey of the books he had
dictated and published, some in the early days of his conversion,
when he was still a layman, some as a priest and some, again, as
a bishop. Whenever he found anything in them that he had
dictated or written when he had had comparatively little knowledge and understanding of the Church's tradition and which
was not in accordance with the Church's mind, he censored and
corrected it himself.

In this way he wrote two volumes entitled *A Survey of my
Books*.[1] He used to complain, however, that some of his books
had been carried off by certain brethren before they had been
properly revised, though he had meant to revise them later.
Some of his books he was prevented by death from correcting.
But in his desire to be of service to all, whether they could read
lots of books or whether they could not, he made a selection
from both the Holy Testaments, Old and New, of precepts and
prohibitions constituting a rule of life. He prefixed a preface to
them and made one volume of them,[2] which anyone who wished
might read, and learn from it how obedient or disobedient he
was to God. He wanted this book to be called *The Mirror*.[3]

[1] Latin, *De Recensione Librorum*. It is the book known to us as *Retractationes*
(" Retractions ") and was published A.D. 427, three years before St. Augustine's
death.
[2] Latin, " codex ", consisting of sheets bound together in the shape of a
modern book and therefore reasonably rendered in modern English by
" volume ", though, in point of fact, " volume " is derived from " volumen ",
the roll, which was the alternative form for books in St. Augustine's day and
therefore precisely what the codex was not.   (" Volumen " is the term used a
few lines further back in connection with *A Survey of my Books*.)
[3] Presumably suggested by the use of the simile in Jas. i. 23–25. The treatise,
under its Latin title *Speculum*, is printed in Migne, vol. 40. The two treatises
with that title, and claiming St. Augustine's authorship, that are printed in
Migne, vol. 34, are spurious. A fourth *Speculum*, printed in vol. 12 of the
Vienna *Corpus Script. Eccl. Lat.*, is probably genuine.

It was not long after this,[4] however, that, by God's will and permission, there poured into Africa from across the sea in ships from Spain a huge host of savage enemies armed with every kind of weapon and trained in war. There were Vandals and Alans, mixed with one of the Gothic peoples, and individuals of various nations. They overran the country, spreading all over Mauretania and passing on to our other Provinces and territories. There was no limit to their savage atrocities and cruelties. Everything they could reach they laid waste, with their looting, murders, tortures of all kinds, burnings, and countless other unspeakable crimes. They spared neither sex nor age, nor the very priests and ministers of God, nor the ornaments and vessels of the churches, nor the buildings.

Our man of God did not view all this running riot and devastation by a ferocious enemy in the same light as other men. He brought to its origin and progress loftier and profounder considerations. He saw in it chiefly the danger and the death it brought to souls and, more than ever, " tears became his bread by day and night "[5] (" more than ever," because " he who adds to knowledge adds to trouble "[6] and " a heart that understands is like a worm in the bones ").

These days, therefore, that he lived through, or endured, almost at the very end of his life, were the bitterest and most mournful of all his old age. A man such as he had to see cities overthrown and destroyed and, with them, their citizens and inhabitants and the buildings on their estates wiped out by a murderous enemy, and others put to flight and scattered. He saw churches denuded of priests and ministers ; holy virgins and others vowed to chastity dispersed, some among them succumbing to tortures, others perishing by the sword, others taken captive and losing innocence of soul and body, and faith itself, in evil and cruel slavery to their foes.

He saw the hymns and divine praises ceasing in the Churches, the buildings themselves in many places burnt down, the solemn sacrifices owed to God no longer offered in the appointed places,

[4] A.D. 429.
[5] Ps. xli. 4 (xlii. 3).
[6] Eccles. i. 18. This is from a pre-Vulgate version of Prov. xxv. 20.

the holy sacraments no longer wanted, and, if they were wanted, ministers of them hard to find. He saw men taking refuge in forests on the mountains, in caves in the rocks, in dens, or in any strong places ; others forced out of them and their escape cut off; others, again, stripped and deprived of all means of subsistence and slowly perishing of hunger ; the very bishops and clergy of the Churches (if, by God's favour, they did not encounter the enemy or escaped from the encounter) robbed and denuded of everything and begging in the utmost need, when there was no possibility of supplying them with all that was necessary for their support.

Of the countless Churches, he saw only three survive, those of Carthage, Hippo and Cirta, which by God's favour were not uprooted ; and their cities still stand, buttressed by human and divine support. (After his death the city of Hippo was burnt to the ground by the enemy after being abandoned by its inhabitants.) And amidst these calamities he used to console himself with the maxim of a certain wise man who said : " No great man will think it a great matter when sticks and stones fall and mortals die."

Over all these events, then, in his own wise way, he daily and deeply mourned. Then, to his other griefs and sorrows, there was added the arrival of this same enemy to besiege Hippo-Regius itself, which had so far been left alone. Their reason was that a certain Count Boniface with an army of allied Goths had taken up his position there to defend it.[7] For nearly fourteen months their investment of the city was complete, for their lines even deprived it of its sea-coast.

I myself, and other bishops from neighbouring regions, had taken refuge there and were in the city during the whole of the siege. We had many talks together, therefore, saying, as we pondered the dread judgements of God that were being executed before our eyes : " Just art Thou, O Lord, and righteous are Thy judgements." [8] And as we sorrowed, sighed and wept

---

[7] Count Boniface, Governor of the Province, a devout Catholic and a friend of St. Augustine, had fallen back on Hippo after an unsuccessful battle against the Vandals.

[8] Ps. cxviii (cxix). 137.

together, we implored " the Father of mercies and the God from whom all consolation comes " [9] that He would see fit to support us in our present tribulation.

XXIX

One day, when we happened to be at table with him and talking about these matters, he said to us :

" You ought to know that, in these days of disaster for us, my prayer to God is that He will either consent to liberate this besieged city or, if He thinks otherwise, will give His servants strength to go through with what He wills for them or, so far as I am concerned, will take me from this world."

Then, using the words he gave us, we joined him in making the same petition to God on high for ourselves and for all our flocks and for those who were in the city with us. And what should happen but that in the third month of the siege he went to bed with a fever and entered upon his last illness. The Lord was not going to withhold from His servant the answer to his prayer. He obtained in due time what he had asked for through his tears both for himself and for his city.[1]

I know, too, that both as a priest and as a bishop, when asked to pray for sufferers from demon-possession, he has petitioned God with many tears and the demons have gone out. Again, when he was ill and in bed, someone came to him with a sick patient and asked him to lay his hand on him, so that he might recover. He replied that if he had any powers of that kind he would surely have used them on himself first. But the man insisted that he had had a vision and had been told in his dream : " Go to Bishop Augustine and get him to lay his hand on him and he will recover." Informed of this, Augustine acted on it without further delay and the Lord at once enabled the sick man to leave his presence healed.

[9] 2 Cor. i. 3.
[1] The siege of Hippo was raised in July, 431, not quite eleven months after St. Augustine's death on 28th August, 430.

XXX

I must certainly record, in connection with these events, how, when the enemy I have been speaking of were threatening us, Augustine was consulted by letter by that holy man, our colleague Honoratus, Bishop of Thiabe,[1] as to whether the bishops and clergy ought to leave their Churches when the enemy were approaching, or not. In his reply he brought out clearly what was most to be feared from these subverters of Romanity.[2] I want his letter to him included in this memoir as a very useful and much needed guide to conduct for God's priests and ministers.

> " *From Augustine, to his holy brother and colleague, Bishop Honoratus, greetings in the Lord.*

1. " I had thought that the copy sent to your Grace of the letter I wrote to our brother and colleague Quodvutldeus would have relieved me of the task you have laid upon me in asking my advice as to what you ought to do in these perilous circumstances in which we are living. For although I wrote only a short letter, I think that I omitted nothing that the writer of the reply needed to say or the questioner to hear. For I said that, while those who wished to withdraw, while they could, to fortified centres, should not be prevented, at the same time we have no right to throw off the fetters of our ministry, with which the love of Christ has bound us, and desert the Churches that we have the duty of serving. These, in fact, are the words I used in that letter : ' I say, then, in conclusion, that our ministrations are so necessary to even the

---

[1] A small town south of Hippo.

[2] Latin " Romania ", a new word that had recently come into colloquial use to denote the Roman world, with its characteristic civilisation and way of life, as distinct from the barbarian world that had lately been making such great inroads upon it, both physically and spiritually. This seems to be only the fourth surviving instance of the use of the word in the written language. It is of some interest to note that of the other three instances, two are from the works of Orosius, another disciple of Augustine, while the third and earliest is from an Arian pamphlet against St. Ambrose written about 383 (see de Labriolle in Fliche and Martin, *Histoire de l'Eglise*, IV, 355), which must have been circulating in Milan just when Augustine went there.

smallest of God's congregations that, when it is staying on in
the place we are in, it ought not to be left without them. It is
for us, therefore, to say to the Lord : Be to us a God who
protects, a city fortified.'[3]

2. " But you are not satisfied with this advice because (you
say in your letter) we would be resisting the teaching and
example of Our Lord, where He advises us to fly from city to
city. And, of course, we remember His words : When they
persecute you in one city, fly to another.[4]

" But who supposes that Our Lord meant by this that the
flocks that He bought with His own blood were to be left without the ministrations necessary to their very life ? Was He himself doing that when He fled to Egypt as an infant in His parents'
arms, before He had gathered any congregations He could be
said to be deserting ? Or when the Apostle Paul, to avoid capture by his enemy, was let down through a window in a sack,
' and so escaped his hands ',[5] was the Church there left without
the ministrations necessary to it ? Were not all that were needed
supplied by other brethren resident there ? Indeed, it was at
their wish that the Apostle was doing it, in order to preserve
for the Church the particular person that that persecutor was
trying to seize.

" Let the servants of Christ, then, the ministers of His
message and His Sacrament, do just what He has commanded
or permitted. By all means let them fly from city to city when
someone is specially wanted by the persecutors, so long as there
are others not so much wanted who are not deserting the
Church and can supply spiritual nourishment to their fellow-
servants, who they know could not live without it. But when
all—bishops, priests and laity alike—are in the same danger,
then those who need the others must not be abandoned by
those they need. Either let them all go off together to fortified
centres or, if some are obliged to remain, let them not be deserted by those through whom their spiritual needs have to be
met. Thus they will either survive together or suffer together,
whichever their heavenly Father wishes to be their lot.

[3] Ps. xxx. 3 (xxxi. 2).   [4] Matt. x. 23.   [5] 2 Cor. xi. 33.

3. " And should it be their lot to suffer, whether in unequal or in equal measure, it will then become apparent which are those who are suffering on behalf of others. They will be those who could have avoided these calamities by flight but preferred to remain and not abandon others in their need. This, indeed, is the great proof of that charity which the Apostle John is recommending to us when he says : As Christ laid down His life for us, so we should lay down our lives for the brethren.[6]

" In other words, when those who take to flight, or are prevented from doing so only by their own concerns, are caught and made to suffer, they suffer, of course, for themselves, not for their brothers. But those who suffer because they were not willing to desert the brethren who needed them for their health as Christians are laying down their lives for the brethren without a doubt.

4. " What, then, of what I once heard a bishop say, that if Our Lord told us to take to flight even in those persecutions in which the crown of martyrdom can be won, we ought all the more to fly from the fruitless sufferings that come from an invasion of barbarian enemies ? That is very true and sound advice for those who have no ties of ecclesiastical duty. But if their reason for not flying from a murderous enemy when they might have done is that they do not wish to desert Christ's ministry, without which men cannot live as Christians or become Christians, then their charity receives a greater reward than if they had fled on their own account and not on their brethren's and had then been caught and suffered martyrdom for not denying Christ.

5. " But what was the point you made in your first letter ? You said : ' If we are to stay with our congregations, I cannot see what good we shall be doing either to ourselves or to the people. All that will happen will be that the slaughter of men, the outraging of women and the burning of churches will take place under our eyes and we ourselves will die under torture when they are trying to get from us something we have not got.' Well, God is quite able to hear the prayers of His children and

[6] I John iii. 16.

ward off these things they are dreading ; and dangers that are, therefore, at the worst uncertain cannot justify us in what would certainly be a dereliction of duty and would certainly inflict fatal injuries on our flocks, not in this life, but in that other life so incomparably better worth our anxious thought and care.

" You see, if those calamities, which we fear may come upon us where we are, were certain, all those for whose sake we ought to stay would have already fled from there and freed us from any obligation to remain. For no one says that ministers have to stay on where there is no one needing their ministry. That is why some of the holy bishops of Spain fled, after their flocks had in some cases melted away in flight, in others had been slaughtered, in others had been starved in sieges or dispersed in captivity. But many more stayed on in the thick of the dangers, because those they stayed for were staying on. And if some did desert their flocks, that is what I say should not be done. For they were not being guided by divine authority but were blinded by human error or in the bondage of human fears.

6. " And how is it that they think they must give undiscriminating obedience to precepts when they read about fleeing from one city to another, and have no horror of ' the hireling who sees the wolf coming and flies, because he is not concerned for the sheep ' ?[7] Here are two pronouncements, both by Our Lord and both true, one permitting and even ordering flight, the other rebuking and condemning it. Why do they not try to find interpretations for them that will show them to be consistent with each other, as indeed they are ? And how can this be found without stressing the point I have just been making, that the time for us ministers of Christ to fly from the places where we happen to be, in face of persecution, is when Christ has no people there who need our ministrations, or the necessary ministrations can be supplied by others who have not the same reason for flight ?

" It was like that in the case I have just quoted, when the Apostle was let down in a sack and fled because the persecutor

[7] John x. 12–13.

was looking for him particularly. Since there were others for whom no such necessity existed and who were responsible for the ministry there, God forbid that we should suppose the Church deserted. It was the same when the holy Athanasius, Bishop of Alexandria, fled,[8] for the Emperor Constantius[9] had given orders for the arrest of him particularly, and the Catholic congregations resident in Alexandria were by no means deserted by the other ministers.

" But when the people stay on and the ministers take to flight and their ministrations cease, what is that but the damnable flight of hirelings who are not concerned for the sheep? For the wolf will come, in the form not of a man but of the devil, who has often persuaded the faithful to apostatize when the Lord's Body ceased to be ministered to them daily; and thus ' the weak, for whom Christ died, will perish,' not ' through your knowledge' but through your ignorance, ' my brother'.[10]

7. " As for those who, in this matter, are not so much deceived by fallacies as overcome by terror, why should they not, by the mercy and aid of the Lord, make a brave struggle against their fears, rather than incur calamities incomparably graver and far more to be dreaded? That is what men do when they burn with the flames of charity, not with the fumes of this world's lusts. For charity says ' Whose weakness is not my weakness? Whose fall is not my shame?'[11] But charity is the gift of God. Let us pray, then, that He who orders it will give it.

" And in our charity towards God's sheep, who must all die some day, some way, we should be more afraid of a butchery of their minds by the sword of spiritual evil than of their bodies by a sword of steel. We should be more afraid of their losing the purity of the faith through the corrupting of the interior life than of women being defiled by violence done to their bodies.

[8] St. Athanasius, Bishop of Alexandria from 328 to 373, was driven out of his see five times by the Arians. The reference here is to his third exile, in 356.
[9] Constantius II, son of Constantine the Great, joint Emperor from 337 and sole Emperor from 350 to 361. He was a supporter of the Arians; see the Life of St. Martin, section VI, and the notes there.
[10] 1 Cor. viii. 11.
[11] 2 Cor. xi. 29.

For violence cannot violate chastity if the mind preserves it. Even the chastity of the body is not violated when she who suffers is not voluntarily abusing her body but is enduring, without consenting, what another is perpetrating.

" We should be more afraid of ' living stones ' being extinguished when we have abandoned them than of the stone and wood of earthly buildings being set on fire under our eyes. We should be more afraid of the members of Christ's body being destroyed, starved of the food of the spirit, than of the members of our own body being tortured, gripped in the clutch of the enemy. Not that such things as these are not to be escaped when they can be ; but when they cannot be escaped without irreligion they are better endured—unless, of course, one is going to argue that a minister is not irreligious who withdraws the ministrations necessary for religion at the very time when the need is greatest.

8. " But perhaps we do not think of the scene when the peril has come to a climax and all chance of flight has gone—of the church packed, as it always is, with a throng of both sexes and all ages, some clamouring for baptism, others to be reconciled to the Church, others, again, to be given penance, and all for consolation and for the consecration and distribution of the sacraments. And if the ministers of the sacraments are not there, what a catastrophe for those who depart from this world either unregenerated by baptism or unabsolved from sin ! What a grief for their Christian relatives not to have them with them when they enter the repose of life eternal ! And lastly, what groans from all, and what blasphemies from some, at the absence of these ministrations and their ministers.

" You see what the fear of temporal calamities can do, and how great an increase of eternal calamities springs from it. But if the ministers are there, they are a help to all, in proportion to the strength which the Lord supplies to them. They baptize some, others are reconciled to the Church, none are deprived of the Communion of the Lord's Body. All are consoled, strengthened and encouraged, so that, when they pray to God, who is able to avert all the ills they fear, they are prepared for either event and able to say, if this cup cannot pass from them, His will be done, who cannot will any evil.

9. " I am sure you can see now what you wrote that you could not see, how much the Christian congregations stand to gain if, in their present troubles, they have Christ's ministers among them. You can see also how much is lost if they are absent ' seeking their own ends and not Jesus Christ's,'[12] not possessing that charity of which it was said ' it seeks not its own ends,'[13] and not imitating the one who described himself as ' seeking to benefit not myself but the many, for their salvation,'[14] and who would never have fled from the plots of that persecuting prince if there had not been others to whom he was a necessity for whom he wished to preserve himself. That is why he says ' I am torn between two desires, to get away and be with Christ— by far the best thing—and to remain in the body—a necessity for you.'[15]

10. " Possibly at this point someone may say that God's ministers ought to flee, when such calamities are threatening, so as to preserve themselves to be of use to the Church in calmer times. It is quite right for some people to do this when there are others to carry on the Church's ministry, so that it is not abandoned by all. Athanasius did this, as I said above. For the Catholic faith, which he defended, by his words and his love, against the Arian heretics, bears witness how necessary it was for the Church, and how profitable, to have him still in the flesh. But when all are in the same danger, the probability is that anyone taking to flight will be regarded as doing it from fear of death rather than from the wish to be helpful and will do more harm by setting an example of fleeing than he can do good by performing the service of living ; and then flight should be out of the question.

" Finally, when holy David would not entrust himself to the chances of battle for fear (as the narrative puts it) that ' the lamp of Israel should be extinguished,'[16] he was taking the course urged by others, not taking it upon himself to

---

[12] Phil. ii. 21.   [14] I Cor. x. 33.
[13] I Cor. xiii. 5.   [15] Phil. i. 23, 24.
                [16] 2 Kings (2 Samuel) xxi. 17.

decide. Otherwise he would have had many imitators among the cowards, who would have supposed him to be acting thus, not out of regard for the good of others, but under the pressure of his own fears.

11. " But another point arises which we have no right to pass over. If we admit that questions of utility cannot be altogether disregarded, so that some ministers ought to escape when some great disaster threatens so as to minister to those whom they find left after the slaughter, what should be done when it looks as if all are going to perish unless some take to flight ? Again, what if the destruction has been checked to the extent that only the Church's ministers are being persecuted ?

" What can one say ? Is the Church to be left desolate by the flight of her ministers because it would be more wretched for her to be left desolate by their deaths ? Besides, if the laity are not being hunted to death themselves, they can hide their bishops and clergy in such ways as God makes possible, who has everything under His control and is able to save by His most marvellous power even those who do not run away— only we are enquiring what we ought to do, because we do not want to be thought to be experimenting with God by looking to Him for a miracle every time.

" Certainly the case when laymen and clergy are in the same danger cannot be compared with one of those storms when merchants and seamen are in the same danger on a ship. God forbid that this ship of ours should be valued at so little that it could be right for the sailors, and even for the pilot, to abandon it in its dangers, just because they can escape by jumping into the ship's boat or even by swimming. For what is it we fear for those who we fear may perish by our desertion ? It is not temporal death, which must come some time or other, but eternal death, which can come if precautions are not taken but need not come if they *are* taken.

" Moreover, if the temporal dangers are really the same for all, why should we suppose that every time the enemy break in, the clergy are all going to die, but the laity are not ? And, if the laity do all die, there will be an end for everyone at the same time of the life for which the clergy are necessary. Alternatively, why should we not hope that, if some of the laity survive, some of the clergy will survive also and be in a position to provide them with the ministrations they will need? 12. " But how much better it would be if the contention between God's ministers were as to who should stay and who should fly to ensure that the Church should be desolated neither by the flight of all nor by the death of all! That will be the contest between them when on both sides charity is the impulse and on both sides charity is the aim.

"And if there is no other way of ending that argument, then, so far as I can see, it must be decided by lot who shall stay and who shall go. For those who say that it is their duty to go will either seem timid because they do not want to face the threatened disaster, or conceited because they think that they are the ones most necessary to preserve for the Church. Then again, the best of them will probably choose to lay down their lives for their brethren, so that the ones preserved by flight will be those whose lives are less useful because they are less skilled as counsellors and rulers. But these, in their turn, if they have a sense of what is fitting, will contest the choice of those who much prefer death to flight but are obviously the ones who ought to live.

"And thus, as Scripture says, ' the casting of lots calms disputes and settles the issue between the strong.'[17] For in these doubtful cases it is better for God than for men to judge whether it is more fitting to call the best to receive the crown of martyrdom and to spare the weak or, alternatively, to give the weak the strength to undergo those sufferings and so take from this world those whose lives could not benefit the Church as much as the lives of the others. No doubt to draw lots would be an unusual course to take but, if it were taken, who would dare to find fault with it? Who, except from ignorance or malice, would not lavish on it the praises due to it?

" But if there is reluctance to take a course without precedent, at least let no one by taking to flight cause the

[17] Prov. xviii. 18.

Church's ministrations to cease, least of all when such great perils make them more than ever a necessity and a duty. Let no one have such regard for himself that, just because he seems to excel in some quality, he says he is the fittest to live, and so to fly. Whoever *thinks* that, is much too pleased with himself; whoever *says* that, is displeasing to everyone else.

13. " There are some, to be sure, who think that bishops and clergy who do not take to flight amid such dangers, but stay where they are, mislead their flocks who, when they see their pastors staying, will not go themselves. But it is easy to avoid these malicious reproaches by addressing these same flocks and saying to them : ' Do not be misled by the fact that we are not leaving this place. It is on your account, not on our own, that we are choosing to stay here, so as not to fail you in the ministrations we know to be necessary to " the salvation you have in Christ."[18] So if you want to leave yourselves, you will at the same time be releasing us from the bonds that hold us.'

" This is what I think *should* be said when it really seems expedient to withdraw to safer localities. But, even after hearing this, all or some may say : ' We are in the hands of Him whose anger no one can escape, no matter where he goes, and whose mercy anyone can find, no matter where he is, if he is reluctant to go elsewhere, either because he is tied by definite obligations or because he is unwilling to spend great toil on finding a dubious refuge and changing the danger without ending it.' If they say this, they certainly must not be neglected by the Christian ministry. But if, after hearing the bishops, they prefer to leave, those who were staying on their account are no longer bound to stay, because there is no one there any longer whom they are bound to stay for.

14. " Whoever, then, flees in such circumstances that the ministrations necessary to the Church are not brought to an end by his flight, does what Our Lord ordered or allowed. But whosoever flees in such a way that the nourishment from which Christ's flock draws its spiritual life is withdrawn from

[18] 2 Tim. ii. 10.

it, is 'the hireling who sees the wolf coming and who flies because he is not concerned for the sheep.'

"I have written to you in this way, dearest brother, in truth and true charity, because you have asked my advice and because it is what I think. But if you can find a better opinion, I claim no priority for my own. But a better thing to do in these dangers we shall never find than to pray to the Lord our God that He will have mercy on us. As for this intention of not deserting the Churches, there are wise and holy men who, by God's grace, have been privileged to entertain it and to act on it, and, in the teeth of obloquy, have persevered in their set purpose."

XXXI

God granted that the life of this holy man should be a long one, for the benefit and happiness of holy Church, and he lived seventy-six years, nearly forty of them as priest or bishop. In the course of them he often told us in intimate conversation that the reception of baptism did not absolve Christians, and especially priests, however estimable, from the duty of doing fitting and adequate penance before departing from this life. And he acted on this himself in his last and fatal illness. For he ordered those Psalms of David which are specially penitential to be copied out and, when he was very weak, used to lie in bed facing the wall where the sheets of paper were put up, gazing at them and reading them, and copiously and continuously weeping as he read.

Moreover, so as not to have his thoughts distracted by anyone, about ten days before his death he asked those of us who were with him not to let anyone go in to him, except at the times when the doctors came to see him or food was brought to him. This was attended to and carried out, and during the whole of that time he gave himself to prayer.

Right up to his last illness he had preached God's Word in the church unceasingly, vigorously and powerfully, with sound mind and sound judgement. Now, with all his limbs and organs unimpaired, and sound in sight and hearing, while we stood by and watched and prayed, he, in the words of Scripture,[1] " slept with his fathers," in the ripeness of " a good old age." In our presence the holy Sacrifice was offered up commending his body to the earth, and he was buried.

He made no will because, as one of God's poor, he had nothing to leave. It was a standing order that the library of the Church and all the books should be carefully preserved for posterity. Whatever the Church possessed in the way of funds or ornaments he handed over in trust to the priest who had been in charge of the Church house in his lifetime.

As for his relatives, whether they were in the religious life or not, neither in life nor in death did he treat them as most people treat their relations. While he was still alive he would give to them, when they needed it, as he would give to anyone else, not so as to make them rich but so that they might not be in want, or be less in want.

To the Church he left an adequate body of clergy, as well as convents for men and for women, full of celibates under their appointed superiors. He left also a library with books containing writings by himself and other holy men. It is through these, thanks be to God, that his quality and stature in the Church is known to the world; and in these he will always live among the faithful. To quote an epitaph that one of the secular poets composed for himself when directing that after his death a monument should be erected to him in a public place :

> Traveller, would you like to know
> How poets live on after death ?
> As you read aloud, it is I who speak ;
> Your voice is sounded by my breath.

His writings, indeed, show us as clearly as the light of truth ever permits one to see, that this priest, so acceptable and so dear to God, lived rightly and sanely in the faith and hope and charity of the Catholic Church ; and no one can read what he

[1] Concerning the death of David see 3 (1) Kings ii. 10 ; 1 Paralipomenon (Chron.) xxix. 28.

wrote on theology without profit. But I think that those were able to profit still more who could hear him speak in church and see him with their own eyes and, above all, had some knowledge of him as he lived among his fellow men. For he was not only " a teacher learned in the law of the Kingdom of Heaven, bringing out of his treasury new things and old," [2] or one of those " merchants who, when they find a pearl of great price, sell all that they have and buy it." [3] He was also one of those in whom is fulfilled the text " So speak and so act " [4] and of whom the Saviour said : " He who keeps them and teaches others to keep them, it is he who will be called great in the Kingdom of Heaven." [5]

And now I earnestly ask you who read these words that in your charity you will join me in giving thanks to Almighty God, " blessing the Lord who gave me understanding " [6] and with it the will and the capacity to bring these things to the knowledge both of those who are with us and those who are far from us, of men of our times and men of times to come. And join me also in praying for me myself, that having been allowed by God to live with this man, no longer with us, in a lovely intimacy without a single bitter disagreement for nearly forty years, I may be his emulator and imitator in this world and may share with him in the world to come the joys promised by Almighty God.

[2] Matt. xiii. 52.   [4] Jas. ii. 12.
[3] Matt. xiii. 45, 46.   [5] Matt. v. 19.
[6] Ps. xv (xvi). 7.

A DISCOURSE ON THE LIFE OF ST. HONORATUS, BISHOP OF ARLES

BY ST. HILARY OF ARLES

PRACTICALLY nothing is known of the antecedents and early life of the author except what he tells us himself in this discourse. He belonged to the same distinguished and wealthy family as St. Honoratus, lived in the same part of Gaul, and received the same kind of literary education. It would appear that he was born in the first year or two of the fifth century, for he was evidently quite a young man with his whole career in front of him when Honoratus made a special journey from his monastery at Lérins to win him for the religious life. He was probably still in the twenties when Honoratus was practically compelled to leave Lérins to become Bishop of Arles and he followed him there, and barely thirty, if as much, when he succeeded him as bishop in A.D. 429. His episcopate of twenty years was notable for his energy, his devotion and his indiscretions. These scarcely concern us here but an adequate account of them will be found in Butler's *Lives of the Saints* (Thurston and Attwater) under May 5th.

Besides this Discourse and a short letter, no certainly authentic writings by this St. Hilary survive. The Discourse is a favourable specimen of the pulpit oratory of the day. It is cast into the conventional mould of the Panegyric, or Eulogy, and bears the stamp of the oratorical training of St. Hilary's youth. But there is evident sincerity behind its artificially balanced phrases ; and an unmistakably authentic portrait of St. Honoratus emerges. The weakest parts of the discourse are the narrative passages, for which neither the style nor the literary form was suited. In these passages the writer seems sometimes to be thrown out of his stride by the necessity of recording hard fact ; and, since he is too honest to distort the facts, the Latin in such cases becomes sometimes very awkward and obscure ; and there are paragraphs in which, I confess, I am still not quite sure that I have got at the writer's meaning, particularly as my interpretation differs at certain points from what some writers seem to have read into the words.

So far as I have been able to ascertain, this Discourse has not previously been translated. The present translation aims at conveying something, at any rate, of the manner of the original, both in its merits and its defects—a thing particularly desirable to do in a case like this, in which the reader is likely seriously to misjudge the work considered as a biography unless he has continuously before his mind the artificial literary form in which the original is cast.

The text used is that printed in Migne, *Patrologia Latina*, volume 50, columns 1249 to 1272 (1863). No more recent recension seems to exist. For convenience of reference I have used the numbering of chapters and sections in Migne's text, which in its turn follows the Bollandists.

A DISCOURSE ON THE LIFE OF ST. HONORATUS, BISHOP OF ARLES, DELIVERED ON THE FIRST ANNIVERSARY OF HIS FUNERAL

BY ST. HILARY, BISHOP OF ARLES

PROLOGUE

1. THIS day, dearly beloved, is known to you as one consecrated among the faithful to public mourning. To me personally, so long as the Lord continues to bestow upon me this life's fleeting years, it will always be a day laden with anguish but replete with grandeur. For this is the day on which this Church's prelate of holy memory —by his virtues, by his priesthood, by his name " the honoured one "[1]—was divested of his body.

Anything I might add to that closing phrase could be adjudged absurd. If I said : " He departed to the stars ", why, he himself, even while he tarried on this earth, was numbered among the most splendid stars of God. Should I add : " He stands in Christ's presence "? But at what time during his life on earth did he *not* stand in His presence? His whole life conformed to the words of Elias : " As the Lord lives in whose presence I stand."[2] Am I to say : " He forsook all earthly things " when I am speaking of one who, as the Apostle says, spent all his time in the fellowship of heaven?[3] And so it is with all that I have in mind to utter, with whatever it occurs to me to say of such a man—from its very immensity it fails to find fit expression. Joy wars with grief. Sweet it is to remember such a man, and an agony to be without him.

2. And so a two-fold topic calls to me. From one side the joy of praising him draws me on to speak ; from the other, the loss we

---

[1] Latin, " Honoratus ", the dead saint's name, but the play on words cannot be reproduced in English.
[2] 3 (1) Kings xviii. 15.
[3] Phil. iii. 20.

all suffer draws me back to sigh. Forgive me, therefore, if, with these two emotions rending my soul, my tongue, like a servant serving two masters, fails in its proper service. Whatever memory proposes as matter for praise, grief claims the whole of it for its record of its losses.

And yet, even if I retained sufficient calm and my tongue did its proper duty to my thoughts, I doubt whether his glories could be manifested by my words more plentifully than they linger in your memories. There can be no one, I fancy, who cannot himself call to mind some more delightful trait of that great man than all the wealth of eloquence could bring before him. But as Scripture says : " Memories of good men bring praise with them ",[4] and those who remember men of shining merits must needs sing their praises. Therefore, beloved, so far as my powers allow me, I will set before you some of those facts concerning him upon which your hearts dwell. And assuredly your memories will aid my efforts ; and whatever strains my powers of expression, your hearts will make eloquent in your own meditations.

3. Someone has written : " Wisdom wins its tribute in the ending"; in other words, the way a wise man conducts his life is praised when his life is finished. Thus we read in another passage : " Praise no man in his lifetime " ; and again : " Praise not any man before his death " ;[5] as much as to say : Keep your praise till after death ; when a living man is praised, the one who is praised is given occasion for vainglory and the one who praises gets the reputation of being a flatterer.

But there are many very good reasons for praising the dead. In the first place, the one whom our praise might gratify is not there, and consequently it has all to be directed to the Giver of grace. Secondly, when flattery cannot be suspected, only admiration for merit is left. When, therefore, the praises of the dead are sung before the holy assembly of the faithful, the effect is wholly to edify, in no wise to puff up. Moreover, he who is praised gains an addition to his reward from the fact that many profit from hearing his praises.

Nor need I fear that I shall be suspected of speaking with undue

<hr>

4 Prov. x. 7.   5 Ecclus. xi. 30.

partiality of one whom I regard as my own. For, setting aside the fact that nothing can be said that is not below the measure of his virtues, there is no one who does not claim him as his own, feel him to be his own, believe him to be his own. Nevertheless, it is not with any confidence in my own talents or in reliance upon eloquence that I set myself to sketch the life of so great a man. For even if the theme were to be attempted by a writer with the old-time mastery of language, not only would all his fluency add nothing to it, but he would sink down vanquished by the immensity of his subject. What urges me on is your love for the man ; it is your affection that gives me courage to talk to you a little about him, in the belief that a discourse vapid in its diction will be enlivened by his virtues, and that what is flat in the telling will be uplifted by the story and seasoned by the love that flows out towards him from its home in your hearts.

I

4. It is a commonplace of oratorical training that those who set out to pronounce a eulogy on any man's life should begin by extolling his birthplace and his origins, so that any deficiencies in his own qualities may appear to have been supplied beforehand by the glories of his ancestors. But we are all one in Christ, and there is no higher rank than to be reckoned among the sons of God ; nor can honours of earthly origin bring us any increase of true dignity except through our contempt for them. None is more glorious in the heavenly places than are those who have ignored their pedigrees and chosen to be reckoned as fatherless except in Christ.

I forbear, therefore, to recall his inherited insignia of worldly honours, and (what the world regards as almost the peak of ambition) a family risen in rank to the consular dignity itself—and all spurned by the higher nobility of his heart.[1] Nor could he have taken pleasure in his family's empty honours, seeing that already for the sake of truth he was turning from his family.

---

[1] For the nature of the office of consul at this period, see note 3 to section XX of the Life of St. Martin in this volume. The family was living in Gaul. But practically nothing is known about it, or about St. Honoratus, except what is derived from this discourse.

5. I hasten, instead, to speak of other things—of the faith he
displayed in his youth when of his own choice he sought baptism,
and the kind of death that, with a mature wisdom, he dreaded
when in full health ; of the way in which before baptism he foresaw a future without life ; of his thirst to be reborn. I would speak
of his sweetness as a child, his modesty as a boy, his seriousness
as a youth ; of how, at all these phases of his life, he was in advance
of his years in his graces and virtues and always seemed to be
older than himself, so that you would undoubtedly have thought
that he was being educated by some sort of divine tuition.

He pursued his studies without any pressure from his parents.
He preserved, with God's help, his baptismal innocence in a way
that no human care for him could ensure. And more than all this,
in the first unspotted radiance of the font, without anyone prompting him, he turned from the world.

I said " without anyone prompting him " ; I did not mention
the fact that his country resisted him, his father strove with him
and the whole family opposed him. For his charm had made itself
felt by all ; and when Christ was calling him to Himself, the
world, in the persons of all his circle, strove eagerly to hold him
back. Some were constrained to do so by his sweet disposition ;
others could not resist the delights of his comradeship ; others
admired too much his prowess in the various sports and pursuits
of young men of the world. Every pleasing trait that had been his
in his former life was made a chain to hold him back from his
renunciation.[2]

All feared to have snatched from them a kind of ornament
owned by the whole family. And indeed, in what attire did he not
seem to belong to it ; what garments did he ever not adorn ? So
it came about that, with one accord, country, friends and relatives
all thought that they were being robbed, as it were, of a most
splendid jewel, an ornament belonging to all. For they could not
believe that all these gifts would be changed and remoulded into
something better, as we have seen them changed ; they believed
that they were about to die.

---

[2] The word rendered by " renunciation " throughout is " conversio ", the
turning from the world spoken of above ; see the Introduction, section II.

Thus it had come about that his father, who had observed how strenuously he practised everything that he undertook, had held him back from baptism as long as he could, for fear that love for his religion would take complete possession of him, as in fact it did. In spite of this, the love and desire for Christ had grown stronger until, routing his father's pretexts, with boyish faith he had set out to take baptism by assault. For while still a catechumen he had formed his mind in the elements of the faith, he had shunned lewdness out of reverence for the baptism he was presently to receive, he had honoured the clergy as fathers, and from time to time had helped the poor with his pocket-money. All that at that age he was allowed to own—and loved all the more for the novelty of ownership—he would give away in his reckless compassion. Already at that time he was practising on a small scale the abandonment of everything and the distribution of all his possessions at once.

6. Thus in these and similar works of piety the catechumen's robust faith had hurried him on to baptism. Thenceforward his far-sighted father, in his earthbound kindliness, had watched over him with a mistrustful eye. He tried to appeal to him with all manner of delights, to allure him to the enthusiasms of youth, to entangle him in various worldly vanities and to renew his own youth in a kind of comradeship with his young son. He spent his days in hunting and in all sorts of games and, in order to appeal successfully to a boy of that age, armed himself with all this world's blandishments. And not without reason did this pagan father fear to have snatched from him by Christ one whom, among all the youths of high accomplishment, Christ was enfolding in His arms as if he had no fellow.[3]

7. As for the youth himself, amidst all these allurements his chief concern was to preserve his baptismal innocence. The boy shrank from what his elderly father enjoyed and constantly plied himself with good advice. " This world delights but deceives ", he would say to himself. " One set of maxims is quoted in church ; quite different injunctions are in my ears all day. There, modera-

---

[3] I have interpolated the words " from him by Christ ", reproducing, in doing so, a gloss inserted in the text by one of its editors (Salinas) to bring out what he regards (I think, rightly) as the meaning of this rather obscure sentence.

tion, self-control, calm and propriety are taught ; here unbridled self-indulgence is encouraged. There, piety is in favour ; here, physical exercise. There Christ invites me to an eternal kingdom ; here the devil tempts me to an earthly one. But ' all that is in the world is ' illusion and ' enticements to the eye ' ; ' and the world will pass away and its enticements with it. But those who do the will of God will last for ever,'[4] just as He Himself will last for ever. We should hurry to escape from these snares while we are still comparatively unhindered. It is hard to loosen what has long been fastened. It is easier to uproot a sapling than to cut down a sturdy tree.

" Save your soul upon the mountain or evil thoughts may take hold of you. The poison of pleasure spreads quickly, and the freedom you have won through Christ's grace should be preserved for Him. Leave it to others to adore gold and silver, and to the metals (as I see it) to master their masters. Leave it to others to own estates and slaves and to their souls to pass into captivity thereby. Let others take delight in distinctions, and trample on the distinction of God's image in themselves. It is freedom enough for me if I am not the slave of vices ; it is health enough to have joy. For a wife, give me wisdom ; for pleasure give me virtue ; for my treasure give me Christ, who will exchange passing joys for better ones and will give me, even in this life, the delights and the advantages of a course of training through which I shall be made fit to enter the heavenly kingdom."

8. Such meditations allowed no long delays. All of a sudden the spark, fed by this kind of fuel, burst into the flame of renunciation. Realising that the licence allowed to youth was the closest kind of captivity, he shook off the yoke of freedom and bowed his neck to take the yoke of the Lord's service. His luxuriant tresses were cut down to short hair. He exchanged his brilliant attire for a radiant mind. Stiff cloaks covered the beauty of his milk-white neck. Gaiety became serenity ; vigour of mind took the place of vigour of limbs ; the powers of the body made way for the power of the spirit. The handsome face grew pale with fasting ; and, formerly full of youthful freshness, it now became full of dignity.

[4] I John ii. 16, 17.

Need I say more? So suddenly did he become a wholly different person that his parent mourned for him as a father that has lost a son. And, indeed, for his body there was a living death but for his spirit there was life. From this time forward his treatment by his relatives was nothing short of persecution. Then for the first and only time he was insubordinate towards his father, when he strove to be God the Father's son, thereby observing already the rule of charity, as Solomon directs. For it was that celebrated prophet, acting as the voice of God, who pronounced the words : " He established in me the rule of charity." [5] And unquestionably he observed the rule and, as charity prescribes, aimed first at loving God and then his neighbour. Thus the father took the youth's renunciation to be a censure upon his own old age. He opposed him, he strove with him and he threatened him. But the boy relied on God, and none of these things could shake his resolution.

II

9. And God was at hand to encourage His recruit. He did not neglect to raise up a comrade for him in the person of one of his own brothers, who saw in his example a call to renounce the world himself.[1] The elder followed the younger ; and in the little time he had still to live he grew with him in virtue as well as in comradeship. From this time onwards there was a delightful rivalry between them in their way of living. Which could feel the more tender devotion and which could eat the tougher food ? Which could use the more soothing language and which could wear the rougher clothes ? Which could speak the more seldom and which could pray the more often ? Which was sooner out of bed and which was longer at his books ? Which less quickly felt annoyed and which more quickly felt compassion ?

Which more readily deprived himself in order to make a gift ? Which more cheerfully gave up to a guest his bed of sacking and that stone that was his usual pillow ? Which of them more

[5] " Ordinavit in me caritatem ", Canticles ii, 4
[1] His name was Venantius, as we see at the end of this chapter.

quickly shed tears over the wayfarer before he gave him alms, or saw Christ in the stranger to whom he gave a meal? In whose talk did the world figure less often and in whose more often Christ? Which, on those heights of virtue, seemed to himself the lowlier and, the higher he climbed by his merits, was the more abased in his contrition?

During this period, through their manner of living, they exercised a kind of private episcopate. Many bishops, if I mistake not, learnt from their entertainment by them how to entertain; for those of them who did not shrink in horror from the austerities of their rule of life took away with them minds stored with memories of kindliness rather than bodies strengthened by refreshment. In this way they ministered to all conditions of their countrymen at once; and there are still many memories of how they watched over the bodies of some and the souls of others, clothing them, feeding them or teaching them as each had need of garments or instruction or money to be spent on them. Any traveller who came there, worn out with the hardships of his journey, came as to his own country and to his family estate. Any traveller who left them, to go further on his way, felt as if he was again setting out from his own home and seemed once more to be parting with his neighbours, once again with his kinsmen.

10. Meanwhile the love of all for them increased and multiplied and spread far and wide; their fame was carried to the remotest regions; and the whole country now strove to render them service and affection and honour. They were simply not allowed to achieve ignominy and poverty. The more they hid their lives, the more their renown shone out. Each tried to make the other the object of this praise and the recipient of the glory, attributing to one alone the spiritual powers they shared between them. But while each wished to hide in the shadow of the other, the effect was that each was lit up by a reflection in the other of his own radiance.

And what serious minds they had already acquired! and, with them, the mature wisdom of old men. How seldom they had visits from women, even from those who were relations! And in spite of all their spiritual powers, how complete was the absence of vanity! How soothing was their sympathy and how careful their watch over the welfare of those who had placed themselves under them for instruction! They lived on earth the life of angels, " in long endurance . . . in nights of prayers, in fasts ; by purity of mind, by insight, by forbearance, by kindness, in their unity with the Holy Spirit, in their unfeigned charity, in the truth they preached, in the power of God." [2]

But at the same time they acquired a dread of their own renown and of this spreading far and wide of the fragrance of a good life.[3] For although they gave the praise for it to God, they were nevertheless afraid that it was putting them in danger of vainglory. They felt that they had been receiving their reward during their lifetime. They began to shrink from human society and human favour, and to be consumed with a yearning for the desert.

11. They laid their plans accordingly for a journey to foreign lands, refugees as it were from their own good name. Once more their country was up in arms ; once more their kinsmen strove with them, fearing, but this time for sounder reasons, to be robbed of their bright star. Ah, good Jesus, what a struggle there was then between faith and affection! What attempts to influence them by advice or by entreaties or by tears! There was no one who did not take upon himself a kinsman's role and add his tears to the father's in waging this war against them. For all their homeland felt that it was losing fathers in these youths. And, indeed, they had attained to an old age that was not white-haired but white with graces, and seen, not in withered limbs, but in lovely dispositions.

Oh, Lord, how marvellous are the dispensations of Thy providence! These lamps of Thine, shining with the flame of faith, were not permitted by Thee to stand fixed in one place, but Thou didst inspire them with the desire to migrate in flight from glory and didst carry them where they would enlighten other regions. And their glory was thereby multiplied, for their spiritual powers grew in the very act of undertaking this journey.

[2] 2 Cor. vi. 4–6. While there is no verbal quotation, in this rendering, from the Knox version, two of the phrases were suggested by it.
[3] Compare 2 Cor. ii. 14–16.

Their possessions had of late been much broken into by various works of mercy, but they were still large and now they were completely dispersed. Kinsmen and strangers alike were allowed to bid for their inheritance. Thus they gave no preference to relatives in respect of making a profit, any more than if they had been selling what was not their own. Ever since it had belonged to them, the property had ministered to the poor; it was now broken up in order to be distributed to the poor. Their country was watered by this flood of compassion and repaid it by a flood of tears.

12. Thus they left their "land and home and kindred," showing themselves true sons of Abraham by following his example.[4] They did not wish, however, to be thought to have undertaken anything out of mere youthful foolhardiness and therefore took with them an old man who had attained to the very summit and perfection of weight and dignity. This was the holy Caprasius, whom they had always regarded as their father in Christ and who is still living the angelic life upon the islands. You, my beloved, will not have heard his name before today, and still know nothing of his life; nevertheless Christ numbers him among His friends.[5] This was the man whom these two, who had themselves been chosen by so many youths as their protector, now took with them as a director of their life in the Lord and a protector of their own youth.

Thus they sought to hide themselves in travel, and fled from the renown of their virtues. Nevertheless, wherever they went, there, whether they liked it or not, a new renown was born. Happy the lands, blessed the harbours, made bright by pilgrims

[4] Gen. xii. 1.

[5] This was St. Caprasius or Caprais, whose Feast is on June 1st. All we know of him, says Fr. Thurston's note in his edition of Butler's *Lives*, is derived from this *laudatio* on St. Honoratus; but in the life printed there he says rather strangely " St. Hilary of Arles who had been present at his deathbed . . . in a panegyric he delivered on St. Honoratus, spoke of St. Caprasius as being already a saint in heaven "—perhaps a possible interpretation of this passage (for the phrase rendered here " who is still living " could in the context be rendered " who had till then been living"), but one that surely somewhat strains the meaning of the last words of the sentence. It may be added that we can gather from a treatise addressed to St. Hilary by St. Eucherius of Lyons (see note 1 to section IV below) that St. Caprasius remained with St. Honoratus until the latter became Bishop of Arles in 426 and was still alive at Lérins a year or two later (*De Laude Eremi*, section 42; Migne, P. L. vol. 50).

thirsting for their heavenly fatherland! Other pilgrims go to Eastern shores or other places full of holy things, to learn from what they see there. These uplifted the places they visited by the good things seen in themselves. Wherever they went they scattered their fortune; and every place at their approach was flooded with the sweet fragrance of Christ.

13. Even at this early date the Church of Marseilles nearly succeeded in securing for itself, before this city, the very man whose memory is our nourishment today. The bishop of that city urged it and the municipality rejoiced at such a prospect.[6] And what might not their zeal have accomplished in a contest of tears and by the persuasions of flattery? Threatened, however, by this new danger, they lost no more time in crossing the seas and made for shores where the eloquence of Rome, in which they were so well versed, was reckoned barbarous.

It would take too long to tell the story of the benefits that each place in turn received from their presence, of the health they brought to Churches without exercising any clerical functions, of the number of teachers they taught without uttering a word.

14. Let it suffice to record their unflinching endurance for the love of Christ of the colds they caught at sea, their arrival at the desolate and barren coasts of Greece, and the immense variety of wind and weather with which they, with their tender and delicate upbringing, had to contend. For the death out there of his brother Venantius, a man most blessed in Christ, and the illnesses of himself and his party, bear witness to the fact that the trial was very severe and more than that delicacy could endure.

At that funeral the town of Modon showed by the numerous attendant choirs how much it felt itself to have been exalted and enriched.[7] Hebrews, Greeks and Latins all showed their joy at this; even the Jews, though they rejected Christ, could admire

---

[6] The bishop was presumably Proculus, a celebrated figure in his day, whose episcopate lasted from about A.D. 380, for perhaps fifty years; see Duchesne, *Fastes Episcopaux*, I, 274.

[7] The Latin for this town is " Methona ". There were at least three towns of that name in ancient Greece but two of them were completely off any probable route, while the one now known as Modon is at the extreme S.W. corner of the Morea, which an eastbound boat skirting the coast would be bound to sight.

Christ's faithful servant. The fervent chanting shook the very stars, and I believe that choirs of angels joined in the strains of human voices and Christ came to meet His faithful servitor. " Well done! Venantius, good and faithful servant " and when you hear the words : " Come and share in your Master's joy," [8] remember those of us whom this world's joys still assail.

Thus the warfare of flesh and spirit came to an end and eternal life and glory made a beginning.

III

15. From this place Christ brought your Honoratus back to you and by His hidden craftsmanship made the journey back a bringer of health.[1] For whatever he touched as he passed by he made bright. Italy welcomed his entry with joy as a blessing. Hallowed Tuscany took him to her bosom and, through the hospitality of her bishops, contrived the most agreeable prolongations of his stay. And then the Providence of God, planning future benefits for us here, overturned everything. The desire for the desert had called him from his fatherland but Christ invited him to a desert not far from this city. So it came about that he sought to go to a certain island uninhabited because of its utter desolation and unvisited for fear of its venomous snakes, lying quite close to the foot of the Alpine range.[2] Apart from the facilities for solitude, he was attracted by the neighbourhood of Bishop Leontius, a holy man most blessed by Christ, and had ties of friendship with him.[3]

[8] Matt. xxv. 21.

[1] The Latin of this and the next paragraph is at several points somewhat obscure and ambiguous, and in more than one place a different interpretation might be given to it from the one given here. But a long discussion would be out of place here and, even if it could be conclusive, would serve little purpose, for the final outcome of these peregrinations of St. Honoratus is clear enough.

[2] This was Lérins, now St. Honorat, the smaller and more remote of two islands, the other of which was Lero or Lerona, now called Ste. Marguérite, after the saint's sister. They lie off the French Riviera, south of the promontory near Cannes. Arles, where this discourse was delivered, is not far from the mouth of the Rhône.

[3] St. Leontius was Bishop of Forum Julii, now Fréjus, on the same coast, and Lérins appears to have been in his diocese. He seems to have been still living when this discourse was delivered; see Duchesne, *Fastes Episcopaux de l'ancienne Gaule*, vol. I, p. 285.

There were many who tried to draw him back from this new venture. For the surrounding population described the island as a terrible wilderness and tried their hardest, with an ambition inspired by faith, to keep him in their midst. But he was finding it hard to endure intercourse with his fellow-men and craved to be cut off from the world by the barrier of the straits. He had ever in his thoughts or on his lips the words that he kept repeating, now to himself, now to his followers : " You shall walk upon the asp and the basilisk ; you shall trample on the lion and dragon,"⁴ and also the promise in the Gospels, made by Christ to His disciples : " I have put it in your power to trample upon serpents and on scorpions."⁵

So he went fearlessly on to the island and dispelled the alarm of his followers by his own unconcern. The terrors of the solitude were put to flight ; the army of serpents fell back. But was there ever any darkness that did not flee from that light or any poison that did not yield to that medicine ? It is a fact, and one unheard of, and to be reckoned (I think) among the miracles to his credit, that not once was he ever in danger or even startled by an encounter with a snake, although encounters are so frequent in those arid wastes (as I can bear witness), especially when provoked by heavy seas.

16. Let me hasten on. Christ, if I may use the phrase, co-operated ; all the obstacles that had at first been a deterrent were overcome ; and your Honoratus established there a kind of camp of God. The place which had recently proved so inhospitable to men was now made illustrious by the rites of angels. The hiding-place was lit up, though the light was concealed. The obscurity of the once unknown place of exile surrendered to the renown of one who was exiled of his own free will.

Do you ask what his coming did, what this reformation brought about ? Wherever Honoratus went, honours had to go also. It was here that he was first bound by the clerical state that he had so long evaded. It was here that the priestly head-band⁶ was

---

⁴ Ps. xc. (xci). 13.
⁵ Luke x. 19.
⁶ Latin, " sacerdotalis infula ", the *infula* being the woollen headband or fillet worn by the pagan priests, which by a characteristic convention of oratory is taken by this very holy Christian bishop as a symbol of the Christian priesthood.

bound around the fugitive, and the dignity came to him who had declined to go to the dignity.

Thus there arose a priest there who was worthy of the honour, not twice over, but many times. Bishops in his presence were unconscious of their fuller priesthood and their higher title. There was never a bishop who went so far as to claim that he was a colleague of that priest. But he himself, a monk who possessed all the virtues of the priesthood, preserved in the priesthood all the humility of a monk.

17. At his instance a temple for the Church's worship was erected, sufficient for the needs of God's elect. Buildings arose suited to be the dwellings of monks. Water, unknown there for ages, began to flow copiously, repeating, in its origin, two miracles of the Old Testament ;[7] for when it burst out of the rock it flowed sweet though surrounded by the saltness of the sea.

Already from all that part of the country those who were seeking God had begun eagerly to make their way there. Whoever wanted Christ sought out Honoratus ; and whoever sought out Honoratus assuredly found Christ. For Christ was there in all His vigour, enthroned in the heart of Honoratus as in a lofty citadel or a splendid shrine. Chastity, which is sanctity, dwelt there and faith and wisdom and spiritual power ; there justice shone, and truth. And thus, as it were, with open arms and outstretched hands he invited men to his embrace, and by this I mean to the love of Christ ; and all men flocked to him eagerly from every side.

For what land remains, what nation, that has not some of its citizens in his monastery?[8] What barbarian ways did he not tame ? And how often he changed, as it were, savage beasts into gentle doves ! Dispositions once all embittered were sprinkled by him with the sweetness of Christ. Men whose depravity had been a burden even to themselves were given graces that have made them a joy to all ; and when they had tasted the sweet savour of goodness they could do no less than hate increasingly the persons they had formerly been. For, once brought out (so to speak) into

---

[7] See Exod. xv. 23–25 ; xvii. 1–7.

[8] St. Patrick was probably among them, recently escaped from slavery in Ireland.

the novel light, they loathed those ancient prison-houses of long-established vices.

A variety of diseases of the soul were dispelled by his exhortations. Bitterness, moroseness and passion gave place to the liberty which Christ offers ; and, after long and burdensome bondage in Egypt, there would come refreshing rest. Stupefying and amazing were the transformations ; but they were not of men into beasts, changed (so the story goes) by the potions of Circe,[9] but of beasts into men, changed by the sweetest of potions, the message of Christ, ministered to them by Honoratus.

For what disorders could resist the pressure of that urgency combined with that eagerness ? What stones would not be turned into sons of Abraham ?[10] Where else was a factory of virtues with such resources in beautifying souls that, when the liveliest exhortations failed to impel men to spiritual health, it compelled God's intervention by prayer ?

The emotional disorders of all were regarded by him as his own and bewailed as his own. The progress and the trials of all were reckoned as his. He knew how to " rejoice with the joyous and weep with the weeping."[11] And their vices and virtues alike went to swell the pile of his own merits. For just as virtue incites to virtue, so pity lavished on the pitiable bears its fruit also. For Honoratus will reap a greater harvest from each of those on whom he took pity than any single one of them will reap for himself ; for the spiritual health imparted to all these separate persons erected a single edifice of glory for him.[12]

Energetic, quick and tireless, he persevered in the course dictated by his insight into the nature and character of each person. With one he would deal privately, with another in front of everybody ; with one he would be severe, with another soothing ; and to bring about a change in one who had to be punished, he would often make a change in the form of the punishment. In this way

---

[9] Circe in Greek and Roman legend was a witch ; and in Homer's *Odyssey* she turns the companions of Odysseus into swine by means of a magic potion.
[10] See Matt. iii. 9.
[11] Rom. xii. 15.
[12] Both the text and the meaning of this passage are somewhat uncertain. I have accepted the verdict of Migne in respect of both and, having done so, I have slightly expanded the original in order to try and bring out the sequence of thought thus attributed to St. Hilary.

it came about that it would be hard to find anyone both so much loved and so much feared. For he implanted these two kinds of feelings towards himself so firmly in each of his disciples that the love the disciple felt for him made him to fear to transgress and his fear of him made him to love to be corrected.

IV

18. You would hardly believe what trouble he took to see that no one became depressed and no one was tormented by thoughts of the world. He discerned what was troubling anyone as easily as if he carried everyone's mind in his own. With kindly planning, moreover, he would contrive that no one was burdened by excessive labour and no one grew slothful with too much inaction. With tender care he weighed out to each of the brethren (if one can say such a thing) their very slumbers. The physically robust he was always spurring into activity ; the ardent spirits he would force to rest. He knew (by divine prompting, I am convinced) everybody's powers, everybody's temperament, everybody's stomach. He was, indeed, the servant of all for the sake of Jesus Christ.

It is astonishing how one man exercised so many functions at the same time, especially in view of the various ailments from which he suffered. With less strength than theirs he would observe the same rule for fasts and night-watchings as the strongest of all, whose renunciation was recent and vigour unimpaired. He visited the sick when he was more sick than they and supplied consolations for souls and bodies at the same time ; and, for fear too little had been done for any one, he was always going back to the cases in his mind. " This one ", he would say to himself " is feeling the cold ; that one broods ; *he* finds the work heavy ; that food doesn't suit *him*; that one there has received an injury from someone else ; what the other man has done to him is serious and what this man has suffered is equally serious." Then it would take great persistence to bring it about that the offence obtained forgiveness, and that one party treated the insults he had received as a light matter or nothing at all and the other party acknowledged sorrowfully that he had been guilty of very serious offences.

He was always at his work and always had his mind set on easing for everybody the yoke of Christ ; on turning aside from them the darts of the devil ; on dispelling the lowering clouds of evil-doing and bringing back the clear skies of grace ; on instilling in others, by his own love, a love for Christ and for their neighbours and tending the minds of others like his own heart ; on bringing joy back again and causing the desire for Christ to burn as brightly as on the day on which the world was first renounced.

19.   Thus it came about that the whole community, assembled around him from all parts of the earth by a desire for the service of God, and differing as much in habits as in language, loved him with one accord. All called him master and all called him father, and reckoned that in him, country, kinsmen and all else were restored to them together.[1] All had learnt, from his sharing of their own sufferings, to count his sorrows as their own. Not without reason did one of those dearest to him, the priest Salvianus, an eminent man most blessed in Christ,[2] compare him in one of his writings to the sun. For just as the whole aspect of the sky changes with the clouding over or the clearness of the sun, so did that community, thirsting for heaven and dedicated to the pursuit of heavenly things, take from him the weather of their minds, cloudy or clear as the case might be, as from a sun that represented Christ. When *he* was troubled, they were troubled ; when *his* spirits revived, theirs revived too.

It was through this that the graces bestowed by the Holy Spirit were (and, thanks to his prayers, still are) diffused through his monastery, strengthened by the example and admonitions of this great teacher and manifested in many kinds of spiritual gifts, in humility and meekness and in unfeigned charity. Thus the unique glory of the head was shared by all the diverse members.

20.   Amid all these activities he had a great solicitude for strangers and guests—and who ever went past without visiting him ? Who would not have disregarded his own convenience and

[1] Compare Mark x. 30.
[2] Salvianus, after leaving Lérins, lived and wrote as a priest at Marseilles. The date of his death has been variously estimated as about 450 and about 480.

broken off the most prosperous voyage and lost the kindest winds through his desire to see so great a man? And if he could not make the island, he would regard the favour of a good voyage as an act of violence and the weather as most foul. No one approached there without hastening. No one, when there, was conscious of the lapse of time. No one set sail from there without a completely carefree mind ; and his host would speed him on his way with affection and provisions and prayers, parting from him as from a disciple of long standing, although he might only have made his acquaintance then for the first time.

In the squalor of the desert he would serve the guests with delicacies, and welcome all with such joy and affection that he might have been waiting for them. Moreover his material resources matched his bountiful spirit and were administered with a faith that matched both. Eagerly had he obeyed to the words : " Sell all that you have and give to the poor and then come and follow Me " ;[3] and those who had dedicated possessions to works of mercy were eager to take them to him to be dispensed. With complete confidence they would entrust their all to the man whose example they had followed in leaving all things.

This was the cause of the continual stream that came to him from so many devastated regions.[4] And assuredly he was one who would not, like a niggardly or timid steward, distribute something and retain more, with an eye on the growing community under his care. But why suppose that he would not do daily with the possessions of others what he did once and for all with his own, which was to keep for himself and his own followers nothing beyond food and clothing for the immediate present ?

21. The wealth to be dispensed was sometimes exhausted, but faith never. On one occasion there remained in the money-chest, so prodigal in its bounty, only one gold coin out of many thousands ; and, though there was very little in the place, he gave this last coin with the utmost firmness to a passing beggar, saying to me and some others standing by : " If our treasury has

[3] Matt. xix. 21.
[4] i.e. those affected by the barbarian invasions.

nothing left to bring out, you may be sure there is someone not far off with something he is bringing in."

Barely three or four more hours of that day had passed when someone arrived who made good these words. Happy generosity, so well served by faith! Happy faith, for which generosity does not wait! And certainly it never occurred to him that all that his faith supplied him with must be dispensed with his own hand. He had a great many tested men in a number of places, through whom what was brought to him was always being distributed. Thus the bounty of one steward employed many stewards; and his faith, like a fountain free to all, was poured out upon many givers and receivers. Those who came to him with a need never went on further with it, and sometimes found that he himself was its satisfaction.

22. As a natural result, while he was doing his best (with what he thought, or at least hoped, was success) to be hidden, letters expressing devotion came to him from every side. To these he would send replies revealing fresh and many-sided sympathies—grave, courteous and charming. One of these was the occasion of a most beautiful comment by the blessed Eucherius, a rival of his in virtue, who shone in the world and still more in Christ.[5] While he was living on the island next to his, he received a letter from him from the desert [6] written on tablets smeared in the usual way with wax. " You have put back its honey into the comb ", said he.

Anyone, indeed, felt that he had been blessed, and his house blessed and his letter-file blessed, if he had been enriched by the great favour of a little gift from his lips. And assuredly there was so much salt and so much sweetness in his writing that they deserved a place, not in letter-files, or book-cases, but in the ark of the heart. Thus it is that there are very many who carry them inscribed in their memory and love to quote them as evidence of

---

[5] This was St. Eucherius, who, after placing his two sons in the monastery at Lérins, eventually went there himself, and from there retired to a hermitage on the neighbouring island of Lero (see note 2 to section III). A few years after this discourse was delivered he was forced to become Bishop of Lyons, where he achieved great eminence both as a bishop and as a writer, dying A.D. 449. His Feast-day is on November 16th. See Butler's *Lives* and Duchesne, op. cit., II, 163.

[6] i.e. from Lérins.

their affection for him. And to conclude, did anyone ever have so many friends bound to him by services he had rendered to them in person as he had friends wholly unknown to him who loved him and longed intensely to see him?

V

23. While I am telling of his great goodness to everybody, I am saying nothing of his infinite solicitude for me. And yet this solicitude did as much to promote my salvation in Christ as his affection did to leave you with someone to love and be proud of. It was for my sake (and it was a condemnation of me, though an act of great goodness in him) that he consented to visit again the fatherland from which he had turned with aversion. He did not shrink from the long and toilsome journey, which was particularly irksome to him in view of his now numerous infirmities. He found me there already at that age overfond of the world and hardened against God,[1] and he tried to draw me to the love of Christ with his caressing hand—a seducer with no falsehood in him.

I would take too long to describe here the characteristic vehemence with which he pressed his arguments. It is enough to say that he who, even before his entry into the religious life, had been able to ply himself effectively with the sharpest incentives to renouncing the world, now, after he had drunk long at the fountains of wisdom, exhausted himself in these arguments many times over. But, when he found that his well-meant words were making little impression on my mind, he turned to his customary weapon of prayer; and his yearning cry, to which I in my hardness of heart was deaf, reached and moved to compassion the ever-kind heart of God.

It was when I was in the act of contending with him and was from time to time confirming my obstinate stand with an oath (as is the very dangerous custom of the world), that he, if I may use the phrase, was filled with the spirit of prophecy and made

---

[1] St. Hilary would appear to have been at this time a little over twenty, having been born perhaps about A.D. 400.

this prediction. " If you ", he said, " will not do this for me,
God will do it."

But oh, how long he strove to soften my stubbornness with a
flood of tears! How he fought with me for my salvation with
fatherly kisses and embraces! But, for the time being, I won, as
he said, a sorry victory. But God's right hand took over the
work of uprooting me and subduing me; for to God he had
handed me over in his prayers.

And then what a turmoil in my heart! What hurricanes of
diverse and conflicting aspirations! How many times " I will "
and " I won't " succeeded each other in my thoughts! Need I
say more? In the absence of Honoratus, Christ carried on the
work Honoratus had been doing in me. After two days, through
his prayers and the mercy of God, my stubbornness was
conquered. For clear thinking had banished dreams, the good
Lord was calling me, and the world with its pleasures appeared
all very remote. Questions as to what it would be advisable to
aim at or abandon I found myself discussing with myself as one
friend with another.

I thank Thee, good Jesus, I thank Thee for yielding to the
devoted entreaties of Thy servant Honoratus and breaking my
chains and binding me with chains of love for Thee. So long as I
am held fast by these, the chains of sin will never grow strong again.

Thus I who had drawn back in my pride drew near in sub-
mission. I laid aside argument and approached in the new role
of suppliant. Thus the saints by their prayers bring their fugitives
back; thus they conquer the stubborn, thus they subjugate rebels.

24. And *now* with what tears he watered my parched soul!
With what fatherly weeping he moved me to weep also! He
received me with such humility, such compliments, as if it were
he who was being received by me! At the same time, all reason
for prolonging his stay had vanished. Then for the first time he
acknowledged as his fatherland what he had formerly regarded
only as a place to escape from.[2] He led me round as his booty,
rejoicing, triumphant, exulting.

[2] Honoratus and Hilary came from the same part of Gaul, which Honoratus
had revisited in order to seek out Hilary. He was still there when, two days
after his parting with Hilary, Hilary came to him to tell him of his acceptance

Then he made haste to shut me in the desert, and I myself, moved by his example, was already eager for seclusion. First he fed me with milk and then with solid food. He allowed me to drink also from that fountain of heavenly wisdom which welled up within himself. And would that my narrow soul had held as much as he strove to pour in! Then indeed he would have equipped me adequately for you, satisfying worthily your desires by training unawares a fit successor to himself.

Even as it was, if I may say this without offence, how much he enlarged in his dealings with me that charity he poured out upon all, and how much lighter he made the light yoke of Christ for me by his honeyed words! Often he called me " his mind ", often " his soul ", often " his tongue ". He could not bear me to be absent ; he was always eager for the sight of most unworthy me! What can I say of all these things except in the prophet's words ? " The Lord has rewarded him on my behalf." [3]

VI

25. In all this, dearly beloved, I have not been giving a complete narrative of events, but touching briefly upon them ; and I have unfolded for preference, concerning your most sagacious pastor, things better known to others than to you. We have, it is true, seen in this Church here his priesthood formally augmented, but, before that, in devotion and in deeds it was already at the summit. But I would ask how it came about that the demand arose here for one so far off and so unknown. Who implanted in your breasts such regard for one not present and not yet seen? Who aroused in you the desire that, leaving orphaned those whom the Lord had allowed to possess him in the desert, he should be born again for you?

He who inspired it was assuredly He who disposes all things —He who, so long as it seemed to Him fitting, allowed his own country to possess him, and then sent His votary travelling over

---

of the call. The meaning here seems to be that he was now proud to acknowledge this region as his own country since it had produced Hilary, whom he now, as it were, exhibited to it in order to stir it to emulation.

[3] Compare Ps. cxxxvii. 8 in the Vulgate.

seas and lands that others might see and profit by his manifold graces.

26. The outcome of it all has been that the short period which has elapsed since he came among you has been enough to make it easy for you to estimate where I have said too much, and where too little about him, in all this. For you have seen for yourselves, dearly beloved, that watchful solicitude of his, that zeal for discipline, those tears of devotion, that continuous and unfailing serenity of mind to which his tranquil countenance bore witness. You have heard, too, those discourses of his that matched his life and in which purity of heart and splendour of language went hand in hand. You have seen that breadth of charity, which in him was so great that it was well said of him by that holy man whose opinion I quoted just now that, if he had to choose a way of depicting charity, he would consider that the best way would be to paint it in the face of Honoratus.

And, indeed, who ever felt that he had seen enough of him? Who felt him out of place in any of his moods? No one else ever so blended caresses with severity nor dealt out discipline with such an admixture of good humour. If he administered correction, there was always joy in it for the one who was corrected. But never did his gaiety savour of frivolity. Never was his sadness anything but salutary. Never did he ever emit a sigh except for sorrow at another's sin. And you always found that he had grown spiritually, since you had last seen him. He was always at the summit of the virtues, yet he always found some means of advancing further.

27. And look at what his admonitions brought about! Those who were worried threw off their distress. Savage characters came to detest their rages. The arrogant loathed their own pride even more than anyone else did. The lewd abhorred their wantonness; need I continue? He made himself, as the Apostle says, "All things to all men"; [1] he was a medicine that suited everybody. He possessed almost every winning trait in such full measure that you would have thought that he had cultivated it specially and cherished it as if he had no other. In every station

[1] I Cor. ix. 22.

of life he displayed such qualities that he seemed to have been especially designed for it.

28. When he first entered upon the government of this Church of Arles, his first concern was harmony and his chief task was to knit together again into one brotherhood of mutual affection those who had been separated, by passions still at white heat, over the choice of a bishop.[2] As a well-tried shepherd of Israel, he knew very well that it is not easy to impose orders on quarrelling factions. He was anxious, moreover, to rule through affection rather than dominate through fear. For he wished reformation to come voluntarily rather than under pressure, so that it should bring with it this further distinction for his subjects, that they should not appear to render him obedience under compulsion.

Thus the speedy banishment of discord made room for charity, the mother of all virtues ; and the Church of Christ flourished under him as the monastery had flourished previously. She increased her stores of precious graces and decreased her store of precious metals. In other words, when discipline was brought into her house, she shut out from it, as from the House of the Lord, " the mammon of iniquity." He assigned to worthy uses, at last, accumulated riches that had long lain idle. He bestowed her treasures on those who had recently died and the donors once again obtained solace from their gifts. He retained no more than sufficed for his own ministrations and, if other uses had demanded it, I think that the ministrations would have had to give way. For he had constituted himself steward of the gifts and intentions of another generation.

VII

29. He did not cease to labour even when the end was approaching. He enriched many on his sick-bed by his stewardship

[2] In A.D. 426 Patroclus, Bishop of Arles, who was accused of simony and was the centre of fierce feuds, was murdered by a high military official (Duchesne, op. cit., I, 112). According to Migne, he was succeeded for a few months by Euladius, whose name appears in an ancient list of the bishops of Arles, but Duchesne, who prints the list (I, 250) declares (p. 253) that Euladius has no right to figure in it and that it is certain that Honoratus was the immediate successor of Patroclus.

of the Word. But it was impossible to keep him long in bed when it had become a habit with him to overcome weakness that was itself not far off death. Finally, struggling with pain, he preached the sermon in the cathedral on the Feast of the Epiphany. For faith so warred against his infirmities that he could never think of yielding to bodily pain in preference to spiritual fervour ; and so he ministered to your desires beyond his strength.

It was not that any form of sickness attacked him from without, nor did any sudden bout of fever take hold of him. It was a long-standing debility resulting from an excessive severity in the past in his way of life, and even now aggravated by too great a reluctance to accept mitigations, that on the eighth or ninth day after the above-mentioned Festival brought about his death through a slow process of weakening. It was scarcely four days since he had taken part with us in the sacred rites of charity ; for he feared, I know, to sadden his disciples by the knowledge that his end was near. Even during the worst of his illness he was never a burden to anyone, nor did his infirmities cause anyone to shrink from him, as is so often the case. It was in this ordered manner that this dwelling-place of the Holy Spirit ceased from his labours.

30. The way in which he kept the vigour of that stainless mind intact to the last is unbelievable, and his first thought was always to give abundant comfort to his disciples. His over-riding fear for them was that they should be worn out by a prolonged wait after all hope for him was gone, for he was well aware that the actual end is easier to bear than the uncertainty. He was ever wiping away the tears of those around him by his piquant talk, but the more he wiped them away, the more he evoked them, so that he reckoned our pain severer than his own.

It was not easy for anyone to preserve such high courage through such a variety of sufferings, cruel and hard to be borne, and neither to desire death at any time nor to dread it. And yet he was quite content to live through any kind of trial in the service of Christ and, at the same time, not afraid to pass to a new life through that gateway to it to which we all must come. For that ultimate necessity for all men had been long in his thoughts and had not come upon him unawares.

Thus it was that, when he was within sight of the end, he began (just as if he were going abroad and were saying goodbye) to make sure that there was nothing he was leaving half-done or for which his arrangements were less complete than he had intended. So he questioned each of us in turn and urged us to remind him of anything that had slipped his memory. He persisted at the same time in confirming everything with his signature and, when we tried to avoid tiring him, he would insist on our completing whatever had to be done, and his insistence would have that authority that was, as always, like a caress.

31.   On one occasion I was struggling to keep back a storm of tears and stem a flood of weeping. " Why are you weeping ", said he, " over the inevitable lot of men ? My departure ought not to find you so unready for it, when it has not found *me* unready." To these words of his I made answer as best I could in words choked with sobs. I explained that I was not now grieving over my own loss, since I felt sure that the support of his prayers would never fail me and, in fact, counted on its being still stronger after his death. What was distressing me acutely was the pain of seeing his sufferings and his difficult struggles in these last hours.

" And what am I having to bear, who am the least of all," said he, " in comparison with those bitter sufferings that most of the saints endured at the end ? " He mentioned several, and added what I think he had read somewhere : " Great men suffer much, and are born to set an example from which others may learn to suffer."

32.   The chief men of the state came flocking to him—the Governor of the Province and ex-governors—and what burning precepts he brought out for them from under what was now the chill of death ! Indeed, he took his own departure as the text for a most vehement exhortation ; and it was assuredly most fitting that one who had always taught a lesson by his life should draw a lesson from his death as well.

" You see ", he said, " what a perishable guest-house we inhabit. To whatever height we climb in our lifetime, death will drag us down from it. From this inevitable end, no one is exempted by his titles, none by his wealth. It is the same for the righteous and for the unrighteous, for the powerful and for the lowly. We owe great gratitude to Christ who, by His own death and resurrection, illuminates our death with the hope of resurrection for ourselves, and dispels the terror of a death that lasts for ever by the offer of a life that lasts for ever.

" Live your lives, therefore, in such a way that you need not fear the end of life ; look forward to what we call death as to a journey to another country. Death is no penalty if it does not lead to punishment. The rending asunder of soul and body is hard, but the joining together of soul and body in the fires of hell will be much harder. Let our spirit throughout our lives realize its own nobility and declare war upon the body, and strive against the vices of the body, so that it may be separated from the filth of the flesh by a happy divorce and preserve both flesh and spirit unstained for the peace of eternity.

" There they will be happily reunited, where ' the saints shall rejoice in their glory and be joyful in their beds,'[1] that is to say, in the bodies that contain them. For if they have consecrated to righteousness the limbs and organs that are now their partners, they will meet them again as their well-remembered hosts.

" Act on this, therefore. This is the legacy that your Honoratus leaves you ; with his last breath he invites you to inherit the heavenly kingdom. Let no one be held too fast by affection for this world. You can see that you will be forced to lose it ; best turn away from it now of your own free will. Let no one surrender himself to riches ; let none be the slave of money ; let the empty show of wealth seduce no one. It is a crime to allow what could be used to purchase salvation[2] to become the instrument of your damnation, or for anyone to be taken captive by what could have been his ransom."

All the time he was speaking he was teaching them even more by his expression, even more by his eyes, even more by all his senses straining towards heaven. No words of a reporter could adequately convey his words of fire ; but the words of the speaker were equally inadequate to convey the spirit that inspired them. Thus in these exhortations, in which he poured out his words with

[1] Ps. cxlix. 5.   [2] i.e. in the sense of Luke xvi. 9.

certain gestures quite unwonted, he imparted a quite unusual kind of blessing.

33. As his limbs began to fail in their service, new beauties of mind kept coming to birth. He had put everything in order (for there were not many of his activities still needing completion) and now he went over in his mind all those who were dear to him. So far as his weariness allowed him to mention them by name, he enriched each one with a greeting sent through those who surrounded him. Moreover, he whispered in my ear :

" Apologize to that holy man for its having been impossible to do what he wanted."[3]

What great and astonishing alertness of mind it shows, for a man labouring in the grip of death to have made sure that he had removed, so far as in him lay, all cause for anyone to be sad, or had at least not let it remain without apologies !

I ask, therefore, seeing that he was leaving in a strange land all those disciples of his whom affection had drawn to this city, why he laid no charge upon any of them either to return to the world or to remain in community-life, and gave none of them definite directions where to live. It was, indeed, as if he foresaw that they would not be dispersed, apart from those who, even while he was alive, had already made up their minds to depart. And in fact it is hard to think of anyone who has been lost to our community except those whose loss he predicted and who felt the call of their homeland too strong, or the discipline too severe.

Meanwhile he was growing drowsier and, in a panic, we kept interrupting his sleep. " I am surprised ", he said, " that, when I am so very weary after so many sleepless hours, you should take such a serious view of my sleepiness ! " Then, when everything had been seen to and we were protesting that he was sitting up too long at the last, he replied with that caressing playfulness that was so characteristic, and with his habitual serenity, that he would allow us to be a nuisance, since we were looking after him !

He had almost used up his life before his sweetness !

34. Then he fell into his last sleep and passed, sleeping, into

---

[3] This is Migne's choice among various readings and requires us to suppose that the dying man mentioned a name, which St. Hilary naturally omitted. It gives a very good sense when read with what follows.

the quiet of death without the usual struggle at the end. He experienced no troublesome delays in passing ; and that holy soul, noble and simple and unstained by any contact with the world, was received by angelic choirs. Many, at the time, had their slumbers broken by various visions, all of which had this common feature, that this saint of ours was met by welcoming saints. And, in fact, at that same hour in the dead of night the cathedral was swiftly filled by those who gathered to meet the hallowed body and who, you would think, could only have been roused by angelic messengers.

The lifeless body was left, still vitalized by the spirit, in all its comeliness ; for the face that had charmed all preserved intact the beauty of its features. But of course you know all this yourselves ; and, much more fully than any words can do, you will depict it in your meditations.

35. There was no one who did not feel that he would suffer a great loss if he did not see the body, if he did not imprint his kiss upon the face or some other member (as reverence or affection moved him) or upon the bier on which the hallowed body lay. At first it lay vested with a great display of faith ; afterwards, on its way to the grave, with a greater display of faith it was almost stripped naked. For faith would not even spare his vestments, hallowed as they were by his use of them, but reckoned that the pulling out of a thread from his garments was something better than the costliest gift. Your affection fought over his funeral.

By his obsequies you put new life into my as yet unnoticed sojourning amongst you. All that charity of spirit poured out on him was food to me. For who on that day was to be found within his house ? Or who within these city walls did not enter this basilica overwhelmed as if by some private sorrow ? It was accounted a great honour to have set a hand or a shoulder to the bier. You saw his glory and, in it, your glory too. For the rites of the funeral were the homage of your faith ; and you were as glad to have had him, as you were sad to have lost him.

It gives no little confidence to be privileged to have his tomb ; for we who treasure his bones here may assuredly count on his pleading in heaven. We saw incense and myrrh carried before his bier ; but there rose to God a sweeter fragrance from your hearts when you showed such great devotion to so great a pastor. When you gave him glory, you gave still more to God ; and, though many tongues clashed in the chanting, love sang with one.

VIII

36. The good Lord, when He impelled your wills to elect insignificant me, enabled me not to be farther than this from his tomb. He will also, if you pray for me, enable me not to depart far from His ways but, instead, to hasten to do without further consideration or argument whatever I find that he used to do himself.

For, as I see the position, God was even then forming me through him for you. It was for you that Honoratus equipped me, in spite of my unworthiness. It was for you, though he knew it not, that he came with such toil to find me. It was for you that, with such intense solicitude and care, he trained me as best he could, hoping to find faith in me, as it might be his blood in my veins. And when I had deserted him at the beginning of his episcopate and returned to the island out of love for solitude, it was for you—I dare not say unconsciously, for perhaps he foresaw it all—that he went to great trouble to get me away from it, attempting it first with much labour through letters and then with much cajolery by journeyings there himself ; and thus he made for me a homeland in your affections near the site of his tomb.

But how shall we manage, now that his premature departure has left me still immature ? It is not for us in any matter to find fault even slightly with the hidden counsels of the eternal King ; you could not easily have realized what a treasure you had lost if your treasure had been restored to you intact.

37. Great and far-famed is your glory, Honoratus ! Your virtue did not need to be attested by manifestations and marvels.[1]

---

[1] " Manifestations and marvels " renders the one Latin word " signa " ; in the remainder of the paragraph the single word " manifestations " is used for it. " Acts of power " in the next line renders " virtutes ", which in the rest of the paragraph is rendered "spiritual powers " or "powers " (or "spiritual power

For your manner of life was itself full of acts of power and pre-eminently something new to wonder at ; in a sense, it was one continuous manifestation. We know, of course (if we have been in close contact with you) that many favours were granted to you by divine intervention ; but you yourself regarded these as the least part of your portion. You took more delight in what Christ set down as your virtues and spiritual powers than in what men recorded as manifestations. And yet what could be a greater manifestation of spiritual power than to shun manifestations and hide the powers ? And, indeed, you spoke to Christ on such intimate terms (as it were) that I think it must have taken the most strenuous prayers to prevent your spiritual power being proclaimed by manifestations.

Peace, like persecution, has its martyrs ; and you, so long as you dwelt in the body, were a constant witness for Christ.[2] It was stupefying to see how day after day without fail the Cross took its toll of the strength you had in your youth, diminishing it through strict and constant abstinence and bringing that meagre look we knew so well, though the comeliness was never lost. Yet you held this course without conspicuous or over-scrupulous observance and shunned all excesses and that thirst for glory that is so closely related to excess.

Your speech was always of peace or of purity, of devotion or of charity. Wherever Christ dwells in the heart, He is the fountain of all these things ; and to you, and through you, He gave the fruits of " charity, joy, peace, patience, good-nature,

---

in the singular). The English word " virtue " (or " virtues ") stands in this paragraph for " meritum " (or " merita "). For these three Latin words I have, in this paragraph, practically reverted, for once in a way, to the old and much-abused method of representing each word in the original by the same word in English every time it occurs. The result, considered as English, is inevitably a little odd ; but it will be pardoned, perhaps, if I have given some idea (a) of the elaborate word-play in which St. Hilary indulges, (b) of the very precise thinking that lies behind it (c) of the almost insuperable difficulties with which a translator into modern English has frequently to contend owing to the ambiguities latent in these words (especially in " virtutes " which may mean either " miracles " or " virtues ", (d) of the possible effect of the use of the ambiguous term " virtutes " (in hands less adroit than those of St. Hilary) on the expectation of the miraculous (e) of the true meaning of " virtue " and its real relation to the miraculous. (See the Introduction, section III.)

[2] The word " martyr ", which is Latin as well as English, is a transliteration of a Greek word meaning " witness ". The word rendered " witness " in this sentence is " testis ".

kindliness, good faith, gentleness, and self-control." [3] These
grew luxuriantly and were multiplied into a rich abundance that
brought salvation and joy to many. With good reason you sang
to the Lord : " Those who fear Thee shall see me and be
gladdened " ; [4] and to Him you unfailingly ascribed every good
thing in your manner of living. Again and again you used to
repeat to yourself or your disciples : " For what do you possess
that was not a gift? And if it was a gift, why boast as if it were
not one? " [5] But the good in your life was all the more yours,
because you denied it was yours.

38. You experienced that solace shared by all who want Our
Lord. There are some who glory in being prosperous in this
life ; you taught, on the contrary, that we should exult in God ;
and you would murmur in that gently modulated voice of yours,
that so well expressed your soul : " Let the hearts of those who
seek the Lord be gay." [6] Nothing ever gave you more pleasure
than prayer and psalms. To such an extent had Christ penetrated
your very tissues that sometimes (and I speak from personal
knowledge) your limbs would be overcome by peaceful slumber
but your tongue would continue to sound His praises in the
accustomed chant, even through your sleep. Often there would
pour from you when sleeping the most rational words of
exhortation, the most affectionate words of prayer. For your
body took its rest in your bed, but your mind in Christ. These
things we all saw if we happened to be present.

But how eagerly and how often you, in whom alone we all
could always rest, would tell us dreams—not dreams fore-
shadowing anything, nor provoked by any anxiety for the future,
but springing from a certain unsatisfied desire, namely for
martyrdom. For that was always in your meditations and Our
Lord used sometimes, I believe, playfully to excite your hanker-
ing for it, so that you underwent it, as if a persecution was raging

[3] This list is identical with the list of nine " fruits of the Spirit " found in
Wordsworth and White's text of the Vulgate (Gal. v. 22, 23) and corresponds
almost exactly to the Greek. It is expanded in the received text of the Vulgate
to twelve fruits (see the footnote in Mgr. Knox's translation for a possible
explanation). The renderings given here (as elsewhere) are my own.
[4] Ps. cxviii (cxix). 74.
[5] 1 Cor. iv. 7.
[6] Ps. civ (cv). 3.

against your faith. And I certainly think that no one would deny that what kept you from martyrdom was not the absence of the will for it, but of the torturers.

Every day, indeed, in discourses of utter sincerity, you bore witness to the faith in the Father, the Son and the Holy Spirit; and it would not have been easy for anyone to have held forth on the Divine Trinity with the emphasis and lucidity that was yours, when you were distinguishing the Persons within It, but making them equal in the eternity and the majesty of Their glory.

39. Remember, therefore, friend of God, remember always us—you who stand stainless before God, " singing the new song and following the Lamb wherever He goes." [7] You are *His* retainer, but you are *our* patron; you are the acceptable interpreter of our prayers. Strong advocate, present the petitions of the flock you fed, which it offers at your tomb. Obtain this boon, that all of us together, bishop and people, inspired by a single purpose, may be privileged to attain in some degree to what you commanded us, what you taught us, through Our Lord Jesus Christ who received you into His glory and who, with His Father and the Holy Spirit, lives and reigns as God for all eternity. Amen.

[7] Apoc. xiv. 3, 4.

THE LIFE OF ST. GERMANUS OF AUXERRE
BY CONSTANTIUS OF LYONS

CONSTANTIUS was born at Lyons about A.D. 415 and spent his life there. He was a monk and may possibly have been a priest. He was devout and learned and a great student of Scripture. He had some literary gifts as a writer, both of prose and of verse. In this connection it has been said with substantial truth : " He writes clearly and vividly and is fond of short and pithy phrases. His style, having been formed by a literary training, is free from the turgid language all too common at that period." He attends to the rhythm of his sentences and commits very few solecisms. Some attempt has been made in the present translation to reproduce the general effect.

He undertook the Life of St. Germanus at the orders of his bishop, Patiens, who had become Bishop of Lyons in A.D. 449, the year after the saint's death. Its most authoritative editor, Wilhelm Levison, suggests the year 480 or a little later as the probable date of its composition. After circulating privately at Lyons, it was given to a wider public at the instance of Censurius, Bishop of Auxerre from about A.D. 470, the third in succession to St. Germanus. It was dedicated by him to these two bishops.

The present translation is made from the text edited by Wilhelm Levison in the *Monumenta Germaniae Historica, Scriptores Rerum Merovingicarum*, vol. VII, pp. 247-283, 1920. Levison rightly eliminated from his text certain fragments from other hagiographical writings (such as the Life of St. Genevieve) interpolated in many MSS. from the ninth century onwards (see pp. 244, 245 of his Introduction) ; but, against certain critics (e.g. Krusch) who proposed to " throw away the baby with the bath-water " and discredit the whole work, he maintained the substantial authenticity and reliability of the remainder.

THE LIFE OF ST. GERMANUS, BISHOP OF AUXERRE
BY CONSTANTIUS OF LYONS

DEDICATIONS
TO HIS MOST BLESSED AND APOSTOLIC LORDSHIP AND MY PERPETUAL PATRON

PATIENS, FATHER IN GOD,[1] FROM CONSTANTIUS, A SINNER

Amongst the virtues, the first place is rightly claimed by obedience; and, though it makes many of us attempt what we cannot accomplish, those who obey orders regardless of their powers merit praise at least for their devotion. Now you, most Reverend Father in God, desiring to secure for a holy man the fame due to his virtues and to publish the witness of his miracles for all to profit by, have again and again commanded me to preserve both for our own and for future generations, in such language as I can, the life of the holy bishop Germanus, hitherto shrouded in silence. In boldly approaching this task I know myself to be guilty of presumption. But grant me your pardon; perhaps some blame attaches to your own judgement; you should have chosen for so great a topic a worthier narrator. But since we have both sinned out of charity, you in thinking me able to do what I cannot and I in deferring with good will to your authority, pray for me that my service may through your intercession earn the favour that it cannot win by its own merits. May you long prosper. Remember me always.

TO HIS MOST BLESSED LORDSHIP, WHOM I REVERE AS AN APOSTLE, CENSURIUS,[2] FATHER IN GOD, FROM CONSTANTIUS, A SINNER

---

[1] Latin, " Papa ", a term then frequently applied to other bishops besides the Bishop of Rome. For Patiens, see the Introductory Note.
[2] See the Introductory Note, towards the end.

It is my first care to preserve intact a sense of humility and, if now I break violently through the barriers it imposes, the blame attaches to those who lay commands upon me, rather than to myself. When I strung together, far from completely, the life and deeds of the blessed bishop Germanus, it was the authority of your holy brother-prelate Patiens that brought it about; I was obeying his commands, if not as I ought, at least as best I could. And now that my obedience has come to the knowledge of your Beatitude, it seems that I must once more be overbold. For you have commanded that my poor pages, which hitherto have been for little more than private circulation, are to go abroad bearing my name; and I am, so to speak, to incriminate myself and surrender myself to execution. For plainly I shall fall under condemnation if my rustic idiom [3] is brought to learned ears. However, I have cast aside the veil of modesty, obeyed your order, and sent you this pledge of the devotion I bear you. I ask only this as a token of your charity, that in your kindness you say two prayers for me: May my readers not scrutinize my words too closely and may my service be brought by your intercession to the knowledge of my holy master Germanus.

PREFACE

MOST people are drawn to writing by an abundance of materials, and wits are supposed to be enriched where there is much to say; but for myself, as I begin to recount, far from completely, the life and deeds of that most illustrious man, Bishop Germanus, I am filled with trepidation at the number of his miracles. Just as the brightness of the sun brought to bear upon stupefied humans blunts the keenness of the eyes, and light throws light into confusion, so my feeble mind shrinks from so much to praise, heaped up before its impotence. Thus, within my breast, two courses are

---

[3] Latin, " verborum meorum abiectio ". This is the conventional modesty of the period. In point of fact, Constantius' style is distinctly literary and artificial and its occasional obscurities are generally due, not to rustic crudeness, but to an undue straining after literary and epigrammatic effect at a period when the language was in a state of transition.

in conflict. On the one side, my knowledge of my impotence says
" No " ; on the other side, the sight of such piety, and the witness
borne by countless miracles, drive me to record and bring to light
matters that it would be impious to hide under a veil of silence
from those who might profit by a knowledge of them. I have
chosen, therefore, to shut my eyes to my own shame rather than
allow the works of God to grow old in a prolonged oblivion. The
materials must excuse the narrator. Those who are displeased by
my rustic idiom will at least find pleasure in the beauty of the
deeds it recounts. Nor need I fear that I shall be regarded as
having pushed myself forward into such a task as this, for so many
cycles of the seasons have gone round that a knowledge of the
facts, dimmed by long silence, can now only be acquired by labour.
Indeed, I should have preferred that another than myself should
have been the historian of such good things, for whoever he was
he would have been more worthy than I. But, since this has not
come about, better myself than no one.

I

Germanus, then, was a native of the town of Auxerre,[1] born of
parents of the highest rank,[2] and was from earliest childhood given
a liberal education. In this, the instruction he received was
matched by the abundance of his talent and together these gave
him learning doubly assured, by nature and by industry. Moreover, that nothing should be lacking to complete his education,
when he had done with the lecture-rooms of Gaul he added in
Rome a knowledge of law to the completeness he had already
attained.

Next, practising as a barrister he became the ornament of the
law-courts. While he was thus engaged and dazzling all by the
praises he drew upon himself, he took a wife, whose birth, wealth
and character were all of the highest. Then, when he was at the
height of his reputation in the legal profession, the state promoted
him to official rank by conferring on him the supreme office of

---

[1] Latin, " Autessiodurum ".
[2] Probably in A.D. 378.   His parents were Christians.

dux[3] and the rule over more than one Province.[4] Assuredly his training was being directed by the hidden wisdom of God so that nothing should be lacking to the completeness of the apostolic pontiff-to-be. Eloquence was provided to equip the preacher, legal learning as an aid to justice, and the society of a wife to witness to his chastity.

II

Suddenly divine authority intervened and universal consent executed its decrees. For all the clergy, the whole nobility, the townsfolk and the countryfolk, with one accord demanded Germanus for their bishop. A war was declared by the people against their magistrate, who was easily overcome, since even his own staff turned against him. Thus he received the fulness of the priesthood[1] under compulsion, as a conscript ; but, this done, immediately he made the change complete. He deserted the earthly militia to be enrolled in the heavenly ; the pomps of this world were trodden underfoot ; a lowly way of life was adopted, his wife was turned into a sister, his riches were distributed among the poor and poverty became his ambition.

[3] The rank of *dux* (afterwards " duke ") was at this period strictly military and, by a rule made by the Emperor Diocletian a century earlier, might not be combined with civil office. Some therefore, including Levison (loc. cit., p. 231), have asserted that Constantius is using the term incorrectly here. Certainly the office of *dux* could not have been the peak of the ladder of civic promotion (" culmen cursus honorum "). Nevertheless it is quite possible that in those troubled times Germanus did actually combine the office with that of civil governor, in which case he would have commanded the armies of his Provinces ; see the *Cambridge Medieval History*, vol. I, p. 30, on the exception sometimes made in the case of a frontier Province, the ruler of which would combine civil and military functions and would be " naturally described " as *dux*. In the present case there seems to be a clear allusion to military functions in the phrase in the next section about deserting the earthly militia, and possible allusions elsewhere (e.g. sections IX, XVII (end)) ; note also the general's cape that formed Germanus' bedspread when he was Bishop (section IV). Constantius certainly seems to be using the term *dux* with intention.

[4] Armorica and Nervica, roughly Brittany, Normandy and Hainault, all of them districts liable to be raided either by sea or by land.

[1] Latin, " sacerdotium ". This term, like *sacerdos*, is used by Constantius in connection both with bishops and with simple priests (see the Introduction, section I). The narrative here suggests that St. Ambrose, was a layman when he was acclaimed a bishop ; but there is evidence from other sources that has led some biographers to think that he had been a priest, perhaps for some years, before the episcopacy was virtually forced upon him. The date of his consecration as bishop was almost certainly 7th July, 418. See Levison in loc.

III

But no words can describe the fierceness with which he did violence to himself and the crucifixions and penances with which he persecuted his own body. I will summarise them briefly, with strict fidelity to the truth. From the day upon which he entered upon the fulness of the priesthood[1] until the end of his life, he persisted in nourishing his soul by starving his body, even to the extent of never taking wheaten bread, nor wine, nor vinegar, nor oil nor pulse nor even salt for seasoning. (It is true that on Easter and Christmas Day a drink was served in which there would have been a taste of wine if it had not been destroyed by excessive dilution in the way one tempers with quantities of water the harshness of vinegar!). At meals he first took a taste of ashes, then bread made of barley which he himself had pounded and ground. And this food, acknowledged to be more trying than fasting, was never served until evening, except sometimes on a Wednesday and generally on Saturdays.[2]

[1] See previous note.

[2] " Et cum hic cibus gravior ieiuniis indicetur, nunquam nisi vespere, interdum tamen in ebdomada media, plerumque die septimo ponebatur ". Many take this sentence to mean that Germanus ate no food at all except sometimes on Wednesdays and generally on Saturdays ; and Prunel, in his *Saint Germain d'Auxerre* (*Les Saints*) supports this interpretation by giving " die septimo " the quite impossible meaning of " on Sundays " instead of " on Saturdays ", Sunday being the natural day for relaxing a fast. (His paraphrase runs : " Cette nourriture, plus mortifiante que le jeûne, était la seule qu'il se permît ; il ne la prenait jamais que le soir, parfois au milieu de la semaine, mais le plus souvent seulement le dimanche ". (p. 33)). He speaks of the famous fast of St. Geneviève of Paris, a disciple of St. Germanus, as an imitation of this fast of his. But even if it is true that St. Geneviève sometimes took food only twice a week, she was virtually an enclosed nun, while Germanus was incessantly engaged in the multifarious work of his episcopal office and, short of a continuing physical miracle, could not have sustained such a fast through an episcopate of thirty years.

All this would be no reason for altering the common interpretation of the Latin if the Latin could bear no other meaning ; but the Latin, admittedly awkward and obscure, seems to me to bear very well the meaning I have given it here. For, in the first place, " hebdomada media " and " dies septimus " cannot reasonably be taken, in such a context as this, as meaning anything but " Wednesday " and " Saturday " and these were both penitential days in the West. It is true that at Milan the Eastern usage was followed that made Saturday a non-fasting day (see the Life of St. Ambrose in this volume, section XXXVIII and note I there) but Saturday in that capacity was associated, not with Wednesday, but with Sunday. Moreover, in the original source for the Life of St. Geneviève (*Vita Genovefae Virginis Parisiensis*, in *Monumenta Germaniae*

IV

His clothing was a cloak[1] and tunic, regardless of the seasons, for winter brought no addition to it nor was summer allowed to lighten it. These two garments continued to be used, unless one was given away, until they fell to pieces from hard wear. Under them there was always a hair-shirt. Narrow rough-hewn planks formed a framework for his bed, the space between them being filled to the brim with ashes. These, by being constantly compressed by his weight, became as hard as unbroken earth. His only bedclothes were a piece of sacking spread beneath him and a single military cape[2] over him ; there was nothing in the way of a pillow to place under his neck to support his head.

Lying flat like this, he condemned his limbs to be stretched out along the ground. He never removed his clothes at night and seldom either his girdle or his shoes, and he always had round his neck a leather strap with a box containing relics. His groans were continual and prayer unceasing, for he could get little sleep in such acute discomfort. Everyone must have his own opinion ; mine is quite definitely that the blessed Germanus, amid all these crucifixions, endured a drawn-out martyrdom. But how wonderful is the power and goodness of our God ! for He gave His servant, travelling faithfully along the true road, a two-fold recompense.

Historica, Script. Rev. Merov., vol. III, p. 220) it is stated that her two days for relaxing her fast were, not Wednesday and Saturday, but Thursday and Sunday ; and the editor, B. Krusch, quotes a sentence from the Life of St. Radegunde (6th century) to the effect that it was on Thursday and Sunday that she broke her Lenten fast. Clearly the natural inference from all this is that any variation that Germanus made in his diet on Wednesdays and Saturdays would have been in the direction of greater austerity, not less : and the explanation surely lies in the opening words of the sentence, that his food was such as to be more penitential than a fast, so that he was aggravating rather than relaxing his austerities when he made an exception to his rule of waiting until evening for his daily meal. The " cum " might, in fact, quite well be rendered " although ", and the " tamen " quite naturally gives the sense of " except ".

[1] Latin, "cuculla", possibly, but, at this period, improbably meaning the distinctive garment of the monk known as the " cowl " (a word derived from " cuculla "). It does not seem likely that St. Germanus became a monk and he only resided intermittently at the monastery he founded near the town (see sections VI and IX).

[2] Latin, " sagulum ", usually meaning a general's cape, presumably the one that Germanus had worn as *dux* ; see note 3 to section I ; also note 1 to section III of the Life of St. Martin in this volume.

Such errors as he may formerly have committed were purged away and in the process a refined sanctity was rapidly acquired ; and, though he may have been a debtor by reason of past sins, he was presently able to draw for the benefit of others upon a stock of accumulated virtues.

V

He was especially punctilious in hospitality. His house was open to all without exception and he entertained them at his table without breaking his own fast. He washed the feet of all his guests with his own hands, following the example of the Lord whose servant he was.

VI

Thus this man of blessings achieved something very difficult : amidst all the coming and going he lived the life of the solitary, and inhabited the desert while dwelling in the world.

Furthermore, for the advancement of religion he provided two roads to Christ, by founding a monastery within sight of the town, across the river Yonne,[1] so that the surrounding population might be brought to the Catholic faith[2] by contact with the monastic community as well as by the ministrations of the Church. This was all the more likely to succeed since the flame of faith was fanned by such a bishop and such a teacher, to say nothing of the miracles. As for these, when, as his holiness grew, he came to make proof of his spiritual powers, his motive was not presumption but mercy.

VII

There was at that time a man of high character named Januarius who was in the Governor's service as head of his office staff and

---

[1] Latin, " Icauna ". The monastery seems to have been originally dedicated to the martyrs Cosmas and Damian but to have been afterwards called after a monk named Marianus who was buried there.

[2] The barbarian tribes who at this period were settling within the Empire either were pagans or had learnt their Christianity from the Arians (see note 2 to section VI of the Life of St. Martin). There must also have been a good many survivals of the older paganism of Gaul so prominent during the episcopate of St. Martin fifty years earlier (see his Life).

used to bring him the gold collected in taxes from the Province. One day he broke his journey to visit the Bishop and mislaid his handbag. It was accidentally found, when no one was looking, by a man who was frequently the victim of demoniacal possession. Presently the traveller resumed his journey and discovered his loss. He filled the city with his lamentations and demanded the money back from the holy Bishop just as if he had entrusted it to him. The latter, as if he had really been his debtor, promised in the name of God that it should be restored.

Now, the day on which the man had rushed all over the city in his frantic search had been a Saturday. The next day,[1] when there was still no trace of the gold, the man who was looking for it clasped the Bishop's knees with tears in his eyes, assuring him that it would mean the death penalty for him if the state's money were not found. The Bishop enjoined patience, promising that all would be well. Soon afterwards, before setting out for Mass, he gave orders for one of the sufferers from demoniacal possession to be brought before him privately; and who should be brought to him but the man responsible for the theft.

He put him through a strict examination, saying that it was impossible for a crime on his conscience to remain concealed. Then he ordered the enemy of souls who had been prompting these evil deeds to admit the truth of the matter without delay. But the wicked spirit, from sheer malice, denied having committed the crime. At this the Bishop, in righteous anger, ordered the liar to be produced in front of the congregation and, without further delay, set out to celebrate Mass.

He gave the solemn salutation to the people,[2] then prostrated him at full length in prayer. All at once the unhappy man, the captive and at the same time the servant of the demon, was lifted high into the air. The church was filled with his screams, the whole congregation was in confusion and the man himself, yelling out the Bishop's name as if he were in the midst of flames, confessed his crime.

[1] Following Levison's interpretation of " post pridie " here.
[2] Namely " Dominus sit semper vobiscum ", followed by the preparatory prayer (Duchesne, *Origines du culte Chrétien*, p. 193 sq.).

Then at last the man of blessings rose from his prayer and came down to the steps of the sanctuary.[3] He called up the raving man, cross-examined him and learnt the whole truth. The coins were brought out of their hiding-place, the acclamations of the people resounded, and with one accord they proclaimed the sanctity of Germanus and the power of God. By one and the same miracle the man who had been robbed had got back his money and the demoniac his sanity. Germanus had, indeed, cured many before this, but always under a veil of secrecy. What made this occasion so notable was its publicity.

VIII

At one time there was a fearful conspiracy of demons to wage a kind of war on the man of blessings himself. When they found him immune, thanks to the breastplate of faith, to all their assaults, they contrived a device for the destruction of his flock. First the children, then their elders, began to succumb to a swelling in their throats which brought death after an illness of less than three days. His congregation was being wiped out as if they were being slaughtered by the sword. No human measures brought any relief and, when it was almost too late, the panic-stricken people appealed to their Bishop for divine aid.

Immediately he blessed some oil and, at its touch, the internal swelling went down and a passage was thereby opened for breathing and swallowing. The heavenly remedy effected a cure as rapidly as the onslaught of the disease had brought death. One of those who had been possessed bawled out when he was being exorcised that all this had been brought about by the entry of demons, and acknowledged that they had been put to flight by the holy man's prayer.

---

[3] Latin, " ad pogium "—" podium ", a word of various meanings in ecclesiastical architecture but always signifying some sort of elevation from which the congregation could be addressed ; see Levison in loc., quoting Boschius.

IX

The man of blessings made it his practice, as general[1] of the soldiers of God, to stay alternately at the monastery and the church, to set the goal of perfection before each of the rivals in this warfare. On one occasion, when he had been invited to the monastery, he was detained by business and excused himself from coming. A little later, however, when the cause of the delay had been disposed of, he set off to give the brethren a surprise. Now, some of them were troubled by demons and it happened that just then one of the sufferers was in the grip of one. Suddenly he announced at the top of his voice : " Germanus is at the river but cannot cross because he has no boat."

For a long time the abbot gave no credence to this assertion, supposing the evil spirit to be lying, since the Bishop had excused himself and would not be coming. But he persisted in his cries[2] and one of the brethren was sent and reported that the demon was right. A boat was sent and the Bishop crossed and was received with the usual fervour. He fell at once to praying and the community knelt with him.

Suddenly the demoniac rose in the empty air, held by invisible cords. There was no more delay than was necessary for the Bishop to rise from prayer, and all that he required of the demon was that it should go out of the man with some bodily weakness of his.[3] Thus adjured it departed, leaving filth behind it and a stench worthy of it.[4]

[1] Latin, " dux ". See note 3 to section I.
[2] For the reference of the pronouns indistinguishably to the demon and the demoniac, see note 4 to section XVII of the Life of St. Martin.
[3] Latin, " cum aliqua debilitate discederet " ; see next note.
[4] See note 4 to section XVII of the Life of St. Martin. The preceding sentence is obscure and many copyists have sought to clarify it by inserting a negative ; but the sense seems to be that some bodily convulsions or disorders are to be expected when a demon is expelled, almost as part of the mechanism of expulsion. This sense is certainly borne out by innumerable stories of exorcism from the Gospels onwards (see Mark i. 26 ; ix. 24–26 (25–27)).

X

He was once making a journey in winter and had gone fasting and weary all day long. It was put to him that the approach of night made it necessary to make a stop somewhere. There was a house at a little distance, obviously uninhabited, with its roof partly fallen in, and all overgrown owing to the neglect of the neighbours. In fact it almost looked as if it would be better to pass the night in the cold in the open air than to face the dangers and horrors of that place, particularly as two old men declared that it was so terribly haunted as to be quite uninhabitable. But as soon as the man of blessings heard this, he made for the horrible ruin as if it had been a most desirable residence. He found in it, amongst what had once been a great many rooms, one that was still something like one, and there his little party and their slender packs were deposited and a short supper was taken ; but the Bishop would eat nothing at all.

Presently, when the night was well advanced, one of the clergy had begun to read aloud, as his duty was, but the Bishop, worn out by fasting and fatigue, had fallen asleep. Suddenly there appeared before the reader's eyes a dreadful spectre, which rose up little by little as he gazed on it, while the walls were pelted with a shower of stones. The terrified reader implored the protection of the Bishop, who started up and fixed his eyes upon the fearful apparition. Then, invoking the name of Christ, he ordered it to declare who he was and what he was doing there.

At once it lost its terrifying demeanour and, speaking low as a humble suppliant, said that he and a companion after committing many crimes were lying unburied, and that was why they disturbed the living, because they could not rest quietly themselves. It asked the Bishop to pray to the Lord for them that He would take them to Himself and grant them eternal rest.

Moved to pity, the holy man told the apparition to show him where they lay. Then, with a torch carried in front, the ghost proceeded to lead the way and, in spite of great difficulties due to the ruins and the stormy night, pointed out the place where they had been thrown. With the return of day the Bishop persuaded some of the neighbours to come, and himself stood by to urge on the work. Rubble that had accumulated haphazard in the course of time was raked up and cleared away. The bodies were found, thrown down anyhow, the bones still fastened together with iron fetters. A grave was dug in accordance with the Church's law, the limbs were freed from the chains and wrapped in winding sheets, earth was thrown upon them and smoothed down, and the prayers for the dead were recited. There was repose for the dead and quiet for the living. From that day onwards the house lost all its terrors and was restored and regularly occupied.

XI

Another incident deserves to be recounted that took place some days later on the same journey. Oncoming darkness had compelled the Bishop to seek hospitality, and his hosts were quite humble people, a thing which he greatly preferred, as he shunned ostentation. When he had spent the night according to his custom in the recitation of the divine office, the sun rose, but no crowing of cocks heralded it, although there were numbers of these birds about the place. He enquired the cause of this novelty and was told that, for a long time now, the natural habits of the cocks had given way to a melancholy silence. Everybody asked for his help, so he made return for their hospitality. He took some corn and seasoned it with a blessing and when the birds had eaten it they wearied the ears of the household almost to distraction by their constant crowing. Thus the power of God reveals its greatness even in the smallest things.

XII

About this time[1] a deputation from Britain came to tell the bishops of Gaul that the heresy of Pelagius[2] had taken hold of the people over a great part of the country and help ought to be

[1] A.D. 429.
See the Life of St. Augustine, section XVIII and note 1 there.

brought to the Catholic faith as soon as possible. A large number of bishops gathered in synod to consider the matter and all turned for help to the two who in everybody's judgement were the leading lights of religion, namely Germanus and Lupus,[3] apostolic priests who through their merits were citizens of heaven, though their bodies were on earth. And because the task seemed laborious, these heroes of piety were all the more ready to undertake it; and the stimulus of their faith brought the business of the synod to a speedy end.[4]

XIII

Thus they embarked upon the ocean under the leadership and inspiration of Christ, who, in the midst of dangers, kept His servants safe and proved their worth. At first, when the ship put out to sea, she ran before light breezes blowing from the Bay of Gaul [1] until she was in mid-channel where, gaze as you might, you could see nothing but sky and water. Then it was not long before the ocean was assaulted by the violence of demons, haters of religion, who were livid with malice at the sight of such great men hastening to bring salvation to the nations. They heaped up dangers, roused the gales, hid the heavens and the day under a night of clouds and filled the thick darkness with the terrors of the sea and air. The sails could not resist the fury of the winds and the fragile craft scarcely sustained the weight of the waters. The sailors were powerless and abandoned their efforts; the vessel was navigated by prayer and not by muscles. And at that point the leader himself, the Bishop, his body worn out, in his weariness went to sleep.

Then indeed did the storm put forth its strength; it was as if a restraining hand had gone. Before long the vessel was actually being swamped by the waves that swept over it. At last the

---

[3] Bishop of Trecassina (Troyes), from about 426 to 478 (Duchesne, *Fastes Episcopaux*, II, 449), another canonized saint, whose feast is on July 29th.

[4] According to the chronicler, St. Prosper of Aquitaine, it was Pope St. Celestine I who sent Germanus to Britain, but there is no essential contradiction between the two accounts. For Prosper's account see Migne, P.L., vol. 51, cols. 594, 595.

[1] They seem to have embarked at Gesoriacum, now Boulogne.

blessed Lupus and all the excited throng aroused their chief, to match him against the raging elements. He, all the more steadfast for the very immensity of the danger, in the name of Christ chided the ocean, pleading the cause of religion against the savagery of the gales. Then, taking some oil, he lightly sprinkled the waves in the name of the Trinity and this diminished their fury. Consulting his colleague, he now called upon everybody; and prayer was poured out by their united voice.

And there was God! The enemies of souls were put to flight, the air became clear and calm, the contrary winds were turned to aid the voyage, the currents flowed in the service of the ship. Thus great distances were covered and soon all were enjoying repose on the desired shore.

There great crowds had gathered from many regions to receive the bishops, whose coming had been foretold by the enemies of souls, for the spirits of evil were heralds of what they feared. And, as they were being cast out of the bodies of the possessed by the prelates, they acknowledged that they had contrived the storm and its dangers, and could not deny that the holiness and the authority of the prelates had vanquished them.

XIV

And now it was not long before these apostolic priests had filled all Britain, the first and largest of the islands, with their fame, their preaching and their miracles; and, since it was a daily occurrence for them to be hemmed in by crowds, the word of God was preached, not only in the churches, but at the crossroads, in the fields and in the lanes. Everywhere faithful Catholics were strengthened in their faith and the lapsed learnt the way back to the truth. Their achievements, indeed, were after the pattern of the Apostles themselves; they ruled through consciences, taught through letters and worked miracles through their holiness. Preached by such men, the truth had full course, so that whole regions passed quickly over to their side.

The teachers of perverse doctrines lay low for a time, lamenting as wicked spirits do, when nations escape from their clutches and are lost to them. In the end, after prolonged consideration, they ventured upon a contest. They came forth flaunting their wealth, in dazzling robes, surrounded by a crowd of flatterers. They preferred the risk of exposure to a silence that would put them to shame in the eyes of the people they had deceived, who would regard them as having condemned themselves if they had nothing to say.

And indeed there was assembled at the meeting-place a crowd of vast proportions, wives and children amongst them, drawn by the occasion. The people were present both as spectators and as jury-men. The two parties faced each other, ill-matched and on unequal terms. On the one side was divine authority, on the other human presumption; on this side, faith, on that side, bad faith; those owned allegiance to Pelagius, these to Christ.

The holy bishops gave the privilege of opening the debate to their opponents, who took up the time of their hearers with empty words drawn out to great length but to little purpose. Then the revered prelates themselves poured out the floods of their eloquence, mingling them with the thunders of the Apostle and the Gospels, for their own words were interwoven with the inspired writings and their strongest assertions were supported by the testimony of Scripture. Empty arguments were refuted, dishonest pleas were exposed; and their authors, as each point was made against them, confessed themselves in the wrong by their inability to reply. The jury of the people could hardly keep their hands off them and were not to be stopped from giving their verdict by their shouts.

XV

Suddenly a man of high military rank, accompanied by his wife, stepped into the middle and put his ten-years-old daughter, who was blind, into the arms of the bishops. They told him to take her to their opponents. But the latter, stung by conscience and much alarmed, joined the parents in begging the bishops to cure the little girl. The bishops, seeing that the people were expectant and their opponents in a humbler frame of mind,

offered a short prayer, after which Germanus, filled with the
Holy Spirit and in the name of the Trinity, took from his neck
the reliquary that always hung at his side and in full view of
everybody put it to the eyes of the child.

Immediately it expelled their darkness and filled them with
light and truth. The parents were filled with joy at the miracle
and the onlookers with awe. From that day onwards the false
doctrine was so completely uprooted from men's minds that they
looked to the bishops for teaching, with thirsty souls.

XVI

When this damnable heresy had been thus stamped out, its
authors refuted, and the minds of all re-established in the true
faith, the bishops visited the shrine of the blessed martyr Alban,
to give thanks to God through him. As they were returning, a
demon, lying in wait, contrived an accident that caused Germanus
to fall and injure his foot. Little did it realise that this bodily mis-
fortune, like those of blessed Job, would advance him in holiness.

The Bishop was detained by his injury in one place for a considerable period, in the course of which a fire accidentally broke
out close to where he was staying. It had burnt several houses,
which in those parts are roofed with reeds, and was being carried
by the wind to the one in which he was himself lying. Everybody
rushed to the prelate to carry him out of danger. But he rebuked
them and, strong in his faith, refused to be moved. The crowd in
desperation ran to meet the flames. But, the better to display the
power of God, everything the crowd tried to save was burnt and
what the injured man on his bed guarded was preserved. Shrinking
from the house where he was a guest, the flames leaped over it
and, although they raged on either side of it, there glittered un-
harmed amid the furnaces a tabernacle intact, preserved by the
occupant within.

The people were overjoyed at the miracle and thankful that
their intentions had been defeated by God's power. Day and
night a countless throng lay around the poor man's hut, some
wanting healing for their souls, others for their bodies. It would

be impossible to record all that Christ did through His servant, who exercised these powers when impotent himself. But, although he would allow no one to bring remedies for his own infirmity, one night he saw before him a shining figure in snow-white garments, which stretched out its hand to him as he lay there and raised him up, telling him to stand firmly on his feet. From that moment the pain left him and he so completely recovered his soundness of limb that, when day returned, he resumed the toil of his journeyings without a qualm.

XVII

Meanwhile the Saxons and the Picts had joined forces to make war upon the Britons.[1] The latter had been compelled to withdraw their forces within their camp and, judging their resources to be utterly unequal to the contest, asked the help of the holy prelates. The latter sent back a promise to come, and hastened to follow it. Their coming brought such a sense of security that you might have thought that a great army had arrived; to have such apostles for leaders was to have Christ Himself fighting in the camp.

It was the season of Lent and the presence of the bishops made the sacred forty days still more sacred; so much so that the soldiers, who received instruction in daily sermons, flew eagerly to the grace of baptism; indeed, great numbers of this pious army sought the waters of salvation. A church was built of leafy branches in readiness for Easter Day, on the plan of a city church, though set in a camp on active service. The soldiers paraded still wet from baptism, faith was fervid, the aid of weapons was thought little of, and all looked for help from heaven.

---

[1] The Saxons had originally been known to the Roman world as sea-raiders but their raids upon Britain were by this time beginning to assume the character of a mass movement. Nothing is known for certain about the site of the victory here described. One tradition places it near Mold in Flintshire, but there are weighty reasons for questioning this, on which see Butler's *Lives*, Thurston and Attwater, under July 31st, p. 445. Confusion between the name of this St. Germanus (in its Celtic form Garmon) and that of his younger contemporary St. Germanus of Man (see Butler under July 3rd) probably accounts for a good many mistaken associations of place-names in Britain with St. Germanus of Auxerre.

Meanwhile the enemy had learnt of the practices and appearance of the camp. They promised themselves an easy victory over practically disarmed troops and pressed on in haste. But their approach was discovered by scouts and, when the Easter solemnities had been celebrated, the army—the greater part of it fresh from the font—began to take up their weapons and prepare for battle and Germanus announced that he would be their general.[2] He chose some light-armed troops and made a tour of the outworks. In the direction from which the enemy were expected he saw a valley enclosed by steep mountains. Here he stationed an army on a new model, under his own command.

XVIII

By now the savage host of the enemy was close at hand and Germanus rapidly circulated an order that all should repeat in unison the call he would give as a battle-cry. Then, while the enemy were still secure in the belief that their approach was unexpected, the bishops three times chanted the Alleluia. All, as one man, repeated it and the shout they raised rang through the air and was repeated many times in the confined space between the mountains.

The enemy were panic-stricken, thinking that the surrounding rocks and the very sky itself were falling on them. Such was their terror that no effort of their feet seemed enough to save them. They fled in every direction, throwing away their weapons and thankful if they could save at least their skins. Many threw themselves into the river which they had just crossed at their ease, and were drowned in it.

Thus the British army looked on at its revenge without striking a blow, idle spectators of the victory achieved. The booty strewn everywhere was collected; the pious soldiery obtained the spoils of a victory from heaven. The bishops were elated at the rout of the enemy without bloodshed and a victory gained by faith and not by force.

[2] Latin, " dux proelii ". See note 3 to section I.

Thus this most wealthy island, with the defeat both of its spiritual and of its human foes, was rendered secure in every sense. And now, to the great grief of the whole country, those who had won the victories over both Pelagians and Saxons made preparations for their return. Their own merits and the intercession of Alban the Martyr secured for them a calm voyage ; and a good ship brought them back in peace to their expectant people.

XIX

All Gaul rejoiced at the return of the revered priests ; the Churches were gladdened, the demons trembled. The return of Germanus, in particular, had been prayed for by his diocese with a double intention, since he was looked to as its protector both in the court of heaven and in the tempests of this world. A burden of taxes beyond the ordinary and countless other exactions had crushed the spirit of his people who, without him, had felt like orphaned children. So he took the destitute under his protection, enquired into complaints, condoled with the sorrowing. And, when he might have claimed quiet and repose after the dangers of the sea, he incurred the toil of a long journey by land, by undertaking to seek remedies for the distresses of his diocese.[1] But, though about to travel right across Gaul, he contented himself with the smallest possible retinue and the poorest of mounts. Better than the amplest riches, he carried Christ in his breast.

XX

I think it worth while putting on record that even the journey itself was notable for miracles. He was still in the territory of his own diocese, making his way without haste, and evening was coming on after a rainy day, when his retinue was suddenly

---

[1] Most bishops at this period exercised under the Imperial government many civic functions in their dioceses and it was in his civic capacity that Germanus had been dealing with some of the troubles of his flock and was now setting out again, his destination being Arles, to which the seat of the Imperial administration in Gaul had been moved from Trier (Trèves). The year was about 435, as is shown by the fact that Auxiliaris, who governed Gaul from about 435 to 439, was then in office. See section XXIV below.

increased by a very scantily equipped traveller, barefoot and without a hood, whose very nakedness moved Germanus to pity. Cunningly passing as one of the party, he shared its quarters in the inn and presently, night robber that he was, went off with the beast ridden by the Bishop, while its unsuspecting guardians were occupied in watching God rather than the animals. When day returned, the loss of the animal was discovered and one of the clergy, in order that the Bishop should have a mount, changed himself from a trooper into an infantryman.

As they proceeded on their journey, those around him noticed in the man of blessings an unusual mirth that he was trying to conceal by covering his face : soon they had all seen it and one of them took it upon himself to inquire the reason for it.

" Let us halt for a little," replied the Bishop, " for the plight of that unfortunate man is both laughable and pitiable. You will see him soon, all hot and bothered."

They stopped and dismounted and soon saw in the distance a man on foot leading the animal he had taken. Before long he had caught them up, hurrying while they waited for him. At once he threw himself at the Bishop's feet and confessed his crime. He described how all night long he had been held fast as it were in a trap. He could not go forward and had found that there was no other means of getting away except to restore the stolen animal. To this the man of blessings replied :

" If yesterday we had given you the clothing you lacked, you would not have been reduced to stealing. Now take this that you need, and restore what is ours."

Thus, for confessing his crime, the man received, instead of punishment, not only pardon but also a reward and a blessing.

XXI

This man so full of God always tried to keep his deeds secret and to be insignificant in men's eyes, but his miracles made him famous, verifying the words of the Gospel that a city set on a hill cannot be hidden. He denied himself the solace of the company of friends and avoided intercourse with strangers, but he shone with a majesty that could not be obscured. In all the places he passed through on his journey—villages, or towns or cities—they flocked to meet him with their wives and children and, most of the time, formed a continuous procession, those who met him mingling with those who followed.

XXII

I would think it a sin to pass by in silence the miracle he worked while stopping at Alise.[1] There was a priest there named Senator, noble by birth and still nobler by piety. He had a wife Nectariola, equally pious. The Bishop for the sake of an old-time friendship sought them out when he passed through the town. They got the house ready for his visit, but the things that had to be provided were inversely proportionate to the importance of the visitor. The lady of the house, however, secretly put some straw under the Bishop's pallet and he lay on it without knowing. He gave the night to prayer and psalms and when morning came resumed his journey.

The whole household were delighted to have had so illustrious a visitor and the good lady collected the remains of the straw and preserved it. Some days later a man of good position named Agrestius, with a household consisting of his wife, children and parents, was entered by a demon, which took possession of him ; and the absence of Germanus was as much lamented by the family as the obsession of the unhappy man himself.

But as there was no cure to be found, the revered lady Nectariola resorted to the power of faith. She brought out the straw she had put by and it was wrapped round the raving man. For a whole night he kept shrieking out the name of the Bishop as if he were in a furnace, for though the Bishop was absent his power was not. In the end the man was delivered from the demon by the divine aid, nor for the rest of his life did he run such a risk again.

[1] Latin, " Alesia ", the modern Alise-Sainte-Reine (Dept. Côte-d'Or.)

XXIII

On this journey to Arles the Bishop was carried down to Lyons[1] on the River Saône.[2] On his arrival the population, in eager excitement, came out together to meet him, regardless of age and sex. All begged his blessing and tried to touch him and those who could not touch him were proud even to have seen him. Maladies of all kinds were cured on all sides by his blessing and the city drew life from his preaching, for although he could only make a short stay he did not fail to refresh a thirsty people from the springs of truth.

But if I were to follow him through the whole of his journey, if I were to record everything, I would weary the reader with my prolixity. May God forgive me for omitting so much that I know!

So, then, the city of Arles received the man of blessings on his arrival with an exultant piety; they might have been receiving an Apostle living in their own day. The bishop and luminary of the city was then Hilary,[3] a man bejewelled with every kind of virtue, a flame of faith, a torrent of sacred eloquence and a tireless worker at the tasks of God. It was with the affection felt for a father as well as with the reverence due to an apostle that he received in honour the revered and holy Germanus.

XXIV

Auxiliaris at that time governed Gaul from the very pinnacle of the Prefecture.[1] He had two reasons for his joy at the Bishop's coming. He wanted to make the acquaintance of a man so famous for his spiritual powers, and his own wife had for a long time suffered from a quartan ague. He advanced to meet him much earlier than etiquette required and was held motionless by wonder.

[1] Latin, " Lugdunum ". Constantius, who lived there, was now probably a young man of about twenty.

[2] Latin, " Arar " ; its other name was Sagonna.

[3] Not of course, the more famous saint, and Doctor of the Church, Hilary of Tours (A.D. c.300–368) but St. Hilary of Arles, bishop there 429–449 and writer of the life of his predecessor, St. Honoratus, which appears in this volume.

[1] i.e., he was Praetorian Prefect, on which see note 1 to section III of the Life of St. Ambrose in this volume.

The majesty of his bearing, his knowledge in discussion, the authority in his preaching, all filled Auxiliaris with awe and he realised that the Bishop's fame did him less than justice ; reality exceeded report. He offered him gifts, plied him with services and asked as a favour of the man of blessings that he would condescend to accept what he had come to ask.

Then he spoke of his wife's illness. The Bishop went to see her and the strength of the malady was so completely destroyed that the shaking that used to precede the attacks, and the fever that followed, both disappeared. Restored to her former health, the good lady partook also of a heavenly remedy which increased both the vigour of her body and the faith in her soul. Thus the Bishop obtained boons from a willing Giver and brought back the desired relief to his diocese. But in the eyes of his flock the best remedy and the greatest joy that he brought back with him was his own return.

XXV

Meanwhile[1] news came from Britain that a few promoters of the Pelagian heresy were once more spreading it ; and again all the bishops joined in urging the man of blessings to defend the cause of God for which he had previously won such a victory. He hastened to comply, since he delighted in toil and gladly spent himself for Christ. The malice of the demons, vanquished by the power of his holiness, had by this time ceased to trouble him ; they dared not make an attempt against one they knew to be a friend of God. So, taking with him Severus, a bishop of perfected sanctity,[2] he embarked under Christ's leadership and the elements permitted a calm voyage ; winds, waves and atmosphere[3] all helped the ship along.

---

[1] Latin, " Interea ". But Constantius, like most biographers of the period, is exceedingly vague in his notes of time, though he preserves well enough the general order of events. This second mission of Germanus to Britain is generally dated A.D. 446.

[2] Bishop of Trèves (Trier) from 426 to 476 (Duchesne, op. cit., III, 37). He had been a pupil and disciple of St. Lupus.

[3] Water, the lower air or atmosphere (" aer ", here " aera ", a form of the plural) and wind were regarded as three elements, water generating the vapour-laden lower atmosphere, which in its turn generated the winds—so St. Isidore of Seville, writing rather more than a century later, in De Natura Rerum.

XXVI

Meanwhile evil spirits, flying over the whole island, made known through the involuntary prophecies of their victims the coming of Germanus, with the result that one of the leading men in the country, Elafius by name, came hurrying to meet the holy men without having had any news of them through any regular messenger. He brought with him his son who had been crippled in early youth by a most grievous malady. His sinews had withered and the tendons of the knee had contracted and his withered leg made it impossible for him to stand on his feet.

The whole Province came along with Elafius. The bishops arrived and the crowds came upon them unexpectedly. At once blessings and the words of God were showered upon them. Germanus could see that the people as a whole had persevered in the faith in which he had left them and the bishops realised that the fallings-away had been the work only of a few. These were identified and formally condemned.

XXVII

At this point Elafius approached to make obeisance to the bishops and presented to them his son, whose youth and helplessness made his need clear without words. Everyone felt acutely for him, the bishops most of all, and in their pity they had recourse to the mercy of God. The blessed Germanus at once made the boy sit down, then felt the bent knee and ran his healing hand over all the diseased parts. Health speedily followed the life-giving touch. What was withered became supple, the sinews resumed their proper work and, before the eyes of all, the son got back a sound body and the father got back a son.

The crowds were overwhelmed by the miracle and the Catholic faith implanted in them was strengthened in all of them. There followed sermons to the people to confute the heresy, the preachers of which were by common consent banished from the island. They were brought to the bishops to be conducted to the continent, so that the country might be purged of them and they of their errors. The effect of all this was so salutary that even now the faith is persisting intact in those parts.[1] And so, with everything settled, the blessed bishops made a prosperous journey back to their own country.

XXVIII

He had hardly got home after his overseas expedition when a deputation from Armorica[1] came with a petition to the weary prelate. For Aetius the Magnificent, who then governed the state,[2] had been enraged by the insolence of that proud region and, to punish it for daring to rebel, had given Goar,[3] the savage King of the Alans,[4] permission to subdue it ; and Goar, with a barbarian's greed, was thirsting for its wealth.

So one old man was matched against a most warlike people and an idolatrous king but, under the protection of Christ, he proved greater and stronger than them all. He lost no time in setting out, for all the preparations for the invasion had been made. The movement of the tribes had already begun and their iron-armed cavalry were filling all the roads. Nevertheless our Bishop rode out towards them till he reached his meeting-place with the King, who arrived soon after him.

Since the march was in progress when the meeting took place, the priest was opposed to a war-lord clad in armour and sur-rounded by his bodyguard. First he made requests, through

---

[1] i.e. in western Britain, where these events had probably taken place. By the time that Constantius wrote, heathen Teutons had overrun the eastern half of the island.

[1] See footnote 4 to section 1.

[2] i.e. the Western half of the Empire, still nominally ruled by the Emperor at Ravenna. " Vir magnificus " was a kind of title for Aetius. It was he who later (A.D. 451) defeated Attila the Hun at Châlons.

[3] Latin, " Gochar ", otherwise Eochar.

[4] Latin, " Alani ", a semi-Mongol people who had moved up the Danube basin during the 4th century. In A.D. 409, under pressure from the Huns, the western section of them, with other peoples, had crossed the Rhine. Some of them went on to Spain, from which (in conjunction with the Vandals) they invaded Roman Africa (see the Life of St. Augustine in this volume, section XXVIII). Others remained in Gaul and taken part in the politics of the Empire. About 440 Aetius had given permission to the Alan tribes ruled by Goar to settle around Orleans, where in 442 they drove out the former inhabi-tants. He was now turning them loose onto Armorica.

the medium of an interpreter. Then, as Goar disregarded them, he went on to rebuke him. Finally he stretched out his hand, seized his bridle and halted him, and with him the whole army.

The wrath of the savage king at this was turned by God to marvelling. He was staggered by such firmness, awed by such dignity and shaken by the strength of such insistent authority. The panoply of war and the rattle of arms gave place to the courtesies of a peaceful interview. Laying aside his arrogance the King dismounted and entered upon negotiations which ended by satisfying, not the desires of the King, but the requests of the Bishop. The King and his army camped peacefully where they were and he gave the most solemn assurances of peace on condition that the pardon which he himself had thus granted to the Armoricans was asked also of the Emperor or Aetius. Meanwhile the mediation of the Bishop, and his holiness, had restrained a king, recalled an army and delivered a Province from devastation.

XXIX

From there Germanus set out for Italy;[1] it was enough for him that he should never be free from toil to enjoy a rest but, in the words of the Prophet,[2] should go on from strength to strength. On the way he paid another visit for old times' sake to his friend Senator, the priest,[3] who brought him a dumb girl, about twenty years old. First he blessed some oil and anointed her mouth and forehead and the rest of her face with it. Then he ordered spiced wine to be brought, in which he steeped three morsels of bread broken off with his own hands. He put one of them into the girl's mouth, telling her before she took it to ask him to bless it. This she did at once, before taking the bread, speaking quite distinctly ; and the power of speech, thus miraculously acquired, remained for the rest of her life.

---

[1] In order to obtain at Ravenna the imperial pardon for the Armoricans that had been the condition of the settlement with Goar ; for at this date Ravenna had been the imperial capital in the West for half a century.

[2] Ps. lxxxiii (lxxxiv). 8.

[3] At Alise ; see section XXII.

On his departure he embraced his friend with more than usual affection, kissing him on the mouth and forehead and eyes. As he clasped him to his breast, his last words were : " Farewell till eternity, my very dear brother ; farewell, part of my very soul. God grant that at the Day of Judgement we may see each other without being put to confusion ; in this world we shall not look upon each other again."

XXX

He made the journey alone, except for his retinue, but he was constantly thronged by the crowds that came out to meet him, so much so, that every eminence associated with his journey is to this day crowned by a chapel, a hermit's cell or a cross erected where he prayed or taught. At Autun[1] in particular, as he passed through its territory, the people came out to meet him regardless of age or sex. Among them were two parents, who knelt in front of everybody and showed him their daughter, whose malady had in the course of time reduced her to a terrible condition. From birth the fingers of her right hand had been bent towards her palm by a contraction of the sinews, so that as her finger-nails grew they pierced her tender flesh and every finger made a wound ; and, had it not been that the bones of the palm to some extent checked the growing points, she would have had ulcers right through her hand.

The Bishop took her hand and felt it and his healing touch brought a blessing. Then he took her fingers one by one and eased the tendons, restoring them to flexibility, and the hand which had caused its own destruction was thus made serviceable. Adding kindness to kindness, he himself with his own sacred hands cut the long nails on the straightened fingers down to the customary length.

XXXI

So he passed through the cities of Gaul. To enter Italy he had to cross the Alps and he lightened the journey by conversation with some workmen who were returning to their own country

[1] Latin, " Augustudunum ".

after a spell of employment in Gaul. As these men, laden with excessively heavy packs, were climbing a pass that rose up into the clouds, they were held up by a mountain stream running through a steep and rocky gorge which gave firm foothold to neither man nor beast. One of these travellers was both lame and elderly and the man of blessings took his pack on to his own shoulders and carried it across amidst the huge whirlpools. Then he crossed again to carry across on his back the man without his bundle. Moreover, in his humility he was most careful to let no one know who he was. When he came to Milan, however, he could no longer conceal his identity or his eminence.

XXXII

He arrived on the solemn festival of its saints,[1] for which great numbers of bishops had assembled. While the sacred mysteries of the Mass were being celebrated at the altar, he entered, unknown and unexpected. Immediately, one of the congregation, who was possessed by a demon, shouted out in a tremendous voice :

" Germanus, why do you pursue us into Italy? Be content that you have driven us out of Gaul. Be content that your prayers have defeated both us and the ocean. Why do you scour the whole world? Take a rest and let us have a rest ourselves."

Amazement and terror filled the congregation. They looked at one another, asking which was Germanus ; and, in spite of the poverty-stricken look of his clothes, he was recognised by the majesty of his face. When asked, he did not deny his position and episcopal rank. Thereupon all the bishops with fitting humility showed their reverence for this saint of God ; and they asked him to treat the demoniac who had proclaimed his name. It was not from swaggering presumption but in a spirit of obedience that he had the man shown to him. He took him aside into the sacristy, speedily exorcised him, and sent him back into the congregation.

[1] The Latin makes it probable though not certain that the saints who were being celebrated were the patrons of Milan. If they were, the day was 19th June, the Feast of SS. Gervasius and Protasius, Martyrs (see the Life of St. Ambrose in this volume, section XIV). The year was probably A.D. 448.

This was the first manifestation of miraculous powers given by Christ through this servant of His in Italy. Crowds came hurrying from all directions, coveting the blessing of a man of such proved sanctity; and when he followed up his miracles by sermons he healed souls as well as bodies.

XXXIII

On leaving that wealthy city, he pursued his journey gently and with much-appreciated pauses. Presently he encountered some beggars who asked for alms. He consulted his deacon as to how much there was in their purse. " Only three gold pieces," was the reply and at once he ordered them all to be bestowed upon the beggars.

" But what are we to live on today ? " asked the deacon.

" God feeds His poor," replied the Bishop ; " give what you have to these who need it."

But the deacon kept one piece back as a precaution and gave away two.

Resuming their journey they noticed behind them some horsemen spurring after them. These soon caught them up, jumped off their horses and went down on their knees.

" Our master Leporius," they said, " a gentleman of rank,[1] lives not far from here. He and his household are down with various illnesses, so that what with his own incapacitation and theirs he is quite prostrated. We have been sent to tell you of his troubles. Will you condescend to come and cure him ? But if you are too much engaged to do as we ask, aid him with your prayers. Let him have the blessing you can obtain for him, even if he cannot have the privilege of seeing you."

This roused the compassion of the holy man and, even though it meant leaving the road, he reckoned that the shortest way was the one that won the reward of a good deed. So, in spite of the protests of his party, he turned aside to pay the requested visit. " Nothing ", said he, " should come before

---

[1] Latin, " vir spectabilis ", an actual title at this period, the second rank in the official hierarchy.

doing the Lord's will." Then the messengers in transports of
joy presented to him two hundred gold pieces that had been
entrusted to them for the purpose. Germanus turned to his
deacon, saying :

" Take what they offer and remember that you have defrauded
the poor ; because if you had given those beggars all you had, our
benefactor would have repaid you with *three* hundred gold pieces
today."

The deacon was appalled at the thought that his guilt had been
no secret from the Bishop.

XXXIV

Meanwhile they had been hastening their pace and presently
reached the house, where the holy man's arrival raised everybody's spirits as if health personified had entered it. He applied
his usual remedies all round. He knelt in supplication to Christ,
to win joy for others by his own tears. Then he visited the master
and his family and the servants as well. Making no distinction he
went the round of the cottages also, visiting every sick-room.
Then he allowed a full day to pass and, so effective was the
celestial medicine, that when he departed the next morning he
left the whole household in the enjoyment of perfect health. The
master of the house, whom he had found in bed when he arrived,
conducted him on his way. Thus the holy man's reputation and
praises preceded him and made all who heard of his coming eager
to see him.

XXXV

Rumour of it was, in fact, already circulating in Ravenna,
where the populace, in their impatience to see him, found fault
with him for the delays on his journey. But, after being long
awaited, he could be welcomed at last. He had, indeed, planned
to make a secret entry into the city by night, under cover of darkness, but his intentions were defeated, for sentinels stayed up to
watch for him.

At that time the bishop of the city was Peter[1], who ruled the Church of Christ there in the tradition of the Apostles. The Empress[2] Placidia reigned over the Roman Empire jointly with her son Valentinian, who was still a young man.[3] They loved the Catholic faith so well that, though rulers of all, they obeyed with the deepest humility the servants of God. All these personages, for the love of God, vied with one another in the reception that they gave to the revered Bishop. Princes courted him, nobles went out to meet him, the body of the faithful were in transports of joy. The revered Empress sent to his lodgings a huge dish of silver laden with many kinds of delicious food, all prepared without meat. He accepted the gift, distributed the food to those who served him and kept the silver, sending back in its place a little wooden platter with a barley loaf on it. The Empress treasured both, immensely delighted, both because her silver had passed through his hands to the poor and because she had received for herself the holy man's food on so humble a dish. Indeed, she afterwards had the wood set in gold and kept the bread to work many miracles of healing.

XXXVI

One day when crossing a wide square and hemmed in by crowds he passed in front of a gaol crowded with prisoners awaiting torture or death. These got to know that he was passing and raised a tremendous clamour, shouting in unison. He enquired the reason and it was explained to him. So he sent for the warders but they kept out of his way, for all these wretched prisoners had been sentenced to that prison by one or another of the great officials of the Palace the night before. His compassion saw no help anywhere.

At last he turned to his old resource and petitioned the divine majesty for the help so difficult to obtain from men. He walked

---

[1] St. Peter Chrysologus, Doctor of the Church, Archbishop of Ravenna from A.D. 433 to about 450.

[2] Latin, " regina ", "queen" ; see note 4 to section II of the Life of St. Martin. Placidia died two years after this.

[3] Valentinian III, who was just 29 at the time. He had come to the throne in A.D. 425 when he was a boy of six and was nominally reigning for thirty years.

up to the gaol and threw himself on the ground in prayer. Then indeed did Our Lord show the crowd, standing by, with what favour He regarded His servant. The gates, secured by chains and bars, flew open ; the iron bolts leapt back. God's kindness undid what man's cruelty had carefully contrived. They came thronging out from chains to liberty, displaying their futile loads of fetters and carrying in their hands the cords with which they had been bound. For once the gaol was harmless, because empty ; and in triumphal procession to celebrate the victory of kindness the throng of unfortunates were restored to the bosom of a rejoicing Church.

XXXVII

Each day men marvelled at the pontiff more and spread his fame. The populace flocked to him, the sick were healed, and Christ continued to enlarge the favours that He granted. Six reverend bishops were continuously in devoted attendance on him and they marvelled as much at the crucifixion he endured from his uninterrupted fasts as at his frequent miracles. Years afterwards they were living to bear witness to his works.[1]

XXXVIII

A man named Volusianus, at that time first secretary to Sigis-vult,[1] the Patrician,[2] had a son who was suffering from a burning fever. The heat of his blood had so wasted the boy's bodily strength that his condition was openly despaired of. The doctors could do no more and gave no hope, and the parents resigned themselves to mourning. Then a belated hope sprang up ; they thought of the man of blessings. They clung to his knees, their friends and neighbours with them, and the attendant bishops added their pleading. With them he hastened to the sick-bed but

---

[1] Taking " suorum " as one of the author's few grammatical blunders.
[1] Latin, " Segisvultus ", clearly a Latinised form of some Teutonic name.
[2] Latin, " Patricius ", a title occasionally bestowed upon the very highest officers of the Empire. Sigisvult had held the (at this time) honorary, but exalted, office of Consul in A.D. 437 and is mentioned as being *magister militum* (at the head of the armed forces) in Italy three years later.

they were met by a runner saying that the boy was dead and that it was useless for the holy man to tire himself.

But the prelates urged him on and the crowd begged him not to leave his work of mercy unfinished. They found the body lifeless, with the warmth of life departed, and already stiffening in the cold of death. With a prayer for his soul they were turning back, when suddenly the bystanders raised a cry of grief and the bishops clung to the hand of their elder to make him petition the Lord on behalf of the bereaved parents for the dead boy's return to life. For a long time he resisted them, full of embarrassment in his humility ; but at last he yielded to pity and to the demands of charity. Girding himself with the weapons of faith, he sent the bystanders out and stretched himself out upon the corpse in prayer. He watered the ground with his tears, his deep groans went up to heaven, he called upon Christ with his sighs. Presently the dead moved and, little by little, the lifeless organs resumed their normal functions. The eyes opened to the light, the fingers twitched, at last the tongue uttered sounds.

Both rose, the one from prayer, the other from death. Germanus lifted the sleeper by the hand and he sat up, drew a breath, pulled himself together and looked about him. Little by little he regained strength, and full health returned. Thus a son was restored to his parents, mourning was turned into joy and the power of God's majesty was acclaimed by the united voice of the people. And Christ continued to show His power through His servant and made him shine more than ever with the glory of miracles, since he was soon to be called to his rest.

XXXIX

A eunuch named Acolus, at that time Imperial Chamberlain,[1] had an adopted son to whom he had given an excellent education but who was now plagued by a demon. It was the kind that strikes down its victims every month at the new moon, by causing them to keep falling to the ground. The Empress through her

[1] Latin, " praepositus regalis cubiculi "—in state documents generally ". . . sacri cubiculi ".

courtiers arranged for him to be taken to the holy man and put into his charge.

After a long examination of him, Germanus put off the exorcism to the next day, although he ordinarily expelled even the most rabid demons at the first laying on of hands. He did this because this demon had entered so deeply into the very inmost parts of the wretched youth that during the periods of possession it practically made his body its own. That night he arranged for the boy to occupy the same room as himself. Then, indeed, the demon burst out openly from its inner lair. As if in torture it revealed how it had first taken possession of its victim in the innocence of early childhood. Now at the Bishop's order it went out of him, and the next day the youth was back in the palace, purged.

XL

It had been the affairs of Armorica that had made this long journey necessary and Germanus would undoubtedly have had them settled as he wished, by obtaining for the Amoricans pardon and security for the future, if it had not been for the treachery of Tibatto, who persuaded that fickle and undisciplined people to rebel again.[1] After that, not even the intercession of the Bishop could do anything for them, for common prudence made it impossible for the Imperial government to trust them ; and their many times perjured leader before long paid the penalty of his reckless treason.

XLI

One day, when the night office had been recited and he was giving a spiritual discourse to the bishops, he made a sorrowful announcement. " Dearest brethren," he said, " I commend my passing to your prayers. In my sleep last night I saw myself as a traveller receiving his provision for the road from Our Lord and, when I asked why I was setting out, He said to me : ' Do not be

---

[1] Levison thinks that Constantius has confused the names here. Tibatto had been the leader of the Armoricans in an earlier rebellion and been captured. But he may have escaped or been released.

afraid. I am not sending you on your travels again but to your fatherland, where you will have quiet and eternal rest.' "

The bishops would have liked to give the dream another interpretation but, more earnestly than ever, he commended his last moments to their prayers. " I know quite well ", said he, " what the fatherland is that God promises to His servants."

XLII

An illness did in fact follow, a few days later. As it grew more serious, the whole city was in consternation. But He who was calling him to glory hastened his journey ; the Lord was inviting the tired hero to receive the reward of his laborious days.

The Empress laid aside the haughtiness of royalty and went visiting the pauper ; she sought out the sick man and promised him anything he asked. But he had only one request to make, and to this she consented most unwillingly, that his dust should return to his native soil. Day and night the crowd of visitors was as much as the house and the forecourt could hold. The chanting of the psalms was kept up continuously ; and the seventh day of the illness saw the passing of his faithful and blessed soul to heaven.[1]

XLIII

Then came the division of what he had left behind him. The Empire and the Church each claimed a share ; and over his scanty possessions there arose a dispute such as we associate with great riches—there was so little for them to seize, poor heirs of a mere benediction! The Empress took the reliquary ; Bishop Peter annexed the cloak with the hairshirt inside it. The six prelates, to make sure of having something associated with the saint, were glad to tear to pieces what remained. One had his pallium,[1] the second his girdle, two divided his tunic and two his soldier's cape.[2]

---

[1] Probably on 31st July, 448.
[1] A kind of stole sometimes given by the Pope to bishops (more usually to archbishops) as a mark of special favour and authority.
[2] His bed-covering ; see section IV.

XLIV

Next came an eager rivalry over his funeral, everyone insisting that no expense should be spared. Acolius had the body embalmed in spices ; the Empress saw to its vestments. When all this was duly accomplished, the Emperor provided the bier and the equipage for the journey and a large body of his own servants to attend them.[1] The clergy were in charge of the chanting of the liturgy, at each stage arranging for it to be carried on by those of the next town—there was one long procession all the way to Gaul.

XLV

The body reached Piacenza[1] on its journey when it was quite dark. It was placed in the church, and, while the liturgical prayers were being recited, a lady of the town who was so badly paralysed that she could use none of her limbs asked as a favour to be placed under the bier. There she remained stretched out till dawn. When, early in the morning, the corpse was taken up again, the woman rose too and astonished everybody by following in the procession on her own feet.

XLVI

Even greater was the devotion manifested in Gaul to its own protector, for there was personal affection as well as reverence. Every kind of person hastened to perform every kind of service. Some smoothed the roads by clearing away stones, others linked them by restoring bridges. Some contributed to the expenses, others chanted the psalms, others again took the bier on to their shoulders. The profusion of torches ousted the sun's rays and provided light for the day. Such were the services of love with which he was brought back to his own see, where his

---

[1] The journey to Auxerre was about 550 miles from Ravenna by road.
[1] Latin, " Placentia ", a town on the Po, about 130 miles from Ravenna.

body is buried but he himself lives on in his daily miracles and his glory.[1]

Of you, my reader, I must ask pardon twice over, first for the solecisms and the rustic idiom with which I have offended your ears, then for a prolixity that must have been wearisome. But we ought not to find it too tedious to read through what Christ did not find it too tedious to do for us—Christ, who when He gives glory to His saints is giving an invitation to us. I call God to witness, who knows all secrets, that the known and attested miracles of my lord Bishop Germanus that I have passed over in silence are more numerous than those I have recorded; and I have to own myself guilty of suppressing marvels that the power of God wrought for the benefit of all. I think that I have written too summarily rather than too much.

[1] The body of Germanus reached Auxerre on Sept. 22nd and was buried there on October 1st.